MW01284776

CONSERVATIVES
AGAINST
CAPITALISM

PETER KOLOZI

CONSERVATIVES AGAINST CAPITALISM

*From the Industrial Revolution
to Globalization*

COLUMBIA UNIVERSITY PRESS

NEW YORK

Columbia University Press
Publishers Since 1893
New York   Chichester, West Sussex
cup.columbia.edu

Library of Congress Cataloging-in-Publication Data

Names: Kolozi, Peter, author.
Title: Conservatives against capitalism : from the Industrial Revolution to globalization /
Peter Kolozi.
Description: New York : Columbia University Press, 2017. | Includes bibliographical
references and index.
Identifiers: LCCN 2016058575 (print) | LCCN 2017022706 (e-book) | ISBN 9780231166522
(cloth : acid-free paper) | ISBN 9780231544610 (e-book)
Subjects: LCSH: Capitalism—Political aspects—United States—History. | Capitalism—Social
aspects—United States—History. | Conservatism—United States—History. | United States—
Politics and government—Philosophy. | United States—Economic policy—Philosophy.
Classification: LCC HC110.C3 (ebook) | LCC HC110.C3 K76 2017 (print) | DDC 330.12/2—dc23
LC record available at https://lccn.loc.gov/2016058575

Columbia University Press books are printed
on permanent and durable acid-free paper.

Printed in the United States of America

Cover design: Lisa Hamm

For my parents

CONTENTS

ACKNOWLEDGMENTS

I am indebted to many people, for without their support and encouragement, this manuscript would not have been possible. First, I would like to thank my editor, Philip Leventhal, and his associates at Columbia University Press. Mr. Leventhal's comments, suggestions, and edits have been vital to improving this manuscript. I also wish to thank the Ph.D. program in political science at the Graduate Center of the City University of New York (CUNY) for giving me the opportunity to pursue my graduate studies.

I especially want to thank Professors Corey Robin and Professor Michael J. Thompson for reading and rereading my work, offering invaluable comments and suggestions, and helping me formulate and engage with my ideas more thoroughly and creatively. I also am grateful to Professors George Gregoriou and Stephen R. Shalom at William Paterson University who inspired and encouraged me to pursue graduate studies in political science.

I wish to thank the Professional Staff Congress (PSC) for securing reassigned time in support of junior faculty doing research at CUNY. I am deeply grateful to my colleagues at CUNY's Bronx Community College (BCC), particularly Ms. Amariliz Gomez-Sanchez and Professors Jawied Nawabi and James E. Freeman, who have been especially supportive during my years of working with them. I am especially grateful to Professor Freeman, my professional mentor and friend, for without his motivation and encouragement I could not have completed this book. I also wish to thank my students at BCC for inspiring me with their energy, intellect, and perseverance.

Finally, I am indebted to my friends and family, in particular Edward and Patricia Kotarski, John Baldino, Maria Pagoulatos, David Gentilella, and Isa Vasquez; my brother, Ladislav, and his family, and, most of all, my mom and dad. I greatly appreciate their patience, understanding, support, and encouragement throughout the ups and downs of graduate studies and in the long journey leading to the completion of this book.

CONSERVATIVES
AGAINST
CAPITALISM

INTRODUCTION

Conservatives Against Capitalism

After the economic crisis that began in 2007 and the jobless recovery that followed, the political debate about capitalism seems to be making a comeback, with economic inequality at the center.[1] Even conservatives now refer to vulture capitalism and the greed of multinational corporations, and they admit that the current levels of economic inequality are a concern. Yet few contemporary conservatives go so far as to critically assess the capitalist system and the economic and political power wielded by the wealthy and corporations in America.[2] Instead, many of their complaints of contemporary America center on "Big Government," the permissive liberal culture, and threats posed by the "other," whether they are immigrants from Latin America or Muslims, and not on a critical analysis of the economic system. This exclusion in contemporary conservative discourse suggests a significant evolution in the conservative intellectual tradition, which for much of its history has had a critical orientation to capitalism, particularly laissez-faire capitalism, the version that is rhetorically dominant among conservatives today.

Although it is commonly assumed that conservatives are consistent supporters of laissez-faire capitalism, and many of them are, this assumption does not reflect the American conservative tradition as a whole.[3] Throughout American history, conservative thinkers have recognized the destructive effects of laissez-faire capitalism on individuals, traditional institutions, communities, the nation, its cultural heritage, and the social order. In fact, since the Industrial Revolution, American conservatives have offered a penetrating criticism of laissez-faire capitalism and endorsed various alternatives to it, ranging from slavery, programs for economic decentralization, and a conservative welfare state.[4] To be sure, the critique of capitalism is no longer as central to conservatives' thinking about the economy as it once was. In fact, the conservative critique of capitalism has evolved from challenges to the economic system as a whole to debates over free trade and protectionism. Both conservatives in general and the tradition in the conservative intellectual movement that has been critical of capitalism have now been reconciled to capitalism as an economic system. Whatever conservative critique remains in the current discourse is now focused on the cultural critique of capitalism, weaving the disparate thinkers that I consider in this book into a tapestry forming a new tradition in American conservative thought.

Many thinkers have embraced free-market capitalism, and not all of them have been self-described conservatives. Some, such as Friedrich Hayek, described themselves as classical liberals.[5] Nevertheless, in the twentieth century, in addition to Hayek, thinkers such as John Bates Clark, Ludwig von Mises, Milton Friedman, Ayn Rand, and Murray Rothbard became part of the conservative pantheon. The current conservative discourse about capitalism has, been dominated, in one way or another, by the ideas of these thinkers, even though many of them showed a discernible ambivalence about laissez-faire capitalism. Indeed, Frank Knight, Henry Simons, Jacob Viner, and Wilhelm Röpke all advocated government intervention in the economy during the Great Depression and "denounced the excesses of laissez-faire."[6] Knight worried that capitalist incentives that reduced all values to monetary measures would undermine morality, which in turn might lead to social collapse.[7] Viner privileged democratic decision making over economic theory (even laissez-faire). Both Viner and Simons were critics of Big Business, and Simons even advocated for regulations to limit business's size, called for the nationalization of utilities and railroads, and insisted on a "steeply progressive" income tax. Hayek, while consistently rejecting economic planning against competition, also rejected laissez-faire and carved out a fairly robust role for the state beyond the framework of a minimalist state. Indeed, these thinkers and how their free-market ideas prevailed, despite their reservations about laissez-faire, have already led to much research.[8] *Conservatives Against Capitalism*, however, is not about them or conservative economic thinkers. Instead, it is about self-described conservative political thinkers and, in some cases, political practitioners, who have wrestled with and tried to reconcile the tension between capitalism and a conservative social order.

In fact, to label conservatives as enthusiastic advocates of laissez-faire capitalism is to overlook a long tradition that has been both critical of it and has offered alternatives. Within this critical tradition, conservative thinkers have challenged capitalism on a number of fronts, including its deleterious social, cultural, and political impacts. The extent of their influence has varied. For instance, James Henry Hammond, John C. Calhoun, Theodore Roosevelt, and the more recent neoconservatives were not only political thinkers but also elected politicians. Men such as Brooks Adams and Irving and William Kristol were close to the levers of power where their ideas influenced public policy. Others, such as George Fitzhugh and the Southern Agrarians, had a minimal influence on public policy but are academically significant as being among the most iconoclastic and sharpest critics of capitalism in the conservative tradition. With the exception of the defenders of slavery, who had an existing alternative at hand, conservative critics of capitalism have been left with no choice but to accept some version of capitalism. Moreover, their ideas about conservatism and their ambivalence to capitalism are important to contemporary debates about the economic organization of a "good" society, to understanding the relationship between an economic system and "conservative" values and institutions, and to conservative intellectual and public policy debates about capitalism and the welfare state.

Writing about the variety of conservative thinking, Patrick Allitt suggested that for some conservatives, "conservatism was, chiefly, the defense of free-market capitalism, even though, paradoxically, capitalism has probably done more to *change* the world in the past two centuries than anything else."[9] For other conservatives, capitalism has been a motor of change, but one that has necessitated offering a theoretical opposition to what it changed.

Conservatives Against Capitalism will, I hope, contribute to the study of American conservatism and political thought.[10] First, I will look at a forgotten tradition of American thought that challenged the core values and normal operating procedures of unbridled capitalism, showing that conservative political thinking about capitalism has not always been libertarian and that a critique of capitalism has not always been the sole property of the Left. Next, I will show how this tradition has changed over time. Finally, I will demonstrate how conservative critics reconciled conservatism with capitalism and gradually removed the most substantive criticisms of capitalism from the conservative discourse. Conservatives have progressed from a robust critique of capitalism into its most ardent defenders while moderating the market through a nuanced vision of a conservative welfare state. In short, I will argue that a whole host of thinkers were both conservative and critical of capitalism.

To explain the evolution of this critical tradition, I will situate the development of ideas in their economic, social, and political contexts and will examine how changing material conditions and class dynamics affected those ideas. Theorists were not only writing about the abstract concept of capitalism but were also reacting to the social reality that capitalism helped create. The historical context also helps explain why certain critiques of capitalism were emphasized at a given moment and why they may have become secondary or completely ignored in another.

I also will argue that this conservative tradition is both critical of capitalism and statist.[11] Although scholars of American conservatism have noted that some conservative thinkers have expressed ambivalence about capitalism,[12] none has identified an ongoing critique of capitalism from the right or has systematically analyzed the development of such a critique. While these individual works offer some insight, none of them fully accounts for the longevity, breadth, depth, and variation of the conservative opposition to, or dissatisfaction with, capitalism in the United States.

Capitalism and its evolution in the United States have been contested even by conservatives. At stake in these conservative debates about capitalism is no less than the core questions about American political economy and the roles of the market and government in American life. These questions include the size, scope, and capability of government, whom it serves and to what end, as well as the extent to which capitalist values and relations pervade both the economic and noneconomic aspects of life. Over the past forty years, there has been a march to the right on economic matters, from the deregulation of business and finance and the erosion of the liberal welfare state to the assault on labor unions. In time, these decades-long trends may be reversed, but in 2017, the economic ideas of conservatives dominate public policy, and their impact is felt in a variety of ways. Perhaps anti-capitalist thought in American conservatism is seldom discussed because the laissez-faire perspective is so dominant in the current conservative discourse. This, however, has not always been the case. Before the U.S. Civil War, the Southern slave system offered an economic model that was rooted in the tradition of half the states in the Union. Then, after the defeat of Southern slavery, lacking an established alternative, conservatives could not reject capitalism outright but they could not completely endorse it, either. In the years following the Civil War, many conservatives were ambivalent economic liberals. President Theodore Roosevelt advocated a regulated capitalism to mitigate class antagonism. Peter Viereck, Clinton Rossiter, and August Heckscher, all highly respected post–World War II thinkers, criticized laissez-faire and defended the New Deal in accordance with their conservative principles.

One of the most detailed analyses of the conservative critique of capitalism is Eugene Genovese's *The Southern Tradition*.[13] Genovese suggests that the conservative critique of capitalism is rooted in the Southern conservative tradition, which includes the antebellum pro-slavery thinkers, the Southern Agrarians, and the paleoconservatives of today. His analysis, however, contextualizes and locates the critique exclusively in the Southern and agrarian tradition, a limitation that excludes key thinkers and their ideas and thereby lends the conservative critique of capitalism a sectionalist, nostalgic, and antimodern orientation. The critiques by Theodore Roosevelt, Brooks Adams, Viereck, Rossiter, and Irving Kristol did not emanate from a longing for the lost Southern tradition or the establishment of a modern-day agrarianism. Instead, conservative critics of capitalism were shaped by the social, political, and economic changes that had accompanied the transformations in American capitalism over the past century and a half. The American economy evolved from being rural and agricultural, in which slave, semifeudal, and wage-labor relations of production coexisted. Post Civil War the economy transformed into a corporate-driven industrial powerhouse with a large industrial proletariat. Then the economy evolved again into a de-industrializing service economy dominated by what John Bellamy Foster called "monopoly finance capital."[14]

These changes have transformed class and power relations throughout society, challenged traditional institutions, undermined established social and cultural practices, and introduced new social and political forces that precipitated wholesale adjustments in the new social order. The conservative critiques of capitalism have been reactions to these changes in social relations and the class rule that accompanied them. Even though certain themes, such as the desirability of economic inequality and a cultural critique, have been consistently maintained in this tradition, the type of capitalism, its specific social relations of production, the elites that are the target of their critique, and, conversely, the elites that these thinkers defend, nonetheless have also changed over time.

WHAT IS CONSERVATISM?

Studies of American conservatism immediately encounter the problem of definition. Alan Brinkley admits that conservatism is "not easy to characterize," since it lacks ideological "consistency and clarity" and encompasses a "broad range of ideas, impulses, and constituencies" that are "conflicting and incompatible."[15] So internally conflicted is the conservative tradition that in the widely praised and influential *The Conservative Intellectual Tradition in America Since 1945*, author George H. Nash refrains from defining conservatism at all, instead writing, "I doubt that there is any single, satisfactory, all-encompassing definition of the complex phenomenon called conservatism, the content of which varies enormously with time and place. It may even be true that conservatism is inherently resistant to precise definition."[16]

In an influential article published in 1957 entitled "Conservatism as an Ideology," Samuel Huntington declared that conservatism is, following the British-Irish political theorist, statesman, and archetypal conservative Edmund Burke, a defense of the established order, reflecting a disposition toward gradual reform rather than radical change.

In contrast, Russell Kirk maintains that conservatism is "an autonomous system of ideas" that is defined by universal values applicable in all historical circumstances.[17] Kirk also argues that conservatism is "a way of looking at the civil social order." Although conservatives have defended a wide variety of social orders and social institutions, there are several general principles to which they "in some degree may be said to have agreed implicitly." According to Kirk, these include beliefs in a transcendent moral order to which society ought to conform; the belief in social continuity or an organic social order; the prescriptive value of tradition or, in Burke's words, "the wisdom of our ancestors"; prudence, which translates into a commitment to slow reform rather than radical change; variety and inequality as essential to social stability; and human imperfectability and therefore the imperfectability of social institutions.[18]

Similarly, for John Micklethwait and Adrian Wooldridge, conservatism is rooted in the Burke's six principles: deep suspicion of the power of the state; a preference for liberty over equality; patriotism; a belief in established institutions and hierarchies; skepticism about the idea of progress; and elitism. American conservatism is exceptional, Micklethwait and Woolridge contend, "in its exaggeration of the first three of Burke's principles and contradiction of the last three."[19] American conservatism's peculiarity, they believe, arises mostly from American conservatives' hostility to the state and from their estimation of rugged individualism, optimism, and, sometimes, populism.

Indeed, Micklethwait and Wooldridge's view of American conservatism points to a combination of both "an autonomous system of ideas" and a situational orientation, as Huntington suggested. Viereck and Rossiter, among others, argued that the defining characteristic of conservatism is a disposition to conserve established traditions and institutions, which in post–World War II America include a regulated capitalism and the liberal welfare state.[20]

Students of postwar American conservatism see it as an amalgam of two "separate and distinct" strands of thought "uneasily coexisting" under one umbrella: traditionalism and libertarianism held together by a mutual aversion to communism.[21] Traditionalist conservatism is a political perspective that privileges social order, hierarchy, and social stability. It promotes traditional values and institutions such as the family, religion, the nation, heritage, and established custom that transmit a sense of continuity across generations and bind individuals together in mutual dependence, responsibility, and duty. These established relations and traditions ground individuals in their communities and give them a sense of belonging, without which they would feel alienated, frustrated, and alone. They also give individuals greater meaning in life, imparting a standard by which they should conduct themselves and evaluate their behavior, institutions, and designs for social change. Most important to *Conservatives Against Capitalism*, this strain of conservativism believes that traditional institutions and culture rein in the excesses of capitalism and individual self-interests and temper the instability caused by the incessant demand for innovation, expansion, and change in the competitive market. For traditionalists, traditional culture and institutions like private property, as well as the notions of fair dealing, trust, and delayed gratification associated with the Protestant ethic rooted in religious institutions, make capitalism possible, both normatively and institutionally. At the same time, traditionalist conservatives' ambivalence about laissez-faire capitalism implies that it is a threat to tradition and traditional values. Though suspicious of political centralization, traditionalists see a role for the state in strengthening traditional values and institutions and guaranteeing social peace and stability. While traditionalists agree that capitalism weakens the traditions and values that they prize, they do not agree on which values and traditions are most urgently in need of conservation. And while they may agree that the state should play a role in defending traditional institutions and culture, they do not agree on what the state specifically should do.

Libertarian-inclined conservatives are most concerned with ensuring freedom and individualism. For them, society is an association made up of self-contained contractual relations among free individuals. Accordingly, any attempt to direct social relations in the name of the common good or transcendent values erodes individual freedom and leads to totalitarianism. For libertarians, the freedom of the individual is threatened by both the state and traditional institutions. In the words of Frank S. Meyer, a pivotal figure in post–World War II conservatism, "Unless men are free to be vicious they cannot be virtuous. No community can make them virtuous."[22] Unlike traditionalists, libertarians oppose state-sponsored social morality legislation as it pertains to the family and culture, and they advocate capitalism largely free of government regulation. They regard the free market as a fundamental component of political liberty and a bulwark against collectivism and the state, which they see as threats to individual liberty and community. Rather than a threat, capitalism is conducive to the development of individual character, as well as being the most efficient mechanism for the allocation of labor, goods, and services. More than any other economic arrangement, capitalism has led to unprecedented economic growth and has enabled large populations to live in material comfort. For libertarians, capitalism is inherently just and natural because it rewards talent, intelligence, ingenuity, hard work, and merit.

Both traditionalist and libertarian conservatives are hostile to the liberal welfare state because they view it as the product of social engineering experiments rooted in abstract rationality and beliefs in equality and human perfectibility. Libertarians contend that the fiscal and regulatory policy of the liberal welfare state is misguided, counterproductive, and an assault on individual freedom. For traditionalists, the liberal welfare state damages the family and local community by substituting liberal values, regulations, and entitlements offered by the state, thereby hollowing out the functions and authority of traditional institutions and the values they impart. Despite their shared opposition to the liberal welfare state, conservatives disagree on whether the free market or the concerns of traditional customs and institutions should take priority. Belief in the sanctity of private property and anti-Communism has been the glue holding traditionalists and libertarians uncomfortably together, particularly in the postwar era.[23] Indeed, the Cold War was a key moment in the evolution of this critical tradition, as anti-Communism transformed the conservative discourse regarding capitalism into a debate between capitalism and Communism and nothing in between.

Despite these disagreements, certain convictions unite conservatives as such and distinguish conservatism from other ideologies. The primary distinction of the conservatives, or those on the right, is their position on human equality and hierarchy and the constitution of a "good political community." According to Italian political philosopher Noberto Bobbio, the Left-Right distinction is that while acknowledging human equality and inequality, the Left believes "that what they [humans] have in common has greater value in the formation of a good community."[24] The Right, however, believes that "diversity," or human inequality, "has greater value in the formation of a good community."[25] For the Left, the inequalities that define our society are social and can be mitigated or removed through social engineering. Conversely, those on the right believe that these inequalities are natural and that society merely reflects these natural inequalities. These inequalities are what generate excellence and distinction in the world, and thus unequal social relations are the necessary condition for excellence and must be preserved.

It follows from this characterization of the Left and Right that conservatives believe that inequalities are natural and fundamental to a good society. As Corey Robin points out, conservatives believe that an egalitarian world will be "ugly, brutish, base, and dull." That is, for excellence to exist in the world, there also must be inequality and hierarchy.[26] Without inequality and hierarchy, and the power to command that comes with it, a world of distinction or excellence is not possible. It is this conviction—that a world of excellence requires inequality, hierarchy, and the power of some to dominate and control others—that unites conservatives. According to James Henry Hammond, a slave owner and an early critic of capitalism,

> In all social systems there must be a class to do the menial duties, to perform the drudgery of life. That is, a class requiring but a low order

of intellect and but little skill. Its requisites are vigor, docility, fidelity. Such a class you must have, or you would not have that other class which leads progress, civilization, and refinement.[27]

Perhaps less crudely but essentially making the same point, Russell Kirk maintained that among conservatism's core principles was a belief that "civilized society requires orders and classes" because "society longs for leadership."[28] What unites the conservatives here is their belief that laissez-faire capitalism distorts and robs the world of excellence. To be sure, capitalism creates its own hierarchy, founded on accumulation of wealth, which conservatives, even those critical of capitalism, defend. Nonetheless, traditionalist conservative critics believed that the organizing principle of capitalist hierarchy founded exclusively on economic laissez-faire was debased.

Beginning in the antebellum period and extending to the present, conservative critics of capitalism have defined excellence differently, criticizing laissez-faire capitalism and alternatives to it rooted in different social bases. Some were slave owners, and others abhorred slavery. Some were nationalists, and others were sectionalists. Some were elitist, and others were populists. Some accepted the concentration of business and industry, and others advocated for the economic decentralization of industry. Some defended the welfare state, and others wanted to see it circumscribed. In other words, over the span of 180 years, conservative critics of capitalism have been fairly heterogeneous. What unites them is their belief that laissez-faire capitalism has undermined an established social hierarchy governed by the virtuous or excellent. The aim of this aspect of the conservative critique of capitalism has been to reconfigure the ruling class and cultural values away from the exclusive rule of economic calculation. The critique of the "Economic Man" and the priority of economic values run throughout this tradition of thought. Even when the "businessman" or the "capitalist" is the representative of the "virtuous ruling class," his economic interests need to be tempered by other concerns, whether this is America's hegemonic role as the "benevolent empire" or the protector of the nation's white-ethnic heritage from free trade and immigration.

Conservative critics of capitalism saw themselves, according to Viereck, as fighting on "two fronts," against both "the atomistic disunity of unregulated capitalism and the bureaucratic mechanical unity of modern socialism."[29] Each of the conservative critics that I will discuss was intellectually engaged in defending a social order based on a specific class hierarchy perceived as being challenged by representatives of "Economic Man" and by workers and racial minorities fighting against inequality via the state. The specter of socialism or communism and the belief that the liberal welfare state put the United States on a "road to serfdom" were crucial motivations for conservatives' defense of the privilege and domination of (various but specific) elites from the demands of greater equality, democracy, and a nonhierarchical social order.

Movements from below were not the only targets of conservatives' criticism. For conservative critics of capitalism, business and industrial elites were targets as well. The defense of paternalistic relations and the idealization of noblesse oblige, which conservatives found wanting in a social order ruled by capitalists, are consistent themes in this tradition. The call for "responsible" leadership was embodied by different elite classes, but even when conservative critics of capitalism embraced the capitalists as the legitimate ruling class, they urged them to step up to the expectations and responsibilities of a ruling class.

Thinkers in this tradition of conservatism believed that the class rule of the specific social order they defended was more effective in preserving the hierarchical power relations of domination and control than was a society ruled by economic interests and priorities alone. They believed that their preferred social order, headed by slave owners, warrior-aristocrats, or white ethnic middle-American populists, offered an opportunity for individual distinction that embodied and transmitted the "best" of Western civilization. Thus, it follows that conservative critics of capitalism were neither reflexive statists nor anti-statists. Instead, their evaluation of the state's role in economic life depended on their belief that the state was oriented to, and acted on behalf of, what they believed to be conservative principles, values, and class interests.

CRITICISM OF CAPITALISM: A CONSERVATIVE TRADITION

The defenders of slavery were the first conservatives to offer a critique of capitalism. The language of their criticism was similar to that of later leftists. Like many leftists, these conservatives viewed capitalism as exploiting, alienating, and immiserating the producing classes. That is, capitalism inculcated a self-centered and self-interested economic individualism; it created a class of dependent but difficult to control "wage slaves"; and it undermined the traditional institutions that historically had restrained individualism and forestalled class antagonism. Critics like George Fitzhugh and James Henry Hammond contrasted what they saw as the social decay and class conflict in the capitalist North with an idealized vision of order, community, and mutual regard located on Southern slave plantations governed by the benevolent, paternalistic hand of the slave owner. Central to these early critics was the belief that purely economic relations separated the various forms of obligation that people (unequals) had to one another and to the social institutions to which they belonged. The class conflict that these exploitative relations caused, along with the capitalist ruling class's priority for profits, threatened the unequal and hierarchical relations necessary for civilization and produced a recipe for revolution.

By the turn of the twentieth century, American capitalism had expanded throughout the continental United States and no longer was a fledgling manufacturing upstart but a corporate industrial economic power dominated by an elite that ruled over a compliant government and a growing and restive industrial working class. In this context, thinkers and politicians such as Theodore Roosevelt and Brooks Adams did not reject corporate industrial capitalism but proposed major reforms to it and challenged the unrestrained rule of economic elites. For Roosevelt and Adams, the selfish pursuit of private interest and economic competition created a culture focused on egoism and commerce that was leading the nation toward internal discord and international weakness. Capitalist greed made capital an "irresponsible sovereign" that created fertile ground for radicals, revolutionaries, and other agitators to prey on people's discontent. Even though Roosevelt and Adams believed that capitalism created the great wealth necessary for a modern, powerful nation, they also held that capitalist rapacity and plutocracy was endangering the capitalist system itself, that corporate capitalism needed to be regulated in order to save itself. To accomplish this, Roosevelt and Adams envisioned a strong, active, imperial state administered by an enlightened bureaucratic apparatus that would channel the financial and industrial power of American capital toward the construction of an American empire that was at once a world-historical civilizing mission, a necessity for America's economic vitality, a safety valve for class conflict, and an arena for elite regeneration.

Later in the century, the Southern Agrarians, including John Crowe Ransom, Allen Tate, Frank Lawrence Owsley, Lyle H. Lanier, Andrew Nelson Lytle, and Donald Davidson, provided a new, more radical indictment of capitalism. In the three decades following World War I, the American South had undergone massive economic, demographic, and social changes. The decline of small farms and the corporate expansion into agriculture, both before and during the New Deal, had had a profound impact on the "Southern way of life," threatening communities, local hierarchies, and the racial caste system. Influenced by slave owners' critiques, the Southern Agrarians indicted capitalism as an economic system that would destroy community and personal relations, that the corporate capitalism that Roosevelt and Adams tried to defend via regulation would destroy an inherently traditional and conservative yeoman class. The Southern Agrarians' alternative called for a radical program of corporate expropriation, decentralization, and the redistribution of land to landless whites based on the model of an agrarian republic. They sought to restore the social, economic, and political landscape dominated by a populist yeoman class of white farmers living according to the rhythms of nature, in awe of God, and rooted to their local community, culture, and heritage. At the foundation of this society was a set of hierarchical race relations of domination and control (legal, social, political, and economic).

Between 1945 and 1965, American conservatism underwent a deep transformation. The liberal welfare state erected in President Franklin

Delano Roosevelt's New Deal was the political context and a real turning point for debates over the direction of modern American conservatism in general and for the conservative tradition critical of capitalism in particular. The conservatives' political critique thus shifted its emphasis to the state as the federal government's size, scope, and capability were drastically increased during the New Deal and World War II. The development of the state during this time ushered in major changes in American political economy, among the most important being the construction of the modern welfare state, which, through the regulatory regime, social insurance, and collective bargaining, softened the harshest effects of capitalism and incorporated the working class into the economic order. To be sure, strikes and other labor actions were commonplace in the 1940s and 1950s, but revolution was no longer on labor's agenda. As the lives of America's white workers improved, at least in part thanks to the welfare state, conservative critics of capitalism also turned from concerns about economic crisis and impending revolution to capitalist culture.

The publication of *The Road to Serfdom* in 1945 (and its subsequent serialization in *Reader's Digest*) by Friedrich Hayek and *Human Action* in 1949 by Ludwig von Mises revived skepticism of economic planning, including the New Deal variety, and resurrected the libertarian defense of capitalism, which had been rendered suspect by the Great Depression. In 1949, Peter Viereck published *Conservatism Revisited: A Revolt Against Revolt*, which sought to divorce conservatism from being merely a legitimization of capitalist wealth, and in 1955, Clinton Rossiter's *Conservatism in America* distinguished American conservatism rooted in the thought of Burke from Manchester liberalism or a defense of laissez-faire capitalism.

Viereck, Rossiter, and other postwar thinkers on the right revived a brand of conservatism that esteemed traditional values, stability, order, and community but distanced themselves from the Southern Agrarians' nostalgia for the Old South. Unlike earlier critics, they seldom addressed the effects of capitalism and the exploitation of workers. Despite the relatively tempered nature of their critiques, postwar conservatives had heated debates over how to contain the threats to community and conservative values posed by both laissez-faire capitalism and the burgeoning liberal welfare state.

Viereck argued that the natural dynamism of the capitalist system destroyed community and produced atomized, alienated individuals who would gravitate to fascism or communism.[30] He observed that the proper task of conservatism was to preserve the established order, which in the postwar era included the regulatory and welfare state. He supported some New Deal programs and the unionization of labor as a means of restoring community within a dynamic capitalist system and a defense against more radical demands.[31] Robert Nisbet, by contrast, focused his criticism on the propensity of the state, rather than the capitalist economy, to centralize and monopolize. For him, capitalism was made possible by the growth of a powerful state, which destroyed centers of authority lodged in traditional institutions and communities.[32] In *The Quest for Community*, Nisbet argued that a centralized state and big capital undermined the communities and associations that helped restrain rapacious and exploitative individualism. In the tradition of Burke, Nisbet felt that capitalism depended on non-capitalistic entities for its survival.[33] Although he recognized that a centralized power like the state or monopoly capital was more efficient at delivering social services than traditional associations were, he worried that the functions of the family, the church, and the local community would inevitably be co-opted and that without these institutions, society would become susceptible to totalitarianism.[34]

In the 1950s, the philosophical tension and the public policy debates within conservatism between economic libertarianism and social traditionalism dominated conservative discourse in the 1950s and 1960s. Philosophical synthesis was the defining project of the new postwar conservatism, and no one was more important in this project than William F. Buckley Jr. and Frank S. Meyer. Buckley was founder and chief editor of the *National Review*, the most important conservative journal at the time. Meyer was the philosophical founder of conservative "fusion," which attempted to synthesize laissez-faire capitalism with social traditionalism. Despite the recent memory of the Great Depression, economic libertarian ideas began to make a comeback on the right in the years following World War II, and critiques of the welfare state intensified as the purported threat of the Soviet Union consumed American politics. Although Meyer's version of conservatism was never universally accepted by traditionalists like Kirk, fusion became the philosophical orientation of both the *National Review* and the conservative mainstream as the journal defined it. Viereck's brand of conservatism, which rejected laissez-faire capitalism and endorsed the welfare state, was far too liberal for Meyer and for Buckley's *National Review*, and by the mid-1950s, Viereck was effectively banished from the conservative movement.[35]

As Michael Lind has written, despite conservatives' attempts at ideological cohesion in the 1950s and 1960s, "the glaring contradiction between social conservatism and radical, destabilizing capitalism had not been resolved—but conservatives pretended it had been."[36] Indeed, conservatives may not have resolved their philosophical disputes, but it became evident that the focus of their criticism had shifted from capitalism and the state to only the state. Postwar conservative critics did not vilify capitalism in the way that earlier conservative critics had done. Nor did they lionize the capitalist as exponents of "democratic capitalism," such as Michael Novak and George Gilder, and as some neoconservatives would begin to do in the 1970s. Beyond the standard defense of private property and the common conservative formulation that economic freedom in the form of free enterprise is the basis of all other freedoms, capitalism was not prominent in the postwar conservatives' narrative. Instead, they focused on the state and, tellingly, the political demands of women and racial minorities, groups that had been left out of the New Deal order, as the principal threats to the established social order.[37]

In the postwar era, conservatives recalibrated their critiques of capitalism. A marked difference between postwar critics like Viereck and Nisbet and more contemporary critics is that the latter viewed the capitalist or "entrepreneur" as doing God's work.[38] They saw capitalism as a force for moral regeneration rather than an arena of coercion.[39] This change in conservative thinking is in many ways attributable to conservatives' reaction to the cultural criticisms of the social, political, and economic institutions offered by the New Left and the black radical movements in the late 1960s. The deindustrialization and financialization of American capitalism, which already were evident in the 1960s and led to major economic crisis in the 1970s, are contextually important, but without a cohesive, militant labor movement demanding substantive changes in the economic system, the threat from the left was primarily to the cultural justification of capitalism rather than to its economic mechanisms of competition, profit, and the exploitation of labor. This led to neoconservatives worrying that capitalism was undergoing a "crisis of legitimacy" that, they feared, would threaten the entire political and economic system. Their remedy was for capitalists to engage in ideological and political struggle to defend the economic system and their class rule. The neoconservatives—and Irving Kristol in particular—popularized the recovery of the Protestant ethic in market relations and rehabilitated the capitalist as the embodiment of the meritocratic society.

Like Theodore Roosevelt and Viereck, the neoconservatives—including Irving Kristol, Daniel Bell, William Kristol, Robert Kagan, and David Brooks—argued that state intervention in economic life is not always antithetical to conservative principles. Unlike Roosevelt, who constructed the early fragments of the regulatory state, and Viereck, who sought to conserve the liberal welfare state of the New Deal, the neoconservatives formulated a specifically conservative welfare state. Irving Kristol was a forceful advocate for cutting many welfare-state programs, especially those of the Great Society, and he was an early convert to supply-side economics, but he would not go so far as to dismantle the New Deal welfare state entirely. "The godfather of neoconservatism," as Kristol was affectionately called, was an early standard-bearer for what came to be known as "Big Government" conservatism.

The neoconservative critique of capitalism had two currents, both of which are in the realm of "cultural critiques of capitalism." The first was offered by Irving Kristol and Daniel Bell, who argued that capitalism weakened its own moral foundations. Specifically, drawing on the work of Max Weber, Bell contended that postindustrial consumer capitalism cut off the Protestant ethic from bourgeois society, thereby threatening such bourgeois virtues as hard work, thrift, saving, and delayed gratification, which reined in capitalist excess and economic inequality. Without the virtues inculcated by the Protestant ethic, capitalism had no cultural justification (for accumulation) beyond hedonism, which, Bell believed, made capitalism culturally bankrupt. Bell continued to believe that the "cultural contradictions of capitalism" had yet to be resolved, whereas Kristol and other neoconservatives were convinced that supply-side economics offered the proper incentives for reviving the Protestant ethic.

The other current in the neoconservatives' "cultural critique of capitalism" contends that an overemphasis on economic values precludes America from its "grand destiny" to advance civilization as the global hegemon.[40] As Theodore Roosevelt observed nearly a century earlier, neoconservatives believe that the nation needs to be rescued from its boredom, decadence, and narrow focus on self-gratification. William Kristol, Robert D. Kagan, and David Brooks continued their predecessors' cultural critique of capitalism, but rather than locating America's regeneration in the recovery of the Protestant ethic, they (particularly Kristol and Kagan) see Americans' "remoralization" as requiring a "remoralization of American foreign policy."[41] Contemporary capitalism, neoconservatives claim, undermines masculinity, martial values, civic responsibility, national unity, and strength. It has created individuals and a national character unbefitting a strong nation and empire.[42] As an antidote, neoconservatives have pushed for a renewed imperial project to mitigate the egoistic values that capitalism fosters, to renew a spirit of national community, and to realize America's potential as the global "benevolent hegemon."[43]

Finally, the other contemporary conservative critics of capitalism are the paleoconservatives, which include Patrick J. Buchanan and Samuel T. Francis. They offer a populist, white-ethnocentric critique of laissez-faire capitalism, the liberal welfare state, and free trade. Like neoconservatives, paleoconservatives do not indict the productive relations under capitalism as inherently exploitative or alienating, and they embrace both economic inequality as natural and the reward of success derived from talent and hard work.[44] Paleoconservatives, however, lament how the free movement of finance, goods, and people under global capitalism—a system they see as orchestrated by international economic elites and compliant liberal-state actors—threatens the ethnic, racial, and linguistic groups that have built and maintained the republican tradition of the United States. Worship of the market and of profits gives capitalism a cosmopolitan ethic that endangers American independence and its culture and ethnic identity, which, in the words of President Donald Trump, "make America great." Moreover, under a "free-trade" regime, multinational corporations are free to pursue profits wherever they find them and to not identify with a sovereign nation. That is, the interests of American-owned multinational corporations are no longer aligned with the nation and instead compete with it while undermining American-based businesses and the white ethnic "Middle Americans" they employ.

True to Viereck's formulation that conservatives "fight on two fronts," the paleoconservatives regard "Middle Americans" as threatened by free-trade, global-capitalist elites; by labor unions and the poor; by immigrants that are "displacing and dispossessing" the native born from employment; and by the liberal welfare state that is robbing them of their earned income.[45] Paleoconservatism embodies the contemporary white populism that has its roots in the backlash to the gains of the civil rights movement and anxieties about the structural changes in the economy since the 1970s. The paleoconservatives' populism, however, stops short of challenging capitalism or hierarchical class relations. Instead, it seeks to preserve those relations by redirecting them in the service of a culturally homogeneous white-ethnic nationalism.[46]

Long a minority proclivity among conservative intellectuals and the Republican Party, paleoconservative ideas, if not the label, surged during Donald Trump's campaign for the presidency, which placed, at least for 2016, economic nationalism and xenophobia at the center of the Republican Party's vision. Whatever Trump's popularity may suggest about the candidate, the party, or the American voter, he has tapped into a deep-seated frustration with the political and economic establishment. Trump's popularity among conservative voters turned out to be more than just a reality-show phenomenon and has prompted much soul-searching among conservative intellectuals and party leaders, and rightfully so.[47] For more than forty years, under both Republican and Democratic administrations, conservative political economy has been hegemonic. It has consisted of tax cuts (largely for the wealthy), privatization, deregulation, a shrinking welfare state, the evisceration of organized labor, and an expanding security-military industrial complex, resulting in stagnant wages, eroding employee benefits, increased employment insecurity, and perpetual war. For decades, working people in America have endured one economic crisis after another. Yet perhaps surprisingly, contemporary conservatives have neglected to critically engage with capitalism as a system that structures the material life of the United States and its people. If the conservative philosopher Richard Weaver was correct—and I think he was—when he wrote that "ideas have consequences," then both the current state of American political economy and the presidency of Donald Trump are consequences of conservative ideas.[48]

In chapter 1, I examine the critiques of capitalism offered by Southern defenders of slavery such as John C. Calhoun, James Henry Hammond, and George Fitzhugh in the decades leading up to the Civil War. Chapter 2 analyzes the critiques of Brooks Adams and Theodore Roosevelt and their commitment to statism and imperialism as alternatives to a disintegrating decadent capitalism. The subject of chapter 3 is the Southern Agrarian indictment of industrial capitalism and the yeoman farmer ideal to which they pointed as an alternative. Chapter 4 examines the critiques of capitalism offered by post–World War II conservatives such as Peter Viereck, Russell Kirk, and Robert Nisbet and their attempt to disentangle conservatism from laissez-faire capitalism and to define a modern conservative alternative to the liberal welfare state. Chapter 5 explores the neoconservatives' cultural critique of capitalism, how they reconciled conservatism with capitalism through supply-side economics, and their critique of how the culture of capitalism undermines the quest for empire. Finally, chapter 6 analyzes the populist, nationalistic, and xenophobic critiques of global capitalism by paleoconservative thinkers Patrick Buchanan and Samuel Francis, whose brand of conservatism (until Trump resurrected it) resided on the fringes of contemporary conservatism.

1

EMERGING CAPITALISM AND ITS
CONSERVATIVE CRITICS

*The Pro-Slavery Critique of Capitalism
in Antebellum America*

Capital is a cruel master.

George Fitzhugh, *Cannibals All! Or Slaves Without Masters*

Defenders of slavery such as John C. Calhoun (1782–1850), James Henry Hammond (1807–1864), and George Fitzhugh (1806–1881) understood that a conservative society, culture, and politics require a stable economic base. They believed that at its core, capitalism, particularly its laissez-faire variant, is unstable, that periodically the capitalist market undergoes what economists call "corrections." These necessary corrections are inherent in a capitalist economy and result in a whole host of social, political, economic, and cultural consequences. Therefore, as Karl Marx, Joseph Schumpeter, and a long line of American conservatives concluded, capitalism is by its nature revolutionary and unstable. With this key insight in mind, the defenders of slavery, the warrior-aristocrats, and the Southern Agrarians were among the most penetrating critics of laissez-faire capitalism in the American conservative tradition. They imagined alternatives to laissez-faire that rejected socialism, promised greater economic stability, and preserved inequality and its accompanying forms of domination and control.

Pro-slavery thought indicates that challenging the hegemony of capitalist thinking in the United States has a long history among thinkers on the political right. Indeed, for decades in the antebellum period, capitalism was questioned not only in the realm of ideas but also in the South's social and economic relations. As Eugene Genovese wrote, the "slaveholders presented the only politically powerful challenge to liberal capitalism to emanate from within the United States."[1] In the realm of ideas, pro-slavery thinkers provided the right's most direct critique of capitalism in American thought.[2] Their strand of traditional conservatism elevated inequality and hierarchy as historically rooted, necessary, and desirable. Pro-slavery thinkers also confronted the central tension in conservatism between the revolutionary nature of capitalism and the stable rootedness of a traditional social, cultural, political, and economic order. Later conservatives attempted to do the same, but unlike them, the defenders of slavery could point to an existing alternative in slavery. Pro-slavery thinkers then tried to resolve this tension by rejecting capitalism outright, as did Fitzhugh, or by circumscribing the expansion of capitalism, as Calhoun and Hammond attempted to do. Either way, for them Southern slave society was decidedly not capitalist. For defenders of slavery, the slave system, and not capitalism, was the economic foundation consistent with a conservative social order on which the progress of civilization depended.

To contemporary readers, it might seem rather shocking to find that Southern intellectuals not only defended slavery as a social good but also believed that it was a social system superior to that of capitalism. Furthermore, such a belief was not a marginal one held by a few cranks but by respected thinkers and statesmen of the antebellum South, the most famous of whom that I will discuss is John C. Calhoun.[3] Calhoun was twice elected vice president of the United States, secretary of war under President James Monroe, and secretary of state under President John Tyler, and in addition, he was an impressive orator and senator from South Carolina. He was also an influential political theorist who championed nullification (the right of states to nullify a federal law that they believed to be unconstitutional) and developed the concept of a concurrent majority as a mechanism to protect the rights of a minority from the legislation of a numerical majority. His *Disquisition on Government* is the most famous and systematic example of his thought on the nature and theory of government.[4]

Lesser known than Calhoun, James Henry Hammond was also an influential pro-slavery thinker and critic of capitalism. He was a planter and elected official from South Carolina, for which he served as the state's representative to the U.S. House of Representatives, one term as governor of the state, and as its U.S. senator until the state succeeded from the Union in 1860. Both Calhoun and Hammond were slave owners.

Perhaps the most iconoclastic of the defenders of slavery and the most ardent conservative critic of capitalism was George Fitzhugh. Like Calhoun and Hammond, Fitzhugh was a slave owner. Unlike the two other men, however, he did not serve in elected office but did serve in various government positions, including some for the Confederacy during the Civil War and for the Freedman's Bureau after the war. Fitzhugh was a tireless writer on behalf of the antebellum South, the institution of slavery, and the conservatism embodied by the two. He published several books, including *Sociology for the South* and *Cannibals All!*, in which he defended slavery not on racial grounds, although he thought that blacks were racially inferior to whites, but on abstract grounds as a superior form of social organization. In addition to his books, Fitzhugh frequently published in *De Bow's Review*, the most important pro-slavery journal of the period, as well as in other publications.

Central to pro-slavery thinkers' critique of capitalism and their defense of slavery was their indictment of the wage system as a key source of social disorder, radicalism, and revolutionary upheaval. At its core, the pro-slavery critique of capitalism is that the domination and control of the stronger class, the one with the right and obligation to rule over the weaker classes, was not sufficiently complete under a free-labor system. The result was that the "front ranks"—to use Calhoun's terminology—did not exert enough control over the laboring masses and that in turn, the working class lost any sense of allegiance to their social superiors and established institutions.

In contrast to the disintegrative effects of the Northern free-labor system, pro-slavery thinkers argued, the paternalistic order of the Old South was better equipped to attenuate the antagonism between the owners of the means of production and the laboring masses. In contrast to the wage system, their model of socioeconomic relations constituted a paternalism characterized by the lifelong reciprocal duties and responsibilities associated with those of an extended family.[5] The defenders of slavery believed that the master-slave relationship embodied these social ties beyond the kin relationship and made the relationship between unequals more rational, humane, mutually beneficial, socially desirable, and necessary.

The Southern slaveholder critique of capitalism had its roots in, and was closely bound to, the defense of slavery from attacks by abolitionist intellectuals, journalists, members of the clergy, and sympathetic elected officials in the United States and Europe.[6] Pro-slavery thinkers used explicitly racist arguments to justify their racial and class domination. Blacks were not thought to be rational, and unless they were coerced into labor by slave masters, they would resort to laziness or criminal behavior. This paternalistic view placed an obligation on the slaveholders of the South to protect blacks from their inevitable destitution in a free, competitive society for which they were, by nature, ill equipped.[7] The defenders of slavery used critiques of the free-labor system against abolitionists who attacked Southern slavery, but they ignored the brutalization, misery, and suffering of the wage laborers in the industrial cities in the North and in England. Needless to say, the slaveholder critique of capitalism and their concomitant defense of the South's "peculiar institution" were arguments of a self-interested ruling class intent on preserving their racial and class privilege. Their analysis of the social consequences of capitalism is insightful, however, because they saw themselves and the Old South as a distinct social order. For them, capitalism fostered class warfare and a spirit of selfish individualism, and it made radical ideas widely appealing, all of which were ingredients for a revolutionary upheaval and a return to barbarism. In the words of Fitzhugh, a "free society," of which the wage-labor system was a central component, "everywhere begets Isms, and . . . Isms soon beget bloody revolutions."[8] In protecting Southern slavery and seeking its expansion to territories and would-be states on the continent, the Caribbean, and Central America, defenders of slavery saw their system as a bulwark of republican freedom and Western civilization defending against the radicalism of both the abolitionists and the working classes that were unleashed by capitalism.[9]

THE EXPANSION OF SLAVERY AND THE EMERGENCE OF CAPITALISM IN THE UNITED STATES

The intellectual and political debate over the issue of slavery and abolition has had a long history in America, stretching back to the colonial era, and slavery has been defended on numerous, sometimes contradictory, grounds. These have included the practical necessity of slavery as essential to the economic development of the South and the United States; slavery as a means of averting race war; ethical and theological justifications for slavery cited in scripture and arguing that it served God's purpose by "civilizing" and "Christianizing" Africans; pseudoscientific evidence contending that blacks are physiologically and intellectually inferior to whites;[10] and slavery justified in the abstract as the proper station for the "inferior," irrespective of race. Beginning in the 1830s, these justifications for slavery were joined with arguments stressing its positive aspects, that it was comparatively more beneficial for slaveholders, slaves, society, and republican institutions than was the system of free labor. According to Peter Kolchin, in the late antebellum period the defense of slavery became "less hesitant, tentative, and apologetic . . . more insistent on the positive virtues of slavery and the society it fostered."[11] Drew Gilpin Faust, one of the foremost scholars of antebellum pro-slavery thought, suggests that the defense of slavery in the 1830s changed in both "style and tone" and "substance."[12] She contends that pro-slavery thought became more "self-conscious and systematic" as a reaction to the strengthening of antislave sentiment following the Missouri debates in 1818 to 1820 and the flood of abolitionist propaganda in the 1830s.[13] Indeed, a key abolitionist argument against slavery following the Missouri Compromise was that as slavery expanded to the western territories, it would shut out free labor from these lands.

But the substantive change in the proslavery narrative had to do with more than defenses against the abolitionists' rhetorical attacks. After 1830, slave-based cotton production became more and more important to the Southern economy because of the demand from merchants and textile manufacturers in Northern cities and, more important, from manufacturers in England. Slaveholders no longer viewed slavery as a "white man's burden" but as a positive good for all.[14] According to historian Eric Foner, "On the eve of the Civil War, it [cotton] represented well over half the total value of American exports. In 1860, the economic investment represented by the slave population exceeded the value of the nation's factories, railroads, and banks combined."[15] Slaveholders saw the South as distinct from the rest of the capitalist world, but they recognized at the same time that it was closely intertwined with the international capitalist market. Indeed, the price of cotton, tobacco, and other agricultural products central to the Southern economy were subject to price fluctuations on the international market. British textile manufacturers were heavily dependent on Southern cotton, and Britain was its largest consumer and the U.S. South was its largest supplier. The growing demand for Southern cotton therefore made the institution and expansion of slavery a lucrative venture.

As Sven Beckert pointed out, increases in the price of cotton resulted in the territorial expansion of the crop. Cotton planters' "migration to Alabama and Louisiana, and eventually to Mississippi, Arkansas, and Texas," he wrote, "was choreographed to the movement of cotton prices."[16] Rather than gradually dying out, as early-nineteenth-century abolitionists believed that it would, the institution of slavery expanded as new states were admitted into the Union. The annexation of huge tracts of territory as a result of the Mexican War, the popular-sovereignty provisions of the Compromise of 1850, and the enactment of the Kansas-Nebraska Act guaranteed the further expansion of slavery nearly to the Pacific coast. The appetite for uncultivated land and thus the expansion of slavery was so great, in fact, that before the Civil War, slaveholders, Southern politicians, and various adventurers envisioned a Southern empire annexing the Caribbean and Central America.[17] "I want Cuba, and I know that sooner or later we must have it," stated Mississippi Senator Albert G. Brown. He continued:

If the worm-eaten throne of Spain is willing to give it up for a fair equivalent, well—if not, we must take it. I want Tamaulipas, Potosi, and one or two other Mexican states; and I want them all for the same reason—for the planting or spreading of slavery. And a footing in Central America will powerfully aid us in acquiring those other states.

Yes, I want these countries for the spread of slavery. I would spread the blessings of slavery, like the religion of our Divine Master, to the utmost ends of the earth, and rebellions and wicked as the Yankees have been, I would even extend it to them.[18]

Thus, at the beginning of the Civil War, the institution of slavery was not gradually fading away but instead was boldly expansionist and central to the American economy, subjugated more people, and governed more territory than ever before in the nation's history.

For the defenders of slavery, the Old South had distinctive characteristics distinguishing it from the free-labor North.[19] Southerners firmly believed that a paternalism rooted in race-based slave-productive relations influenced all other forms of social life in the antebellum South. Therefore, an attack on slavery was perceived as a direct attack on all of Southern civilization. As Kolchin observes, in the half century before the Civil War, slavery, racism, and the idea of the South were inseparable in pro-slavery intellectual discourse.[20] Indeed, many pro-slavery thinkers argued that the virtuous character and distinction of gentlemen and ladies of the South were directly linked to the existence of slavery. Writing about the courage, intellect, and hospitable nature of the Southern gentleman and the chastity and devotion of Southern ladies, Hammond stated, "My decided opinion is that our system of slavery contributes largely to the development and culture of those high and noble qualities."[21] While few defenders of slavery would go so far as Fitzhugh and Hammond did to defend slavery in the abstract as an appropriate system regardless of race, the even more tempered pro-slavery critics of the free-labor system, like Calhoun, highlighted the benefits to civilization resulting from the slave system in the South.

In the years between the War of 1812 and the Civil War, the United States was a nation in the midst of significant economic and political transformation. Advancements in the areas of machine technology, transportation in the form of canals and railroads, and communication (telegraph) all changed the nature of the American economy. In particular, an improved power loom transformed the manufacture of textiles from a cottage industry into America's first factory system.[22] Many of the factories that adopted the new technology were located in New England, making the region the nucleus of the domestic textile industry for decades to come. In this way, a predominantly rural agrarian nation was becoming urban and industrialized. The populations of established East Coast cities like New York, Philadelphia, Boston, and Baltimore multiplied, thanks to the large number of immigrants fleeing the European Continent and the marked decrease in death rates as a result of a more stable food supply.[23]

As the North began to industrialize, its manufacturing output and wage-labor employment surged dramatically. Between 1800 and 1860, the self-employed and the slave labor-force in the United States quadrupled, but the wage-earner labor force grew twentyfold.[24] According to Eric Foner, by 1860 the number of wage earners outnumbered the self-employed members of the American labor force.[25] The changing character of American capitalism, especially in the North, from one characterized by small independent producers to one that was becoming industrial and based on wage labor signaled the social and political changes to come and caused a further rift between the North and South.[26] The tariff issue became particularly contentious as manufacturing concerns in the industrializing North welcomed tariffs while the South grew more dependent on the export of cotton. Owing to the profitability of Southern cotton on the international market, Southern interests concerning slavery and the tariff had many influential advocates in the North. New York City bankers and merchants like August Belmont were politically connected supporters of the South right up to the Civil War.[27] Whereas Northern manufacturers viewed the tariff as essential to protect the development of U.S. industry, cotton merchants and slave owners perceived it as impeding international trade and impoverishing the South through British retaliation in the form of duties on Southern cotton. "The American Tariff," wrote Hammond, "is neither more or less than a system by which the slave states are plundered for the benefit of those states which do not tolerate slavery."[28]

Thinkers from across the political spectrum sensed that the social, political, and economic world that they had known in the first few decades since the nation's founding was being radically altered by the expansion of the market and wage-labor capitalism. The late-eighteenth-century economy, characterized by home manufacture, small artisan shops, and family farms, was gradually replaced by machines and the cheap unskilled labor needed to operate them. Open conflict between a rising capitalist class and a growing wage-earning working class became more frequent and intense.[29] Workers banded together to form laboring societies and organized working men's political parties. Through these associations, the working class participated in labor actions with increasing frequency, demanding higher wages, a right to strike, a ten-hour workday, restrictions on monopoly, a redistribution of property, as well as political rights.[30] These popular democratic movements pushed the political system toward greater inclusiveness and political equality by winning universal white manhood suffrage. In the four decades before the Civil War, the states amended their constitutions by dropping property qualifications for the franchise. By 1860, every state in the Union had eliminated property qualifications for the vote.[31] Radical republicans' indictments of capitalism emphasized the ways in which the wage system robbed the laborer of the fruits of his labor and made his condition miserable while enriching the owners of capital. They warned against the danger to republican institutions resulting from the vast inequality of wealth and power produced by emerging capitalism. For them, emerging industrial capitalism signaled a form of domination and dependence characteristic of European feudalism and Southern chattel slavery.[32]

Radical reformers in the mid-nineteenth century sought to liberate workers from the oppression of capitalist domination by taking on the banks, breaking up large industrial enterprises, and advocating for policies directed toward greater economic equality. Their schemes were informed by the Declaration of Independence and the civic republicanism of the anti-Federalists. For conservative thinkers, however, liberal ideas of natural rights, equality, the contractual nature of society, and government were erroneous philosophical abstractions with no basis in experience. According to Hammond in *A Letter to an English Abolitionist*, "I repudiate, as ridiculously absurd, that much lauded but nowhere accredited dogma of Mr. Jefferson, that 'all men are born equal.'"[33] Indeed, some pro-slavery thinkers like Fitzhugh rejected the totality of liberal social contract philosophy and grounded their arguments in the ancients and their more modern progenitors like Robert Filmer. Others, like Calhoun, who did not discard all of liberal theory, worried that notions of equality and liberty, combined with the miserable conditions of the Northern working class, would lead to popular inroads against property and all established institutions.[34] According to Fitzhugh,

> All modern philosophy converges to a single point—the overthrow of all government, the substitution of the untrammeled "Sovereignty of the Individual" for the Sovereignty of Society, and the inauguration of anarchy. First domestic slavery, next religious institutions, then separate property, then political government, and, finally, family government and family relations, are to be swept away. This is the distinctly avowed programme of all able abolitionists and socialists.[35]

Southern defenders of slavery worried that the insecurity, misery, and exploitation experienced by the laboring classes under capitalism would lead them to communitarian or associationalist, radical agrarian, and socialist ideas that were gaining a foothold in Britain and in the United States. Unlike the North and western Europe, the slaveholding South was protected from the "remarkable religious Isms . . . Mormonism and Millerism . . . Shakers, Rappists, Dunkers, Socialists, Fourrierists, and the like" because, as Hammond wrote, the South offered "no material here for such characters to operate upon."[36] Were these doctrines to gain a mass following, as conservatives continually worried they might, then the whole edifice of Western civilization would crumble.

THE CONSERVATIVE CRITIQUE OF CAPITALIST EXPLOITATION AND IMMISERATION

The pro-slavery critics of capitalism were not philosophically united. Some expounded a racial theory of slavery suggesting that it was appropriate only for an inferior race of people. Others repudiated the race theory of slavery and defended it in the abstract as "the natural and normal condition of labor whether white or black."[37] Most pro-slavery thinkers rejected the assumptions of Lockean liberalism and erected their defenses of slavery on the basis of experience, tradition, and natural inequality. Even Calhoun, who retained liberal assumptions regarding progress, concurrent majorities, and the contractual nature of American political institutions, qualified the notion that "all men are created equal" to mean equality under the law, for white men, at least.[38] Likewise, many believed that slavery and capitalism were not mutually exclusive. Despite their differences, pro-slavery thinkers were united in regarding capitalism as exploitative and leading to social upheaval. They were united, too, in believing that the less exploitative nature of slavery versus wage labor and the near total domination and control of slave owners were the socioeconomic arrangements that not only persevered in society but also created the conditions for it to flourish.

Along with classical liberals, republicans, and socialists, Southern conservatives believed that wealth and value were the products of the labor that had been expended to create them. According to Calhoun:

> Let those who are interested remember that labor is the only source of wealth, and how small a portion of it, in all old and civilized countries, even the best governed, is left to those by whose labor wealth is created. Let them also reflect, how little volition, or agency the operatives in any country have in the question of its distribution—as little, with a few exceptions, as the African of the slave holding States has in the distribution of the proceeds of his labor.[39]

For the defenders of slavery, the exploitation of labor had existed in every form of civilization. In their view, the inequality and exploitation in the slave South were no worse than the exploitation of labor in any other civilization. Indeed, pro-slavery thinkers saw slave owners as model Christians and accomplished humanitarians for civilizing and protecting those under their charge whom they viewed to be racially inferior. History and experience had shown, they argued, that economic exploitation, inequality, and hierarchy were the bedrock of the timeless accomplishments of the greatest civilizations of the Western world, including those of the Egyptians, Greeks, and Romans. According to Calhoun:

There never has yet existed a wealthy and civilized society in which one portion of the community did not, in point of fact, live on the labor of the other. Broad and general as this assertion [is], it is fully borne out by history. This is not the proper occasion, but if it were, it would not be difficult to trace out the various devices by which the wealth of all civilized communities has been so unequally divided, and to show by what means so small a share has been allotted to those whose labor it was produced, and so large a share to the non-producing classes.[40]

Egalitarian-inclined thinkers pointed to the exploitation of slave labor as the source of oppression that transformed economic, social, and political relations into domination and control that retarded social progress. In contrast, Southern conservatives insisted that it was the inequality of condition "between the front and the rear ranks," according to Calhoun, "which gives so strong an impulse to the former to maintain their position, and to the latter to press forward into their files . . . this gives to progress its greatest impulse."[41] In other words, civilized society rests on the inequality and the exploitation of the vast majority of the people. And according to the defenders of slavery, Southern slavery represented the most thorough, enlightened, and humane form of inequality on which civilized society is based. Despite the differences in their philosophical orientations, Fitzhugh and Calhoun agreed on this point, as did many other pro-slavery thinkers. In a 1858 speech in the U.S. Senate, James Henry Hammond claimed that progress and civilization required class exploitation, dubbing this exploited class of laborers as the "mud-sill of society":

In all social systems there must be a class to do the menial duties, to perform the drudgery of life. That is, a class requiring but a low order of intellect and but little skill. Its requisites are vigor, docility, fidelity. Such a class you must have, or you would not have that other class which leads progress, civilization, and refinement. It constitutes the very mud-sill of society and of political government; and you might as well attempt to build a house in the air, as to build either the one or the other, except on this mud-sill.[42]

Yet despite having accepted social hierarchy and class exploitation on principle, the defenders of slavery saw in capitalist productive relations a harshness and dehumanizing quality that was distinct from what they believed to be a milder form of exploitation under feudalism and Southern slavery. This perspective was ubiquitous among Southern pro-slavery critics of capitalism. In *Exposition and Protest*, Calhoun recognized how capitalist productive relations tended toward increasing exploitation and making the condition of workers more miserable: "Under the operation of the system, wages must sink more rapidly than the prices of the necessaries of life, till the operative will be reduced to the lowest point—when the portion of the products of their labor left to them, will be barely sufficient to preserve existence."[43] William J. Grayson, a poet and U.S. representative from South Carolina, compared the existence of the feudal serf and the Southern slave with that of the European wage laborer. He concluded that the misery and pauperism so commonplace in western Europe was the consequence of the free-labor system:

> There, unconcerned, the philanthropic eye
> Beholds each phase of human misery;
> Sees the worn child compelled in mines to slave
> Through narrow seams of coal, a living grave,
> Driven from the breezy hill, the sunny glade,
> By ruthless hearts, the drudge of labor made,
> Unknown the boyish sport, the hours of play,
> Stripped of the common boon, the light of day,
> Harnessed like brutes, like brutes to tug, and strain,
> And drag, on hands and knees, the loaded wain.[44]

In *The Political Economy of Slavery*, Edmund Ruffin explained how Northern industrialization and the accumulation of capital were predicated on the ever increasing impoverishment of the producing class:

> When the greatest possible amount of labor is thus obtained for the lowest amount of wages that can barely sustain life and strength of labor, there has been attained the most perfect and profitable condition of industrial operations for the class of capitalists and

employers, and also for the most rapid increase of general and national wealth. But these benefits are purchased only by the greatest possible amount of toil, privation, and misery of the class of laborers under which they can live and work.[45]

For his part, Fitzhugh understood that the exploitation and pauperization of labor were the source of wealth inequality under capitalism. "All capital is created by labor," he declared, "and the smaller the allowance of the free laborer, the greater the gains of his employer."[46]

Pro-slavery thinkers also understood that the exploitative nature of the free-labor system reached beyond the workplace. Among the repercussions were the appalling conditions of poverty and misery that were widespread in cities in the North and in England. Hammond argued that one "would meet more beggars in one day, in any single street of the city of New York, than you would meet in a lifetime in the whole South."[47] Grayson held that capitalist Europe was marked by social ills such as drunkenness, prostitution, disease, and pauperism, in which "unburied corpses taint the summer air, and crime and outrage revel with despair."[48] Likewise, Fitzhugh argued that the material misery of free laborers degraded their virtue.[49] Although he traveled outside the South only once in his lifetime—a short trip to New Haven, Connecticut, to debate abolitionist Wendell Phillips—Fitzhugh learned only at second hand about the exploitation and misery of the laboring classes. He read British parliamentary reports on the conditions in England's textile mills and iron mines, as well as criticisms of industrial capitalism by English Christian Socialists, and he drew heavily on British conservative journals such as the *Westminster Review*, *Blackwood's Magazine*, the *North British Review*, and the *Edinburgh Review*, which he quoted extensively in *Cannibals All!*. Fitzhugh was most profoundly influenced by Thomas Carlyle's critiques of laissez-faire of Manchester economics.[50] Reminiscent of a famous passage from the *Communist Manifesto*—and there is no indication that he read it—Fitzhugh suggests that the free laborer's troubles do not end once his hours of toil are over:

Capital, irresponsible capital, begets, and ever will beget, the immedicable vulnus of so-called Free Society. It invades every recess of

domestic life, infects the food, its clothing, its drink, its very atmo-
sphere, and pursues the hireling, from the hovel to the poor-house,
the prison, and the grave. Do what he will, go where he will, capital
pursues and persecutes him.[51]

Many conservatives thought that capitalist exploitation was both
materially and morally worse than feudalism and chattel slavery. The
impersonal nature of capitalism created a social ethic in which the
measure of value and success was determined by the bottom line and
the personal relationship on which human sympathy, generosity, and
benevolence is founded was lost. Under capitalism, the relationship
between the strong and successful, or the owners, on the one hand,
and those who toiled, on the other hand, had been reduced (to use
Carlyle's phrase), to the "cash nexus." In her study of Hammond's trav-
els to western Europe in 1836/1837, Drew Gilpin Faust emphasized his
abhorrence of how his relations with innkeepers, drivers, and personal
servants were dominated by financial transactions, which he took as
"ego-threatening" and "anxiety-provoking" for fear of being taken
advantage of and cheated.[52] Pro-slavery thinkers demonstrated that
the material productive relations of a society are at the root of its cultural, social, and political fabric. Without a conservative economic
foundation, as they saw slavery to be, a conservative society, culture,
and politics were impossible.

For defenders of slavery, the capitalist was a primary revolutionary
agent who threatened the conservative social order. The capitalist was
often portrayed as the embodiment of unadulterated mechanistic bru-
tality. According to Senator Hammond:

The primitive and patriarchal, which may also be called the sacred
and natural system, in which the laborer is under the personal control of a fellow-being endowed with the sentiments and sympathies
of humanity, exists among us. It has been almost everywhere else
superseded by the modern artificial money power system, in which
man—his thews and sinews, his hopes and affections, his very being,
are all subjected to the dominion of capital—a monster without a
heart—cold, stern, arithmetical—sticking to the bond—taking over
the "pound of flesh"—working up human life with engines, and
retailing it out by weight and measure.[53]

The capitalist was vilified as cold, hard, competitive, and calculating. As Fitzhugh exclaimed in typically bombastic fashion:

> You are a Cannibal! and if a successful one, pride yourself on the number of your victims quite as much as any Fiji chieftain, who breakfasts, dines, and sups on human flesh—and your conscience smites you, if you have failed to succeed, quite as much as his, when he returns from an unsuccessful foray.[54]

The capitalist was the prime destructive and conquering agent of the epoch. "We contend," wrote Fitzhugh, "that it was the origin of the capitalist and moneyed interest government, destined finally to swallow up all other powers in the State, and to bring about the most selfish, exacting, and unfeeling class despotism."[55]

Pro-slavery thinkers made much use of the contrast between atomistic capitalism and paternalistic and protective Southern chattel slavery. In a passage that captures the essence of this contradistinction Fitzhugh stated:

> Capital commands labor, as the master does the slave. Neither pays for labor; but the master permits the slave to retain a larger allowance from the proceeds of his own labor, and hence "free labor is cheaper than slave labor." You with the command over labor which your capital gives you are a slave owner—a master, without the obligations of a master. They who work for you, who create your income, are slaves, without the rights of slaves. Slaves without a master![56]

Having indicted Northern capitalism for its exploitative productive relations and for the miserable conditions in which much of its population lived, Southern defenders of slavery also illustrated how the institution of slavery protected those most likely to be victimized by capitalist relations. Ironically, key to the slaveholders' contention that the free-labor system was more exploitative than slave-productive relations were arguments regarding capitalism's efficiency and profitability. Fitzhugh lambasted Northern capitalists for boasting of their efficiency and profitability, seeing this as an unequivocal admission of their exploitation of the laborer and indifference to the miserable state in which the laborer is left when his labor has been used up.

Rather, he maintained, slavery was less efficient and less profitable precisely because it allowed slaves to keep a larger reward for their labor while they were capable of work and afforded protection and aid when they were no longer able to work.[57] Thus defenders of slavery distinguished themselves from the owners of wage laborers by spurning the priority of profitability and efficiency.[58] They thought of slave owning as a selfless contribution to the human race. "We [slave owners] must, therefore, content ourselves," wrote Hammond, "with our dear labor, under the consoling reflection that what is lost to us, is gained to humanity; and that, inasmuch as our slave costs us more than your free man costs you, by so much is he better off."[59]

Even Calhoun could not refrain from stoking the paternalistic self-image of the slaveholder. In a speech on the Senate floor in 1837, Calhoun compared the condition of the Southern slave and the Northern free laborer:

> I may say the truth, that in few countries so much is left to the share of the laborer, and so little extracted from him, or where there is more kind attention to him in sickness or infirmities of age. Compare his condition with the tenants of the poor houses in the most civilized portions of Europe—look at the sick, and the old and infirm slave, on one hand, in the midst of family and friends, under the kind superintending care of his master and mistress, and compare it with the forlorn and wretched condition of the pauper in the poor house.[60]

Despite their self-congratulation, it could not have escaped the proslavery thinkers that it was in the economic interest of slaveholders not to work the slaves to death (at least not in a short span of time). Moreover, with the end to the legal importation of African slaves in 1808, the market became limited to the domestic slave trade. The purchase of a slave was a considerable investment. According to historian Eric Foner, "The price of a 'prime field hand' rose from $1000 in 1840 to $1800 in 1860 (the latter figure equivalent to around $40,000 today)."[61] Thus it made economic sense not to work slaves to exhaustion and early death. And indeed, when not waxing idyllic about the "peculiar institution," the defenders of slavery admitted as much. "It is certainly in the interest of all, and I am convinced that it is also the desire of every one of us," wrote Hammond, "to treat our slaves with proper kindness. It is necessary to our deriving the greatest amount of profit from them."[62]

The central point in the comparison of capitalism with chattel slavery was not merely that the latter was less exploitative of the laborer than capitalism was. It was taken for granted by pro-slavery thinkers that laborers are exploited under all systems of production. Instead, Southern chattel slavery bound the laborer to his superior (slave owner) in a paternalistic relationship of domination and control that obligated the lord or master to protect and provide for his subjects in times of both plenty and scarcity. Under capitalism, these bonds did not exist. The capitalist's obligation to his workers ended with paying compensation for their labor in the form of wages. If the laborer was unable to find employment for any reason, whether it was because he was too sick, too old, or too infirm for gainful employment or because there was no work to be found, it was not the fault of the capitalist or his obligation to offer aid. Fitzhugh found this arrangement to be the cruelest of all deceptions:

> Now, under the delusive name of liberty, you work him [the laborer] "from morn to dewy eve"—from infancy to old age—then turn him out to starve. You treat your horses and hounds better. Capital is a cruel master. The free slave trade, the commonest, ye the cruelest of trades.[63]

In the nineteenth century, it was not uncommon for republican and socialist critics of capitalism to employ the concept of wage slavery to describe the dependent condition of the factory worker. For these critics, wrote Eric Foner, "the metaphor of wage slavery drew on immediate grievances, such as low wages, irregular employment, the elaborate and arbitrary work rules of the early factories. . . . But at its heart lay a critique of economic dependence."[64] Indeed, the idea that emerging capitalism was producing a state of economic dependence was essential to the economic critique of radical republicans at that time. According to these radicals, republican institutions required that its citizens be economically autonomous agents acting in the interest of the common weal in an environment of independence, relative equality, and public-spiritedness. But radicals were not the only ones employing the concept of wage slavery in their critique. As was the case for radical republicans and for conservatives like Calhoun and Fitzhugh, the idea of wage slavery, or comparing capitalist labor with slave labor, implied economic relations of dependence and domination. Unlike later conservatives, who imagined the capitalist market as an arena absent of coercion, antebellum Southern conservative critics saw coercion taking place in capitalist economic relations. They pointed to the very real prospect of eviction and starvation as compelling the "free laborer" to be exploited by capital in a competitive market economy. "Capital exercises a more perfect compulsion over free laborer than human masters over slaves," declared Fitzhugh, "for free laborers must at all times work or starve."[65]

Unlike radicals who sought to liberate the laboring classes from these despotic relationships with employers, conservative critics argued that the combination of despotism and "liberty" emerging out of capitalist relations was detrimental to the livelihood of working-class individuals and the social order. The problem with capitalism was not that it created economic relations of domination and subordination in the workplace. Instead, the problem was that capitalist economic relations were based on a contractual relationship that bound the employer and the employee, albeit in a very unequal relationship, to a time-bound exchange of labor for wages. Beyond that arrangement and other rules and regulations that governed the behavior of the employee during employment hours, the employer and the employee had no other obligations to each other. As a consequence, under a contractual relationship, an employer could not exert adequate governance over his laborers after the workday was over, as opposed to the power of a feudal lord or a slave master. Hence, the defenders of slavery consistently regarded the North and capitalist Britain as pools of human degradation, drunkenness, prostitution, and markets of dangerous "isms" and other ideas. These were the products of "liberty" arising from inadequate domination of the laboring or "mud-sill" classes by their social superiors. Essentially, the proslavery critique centered on the failure of the capitalist ruling class and on the liberty of contract that allowed employers to fire and hire employees at will, which contributed to capitalist profits but granted the wage laborer freedom from the personal domination of a particular employer.

Another conservative criticism of capitalism in the antebellum period pertained to the ethics of the economic system. The morality of capitalism is "simple and unadulterated selfishness," Fitzhugh stated.[66] Pro-slavery thinkers argued that plantation life created a social environment conducive to personal intercourse between master and slave, through which bonds of mutual affection, goodwill, generosity, and respect were established. These paternalistic relations of dependence and control, they maintained, provided a less harsh and exploitative labor system. In return for their labor, the master's obligation was to protect the slave from the dangers of the world beyond the plantation. Only in this hierarchical relationship could the exploitation and misery of the weak (the slave) be minimized. For defenders of slavery, these paternalistic relations were justifiable on grounds beyond the belief that they were less exploitative of labor and afforded a more secure material existence for the producing class than in the free-labor North. In a competitive labor market, the relationship between the employer and the employee is devoid of human significance. The defenders of slavery agreed that slavery's most morally redeeming characteristic was that it was an institutional arrangement that obligated the strong to protect the weak.

Moreover, not only did the slave owner give a greater share of the slaves' labor back in the form of daily sustenance, shelter, care and protection in old age, but he established personal relations with his slaves. Slave owners knew their slaves' names and families, marked occasions such as weddings and harvests, and commonly took a great interest in their religious instruction. Of course, this was only one-half of a slave owner's paternalistic relationship with his slaves. The other side of it—the sexual exploitation of female slaves, the cruelty of corporal punishment, and the trauma of family separation—was dismissed as wild exaggerations and untrue or was blamed on abolitionists' incitement.[67] An economy based on chattel slavery, the pro-slavery thinkers contended, allowed for the practice of Christian morality of caring for the weak, the sick, the old, the helpless, and the infirm. Northern wage labor, Fitzhugh and other defenders of slavery suggested, made Christian morality impracticable.

Christian morality can find little practical foothold in a community so constituted that to "love our neighbor as ourself" or "to do unto others as we would they should do unto us" would be acts of suicidal self-sacrifice. Christian morality, however, was not preached to free competitive society, but to slave society, where it is neither very difficult nor unnatural to practice it.[68]

Capitalist morality, in contrast, valued the vices of "avarice, circumspection, and hard dealing" as virtues.[69] The capitalist morality of "let us alone, save who can, and the devil take the hindmost" created relationships between individuals and classes that made it nearly impossible for individuals to act morally toward one another. "Neither the Epicurean, nor the Sadducee professed as low, selfish and groveling amorality as that which our prevalent political economy inculcates," wrote Fitzhugh.[70] Consequently, the sheer misery, poverty, and atomistic condition of the masses made inevitable an environment in which there was widespread violation of Christian strictures governing licentiousness and crime. Defenders of slavery were fond of reminding their readers of the prevalence of crime in Great Britain and in the Northern states of the Union, contrasting those morally corrupting environs with the absence of immoral behavior among the producing classes under European feudalism and in the slave states of the Union.[71] Pro-slavery thinkers believed that it would come as no surprise that liberating the laborer from the personal authority of his master, which included the authority to compel moral and religious instruction, and instead enslaving the laborer to the impersonal rule of the competitive capitalist market would entice workers to gravitate toward licentiousness, vice, and moral degradation, all of which were gateways to radicalism.

CAPITALISM, CLASS CONFLICT, AND THE THREAT TO SOCIAL ORDER

The culmination of the conservative indictment of capitalism in the antebellum period lay in capitalism's tendency to exacerbate class conflict. Pro-slavery thinkers understood the essential conservatism of paternalism and its role in maintaining social order. "Wherever paternalism exists," Genovese pointed out, "it undermines solidarity among the oppressed by linking them as individuals to their oppressors."[72] The Northern contractual wage system lacked this stable, long-lasting paternalistic relation. Since workers' wages were inadequate and their employers were under no obligation to offer aid and protection in times of crisis, workers turned to mutual aid societies, unions, and political associations for protection, aid, and, ultimately, identity. It was in these organizations that workers built solidarity and grew conscious of their collective strength. In these associations, the seeds of radicalism germinated.

Theodore R. Marmor correctly argues that Calhoun's critique of Northern wage slavery was concerned primarily with its effects on the stability of society.[73] In a letter to James F. Simmons in 1847, Calhoun warned, "Where wages command labor, as in the non-slaveholding States, there necessarily takes place between labor and capital a conflict, which leads, in process of time, to disorder, anarchy, and revolution."[74] For pro-slavery thinkers, the exploitation and misery of wage labor, capitalist imperatives toward hard dealing, profitability, efficiency, and, in the words of Fitzhugh, a social organization of "slaves without masters" described the social and economic environment of the antebellum North. These conditions brutalized the laboring masses and resulted in extreme material deprivation and misery, which in turn produced a political and social environment conducive to the popularization of radical ideas.

The comparisons of the level of exploitation or cooperation afforded by capitalism and the slave system were meant to illustrate how the competing economic systems averted or aggravated class conflict. Writing to Thomas Clarkson, an English abolitionist, Hammond declared,

> Stability and peace are the first desires of every slave-holder, and the true tendency of the system . . . scenes of riot and bloodshed, as have within the last few years disgraced our Northern cities, and as you have lately witnessed in Birmingham and Bristol and Wales, not only never have occurred, but I will venture to say, never will occur in our slave-holding States.[75]

What Hammond, Calhoun, Fitzhugh, and others feared was that the misery that capitalism wrought on the laboring classes in the North made them susceptible to the radical ideas then in circulation, of which abolitionism and socialism were a part. They believed that the movements spawned by these ideas were threats not only to Southern slavery but also to all the institutions that embodied and protected hierarchy and restrained humans from constant conflict. In the preface to *Cannibals All!*, Fitzhugh warned that "the banners of Socialism and, more dangerous because more delusive, Semi-Socialism, society is insensibly and often unconsciously marching to the utter abandonment of the most essential institutions—religion, family ties, property, and the restraints of justice."[76]

Calhoun feared that the 1848 revolutions that swept across Europe might infect the consciousness of the American working classes.[77] The defenders of slavery worried that as capitalist exploitation spread throughout the country and enveloped greater numbers of people, class conflict would inevitably intensify. "Every city," he wrote, "was destined to be the seat of free-soilism . . . Socialists, Communists, Anti-Renters, and a thousand other agrarian sects that . . . threaten to subvert the whole social fabric."[78] The fear was that as the material condition of wage laborers was gradually made more miserable, socialist ideas challenging the growing inequality in wealth might sound more appealing to the dispossessed masses and result in a revolutionary assault on inequality, whether based on slavery or on capital.

> So rampant and combative is the spirit of discontent wherever nominal free labor prevails, with its ostensive privileges and its dismal servitude. Nor it will be long before the "free States" of this Union will be compelled to introduce the same expensive machinery, to preserve order among their "free and equal" citizens. . . . The intervention of their militia to repress violations of the peace is becoming a daily affair.[79]

The way the defenders of slavery saw it, the greatest threat to order and stability was the conditions in the free-labor North that inspired radical ideas and movements. Slavery, they believed, offered an alternative to Northern instability.

Despite their critique of capitalism, which in some ways rivaled those of American egalitarians and European socialists, pro-slavery critics of the system of free labor were not wholly anticapitalist.[80] None wanted to see it overthrown by revolutionary upheaval. Even critics like Fitzhugh and Hammond who defended slavery in the abstract thought that enslaving white wage laborers was impracticable and would require a revolution in its own right. Both Southern slavery and Northern capitalism were inegalitarian hierarchical systems reflecting a natural inequality in which the few are "by nature born to command and protect, and law but follows nature in making them rulers, legislators, judges, captains, husbands, guardians, committees and masters."[81] Abolitionism, like socialism, sought to invert this natural order of things by making all equal and, as a consequence, enable the weak, the unfit, and ignorant masses to rule. The socialists, according to Fitzhugh, have "point[ed] out distinctly the character of the disease under which the patient in laboring, but see no way of curing the disease except by killing the patient."[82]

To avert revolution, antebellum-period pro-slavery thinkers took pains to remind the Northern elite of their mutual interests. "Looking to the future," wrote Calhoun, "I can see no hope of a complete restoration of our system, till the men of wealth and talents in the North, shall become convinced, that their true interest is to rally on the South and on Southern doctrines."[83]

Southern elites attempted to devise constitutional mechanisms like nullification and the concurrent majority to arrest democratic inroads on property. In his *Disquisition on Government,* published posthumously in 1853, Calhoun explored a constitutional mechanism that would preserve the rights and interests of a minority facing the will of a democratic majority. Calhoun's proposed concurrent majority was a constitutional mechanism intended to preserve the interests of Northern capital from popular democratic inroads and to safeguard Southern slavery. While the argument in the *Disquisition* is theoretical, without reference to the American social, political, and economic scene, Calhoun was clearly reflecting on the impact of contemporary social transformations:

> For as the community becomes populous, wealthy, refined, and
> highly civilized, the difference between the rich and the poor will

become more strongly marked, and the number of the ignorant and dependent greater in proportion to the rest of the community. With the increase of this difference, the tendency to conflict between them will become stronger; and as the poor and the dependent become more numerous in proportion, there will be in governments of the numerical majority no want of leaders among the wealthy and ambitious to excite and direct them in their efforts to obtain the control.[84]

His remarks regarding the exploitation of labor by capital and the various radical movements threatening the "social fabric" in the North were indicative of his fear of the laboring classes' potential political power in a democracy.

Similarly, in the "Mud-sill" speech, Hammond warned the Northern elites of the dangers of an exploited and politically empowered class of wage slaves:

Our slaves do not vote. We give them no political power. Yours do vote, and, being the majority, they are the depositaries of all your political power. If they knew the tremendous secret, that the ballot-box is stronger than "an army with banners," and could combine, where would you be? Your society would be reconstructed, your government overthrown, your property divided.[85]

In his more sober moments, Fitzhugh called for a coalition of Northern and Southern property: "We think that by a kind of alliance, offensive and defensive, with the South, Northern Conservatism may now arrest and turn back the tide of Radicalism and Agrarianism."[86]

Pro-slavery thinkers' defense of the slave system was based on the belief that it was the most effective social, political, economic, and cultural arrangement to preserve existing hierarchies. For them, if social order was to be preserved in the United States, slavery did not need to be expanded to the whole of the nation, but it did need to have a major stake in it, not merely for the sake of the South and its way of life, but for the sake of hierarchy, on which the progress of civilization depended.

What the defenders of slavery said and wrote about the condition of workers and the relations between capitalists and free laborers was, for the most part, true. Whatever their motivation was for making these indictments, the defenders of slavery were the first and most direct critics of capitalism in the nation's conservative tradition. Pro-slavery thinkers confronted a tension that has always plagued American conservatives, a tension between a capitalist economic system and a conservative culture, society, and politics. For the defenders of slavery, capitalism bred class warfare, a spirit of selfish individualism, and radicalism, all of which were ingredients for a revolutionary upheaval, which would inevitably lead to barbarism.

The argument that capitalism posed a fundamental threat to a specific and, in their view, elevated social order was not unique to the defenders of slavery. With variations, it is a principal tenet of the conservative critique of capitalism to which right-wing critics of the economic system return time and again. No other conservative thinkers in the American tradition come close to the pro-slavery thinkers in challenging capitalist productive relations as explicitly as they did in the antebellum period. Antebellum Southern critics of capitalism were able to do so because they had an existing and viable alternative in the form of chattel slavery. To be sure, critiques of the capitalist ethic and capitalism's tendency toward instability and class conflict would recur in the conservative discourse, as would concerns about the threat posed by radical doctrines. But these critiques would gradually be divorced from the social and productive relations wrought by capitalism. By the middle of the twentieth century, in the thick of the Cold War, aspects of pro-slavery thinkers' cultural critiques of capitalism remained in the conservative discourse. But crucially, perhaps for lack of an alternative, the material productive relations of capitalism would not be challenged.

Following the Civil War and the defeat of Southern chattel slavery, the social base of the pro-slavery critique of capitalism was destroyed, and the conservative critique of capitalism rapidly declined. Among the defenders of slavery, many remained nostalgic for the old slave South but had to reconcile themselves to the new order. Economic domination and a century of segregation, discrimination, political and legal disenfranchisement, intimidation, and terrorism against blacks has proved that the white elite was able to retain much of their domination and control well after abolition. Even an uncompromising proponent of slavery like Fitzhugh accepted the Confederacy's defeat in the Civil War and worked for the Freedman's Bureau as a local court agent charged with supervising labor contracts between free men and farm employers. Like many in the postbellum South, Fitzhugh underwent an "ideological transformation" with the changing social order.[87] He came to terms with monopoly capitalism as embodying the "attractive feudal ideals" of the paternalistic orders, which he so admired and defended.[88] Indeed historian Laura F. Edwards points out that

> the law of master and servant continued to structure all labor rela-
> tions [in the South] . . . both law and practice positioned all common
> laborers as nominal dependents within their employers' households.
> When workers lived on their own their employers legally could and
> actually did exercise broad supervisory powers over their lives on as
> well as off the job.[89]

This is not to say that nothing changed following the end of the Civil War and the abolition of slavery. Much certainly did. The freedom from slavery, the right to own property, and the right not to be forcibly sold to another, among other previously denied basic rights and freedoms, were revolutionary achievements. But property relations did not change much. Former slaveholders became capitalists, and their former slaves became their employees. Denying former slaves access to productive land answered the all-important question on the minds of Southern planters, British and Northern cotton merchants, manufacturers, and financiers of how to maintain control over black labor, feed the international market's demand for Southern agricultural goods, and protect "the front ranks" from the mudsill in a post-slavery society.[90] Years later, in his landmark study of Reconstruction, W. E. B. Du Bois wrote, "The slave went free; stood a brief moment in the sun; then moved back again toward slavery."[91] This statement does much to explain why antebellum proslavery critics of capitalism, like Fitzhugh, adapted to the postbellum capitalist order.

In the decades following the Civil War, the U.S. economy changed at breakneck speed. Manufacturers, railroad tycoons, and financiers became central to the America's political economy, having supplanted merchants and plantation slaveholders as the drivers of the nation's economic framework and development. Native Americans were cleared from the frontier and herded into reservations as railroad tracks crossed the nation; vast stretches of prairie were plowed into huge agricultural fields or fenced off into livestock ranches; oil fields sprouted in Pennsylvania and California; huge manufacturing firms employed thousands of people and churned out millions of dollars in goods every year; gigantic financial institutions controlled investments from coast to coast; and millions of people immigrated to the United States, adding to the population of America's cities. A thoroughly individualistic social philosophy (social Darwinism) took hold of the elite's imagination, which, although serving the interests of the capitalist class, kept the federal government relatively small compared with those of other modern, Western capitalist powers such as Britain, France, and Germany. With the assistance of the state in the form of "Indian removal," suppression of strikes and other labor actions, land grants and other corporate subsidies, hard-money policy, vagrancy statutes and other coercive employment laws, and a Supreme Court fully on the side of private property and corporations, great fortunes were made in steel, oil, railroads, banking, insurance, real estate, retail merchandise, and, later, automobiles. But as industrialization proceeded unabated and as the size and concentration of businesses grew and became national in their scope and operation, the instability of the market became more extensive and severe. Before the Great Depression of the 1930s, the worst depression on record (also known as the Great Depression) lasted from 1873 to 1879. In fact, in the twenty-five years from 1873 to 1897, there were three major depressions, in which millions of workers and their families went jobless, hungry, and homeless while the wealthy accumulated greater riches along with the economic and political power that accompanies great wealth. As the conflict between labor and capital grew more intense in the second half of the nineteenth century, the pro-slavery conservatives' warnings of the incompatibility of the capitalist wage system and social stability proved to be more than the ravings of an overzealous self-interested ruling class. To be sure, pro-slavery thinkers were protecting their interests, but in doing so they also saw something inherent in capitalism that would only get worse in the decades ahead. Capitalism failed to solve the perennial problem that class conflict posed for the preservation of a stable, hierarchical, and conservative social order. As the great Pullman and Homestead strikes, along with thousands of other labor agitations, indicated, class antagonism was a perennial reality of American social, political, and economic life. Indeed, the "labor question" was the main political problem in the decades between the end of the Civil War and World War I. The social upheavals in these years forced some conservatives to rethink the discarded paternalist ideal of the defenders of slavery and to try to change it for a modern, industrial, capitalist, and imperial nation.

2

IN SEARCH OF THE WARRIOR-STATESMAN

*The Critique of Laissez-Faire Capitalism
by Brooks Adams and Theodore Roosevelt*

> If we want everything to stay as it is,
> everything has to change!
>
> Tomasi di Lampedusa, *The Leopard*

n *Rebirth of a Nation*, historian Jackson Lears calls the period between the end of Reconstruction and World War I an "age of regeneration." "Seldom if ever in our history," he wrote, "have longings for rebirth played a more prominent role in politics."[1] Historian Robert H. Wiebe described the political project of the time as a "search for order."[2] Indeed, some people believed that the United States was in a state of disarray and decline resulting from the ascendance of a decadent business mentality, a lack of public-spiritedness, a corrupt political class, and bitter class conflict. Others worried that as the United States urbanized and attracted more immigrants of so-called inferior races from southern and eastern Europe and China, its Anglo-Saxon heritage and cultural superiority would be threatened. For many, political life had lost its ennobling character as political machines dominated the governments of many cities and elected officials used public resources for their own personal fortune and aggrandizement. The federal government was hardly better; the U.S. Senate came to be known as the "millionaires' club," and "special interests" commanded all three branches.

During this period, the United States underwent rapid economic and territorial expansion, stretching to the Pacific Ocean and beyond as the Philippines, Guam, and Puerto Rico were incorporated as colonies in the new American empire. Meanwhile, industrial consolidation and centralization, technological innovation, and dramatic economic fluctuations in the United States were met with violent clashes of class between the owners of capital and their government allies, on the one hand, and an increasingly class-conscious industrial working class, on the other.[3] Perhaps in no other period in American history was such revolutionary economic transformation accompanied by such intense social unrest than the half century leading up to World War I. Railroads tied the country into one large production and consumer market as it never had been before. Innovations in business management strategies created a new kind of business enterprise. Nationally organized and vertically and horizontally integrated firms employed the latest in scientific strategies to squeeze the maximum amount of productivity out of labor and at the lowest cost. National mail-order merchants delivered goods to the most rural outposts, while department stores in urban areas offered thousands of items under one roof. All these novelties contributed to the development of a national consumer market in which standardized goods were both produced and consumed by Americans who resided in New York, California, and everywhere in between.

Through these developments in communication, transportation, business management techniques, and mergers, businesses grew exponentially. Some employed tens of thousands of workers around which entire towns and communities were organized. Great fortunes and economic power were acquired in oil, coal, iron, steel, railroads, banking, retail, and the like. Indeed, the captains of industry and finance accumulated wealth and resources that surpassed the total revenues of many states in the Union. Yet despite the prosperity, the American economy regularly spiraled into crisis, in 1873–1877, 1883–1885, 1893–1897, and 1905. These market fluctuations enriched some and ruined many more. The 1893–1897 depression, then called the "Great Depression," was the worst to date. Twenty percent of the working population was unemployed, 642 banks failed, and 16,000 businesses were forced to close.[4] Each time the economy began to recover, a wave of business mergers and acquisitions followed. By the late 1890s, the concentration of business enterprises was unprecedented. Of the seventy-three largest companies in 1900, fifty-three had not existed three years earlier.[5] By 1910, notwithstanding the publicized "trust-busting" campaigns of Presidents Theodore Roosevelt and William Howard Taft, 1 percent of the nation's manufacturers accounted for 44 percent of the nation's total industrial output.[6] The price of this boon for the wealthiest and most powerful of Americans was steep, paid for by the working classes whose wretched living and working conditions were the subject of exposés by such journalists and authors as Jacob Riis, Upton Sinclair, and William Hard.

The socially explosive potential of these conditions worried thinkers across the political spectrum. The conflicts between capital, on the one hand, and farmers and laborers (the two latter groups were by no means united), on the other, were a serious threat to the hierarchical social order and relative stability that conservatives prized. The Granger movement, the radical unionism under "Big" Bill Haywood and the Wobblies, along with the popular electoral campaigns of the Socialist Eugene Debs, the radical reformer Henry George, and, in particular, William Jennings Bryan's popular presidential candidacy in 1896, instilled in conservatives a fear of revolution. The rise of radical political movements, combined with the increasing frequency and level of violence of labor actions—most notably Haymarket in 1886, Homestead and Coeur d'Alene in 1892, Pullman in 1894, and hundreds of others—confirmed their fear. The nationally disruptive nature of these labor actions and the inability of the capitalist ruling class to resolve these conflicts without resorting to the state's means of violence convinced some conservatives that to preserve the established social, political, and economic order, reforming capitalism, its culture, and the state must be their principal project.

In reaction to the upheaval during this transformative period in American history, a distinctive type of conservative political thought emerged. It was elitist, anti-egalitarian, and anti-socialist like other strands of conservatism. But it was also reformist, critical of laissez-faire capitalism, imperialistic, and statist.[7] This strand of thought was best expressed by the historian and social theorist Brooks Adams (1848–1927) and the adventurer and president Theodore Roosevelt (1858–1918).[8] Influenced by evolutionary theory, Adams and Roosevelt believed in the evolutionary hierarchy of nations and people but were not convinced by the individualism of social Darwinism and its defenses of laissez-faire capitalism. They believed that the underlying assumptions of individualistic capitalism emphasizing the selfish pursuit of private interest were a recipe for domestic discord and international weakness that threatened capitalism's very existence. In fact, for Adams and Roosevelt, it was the emphasis on commerce and egotism that permeated America's politics and culture, especially in its ruling class, that pointed to the regression and decay of the nation and its people.

Brooks Adams and Theodore Roosevelt were friends who greatly influenced each other. Indeed, historian Daniel Aaron has written that Adams had more influence over Roosevelt's thought than anyone else did. The two men reviewed each other's published works, corresponded often, sought each other's advice, and shared powerful mutual friends such as John Hay and Henry Cabot Lodge.[9] Adams was the theorist and Roosevelt the practitioner. According to Matthew Josephson, "the terms in which [Adams] defined the dilemma of society, faced with the choice of violent proletarian revolution or social decadence eating at the top of the society, were always present in [Roosevelt's] writings and speeches."[10] They were both, as Aaron has argued, "pseudo-progressives" for their belief in the necessity of reform. Both men's reformism was animated by deeply conservative assumptions, with both believing that their prescriptive reforms were "not wild radicalism . . . but the highest and wisest kind of conservatism."[11]

For Adams and Roosevelt, the fundamental threat to the nation's survival and strength was that its capitalist society had failed to generate a stable and virtuous elite whose dedication to the national interest would triumph over its own self-interest. The capitalist class's inability to lead and to rule created the space and the conditions for agrarian, labor, and radical movements from below to challenge the social order. Adams and Roosevelt sought to regenerate an elite whose authority and learned statesmanship would save capitalists from the consequences of their misrule and avert radical challenges to the social order and national decay. Their critique of capitalism, in essence, was an elite theory of capitalist deformation, and their prescription for national regeneration was based on the invigorating spirit of the martial man, the guiding hand of the regulatory state, and the American empire.

As historian Jackson Lears notes, this narrative of elite deformation was not a marginal sentiment. "For many conventionally wise Americans, the martial ideal emerged as a popular antidote to over-civilization."[12] America's global Manifest Destiny, its world historical task as the new standard-bearer of Western civilization, the necessity of imperial expansion wrought by the impending social upheaval as industrial production outstripped the domestic market's ability to consume, and the regenerative prospect of war and empire were accepted ideas among statesmen and writers, including Senators Henry Cabot Lodge and Albert Beveridge, Secretary of State John Hay, Admirals Stephen B. Luce and Alfred Thayer Mahan, and writers Charles A. Conant and Homer Lea.[13] Like Roosevelt and Adams, Lea and Mahan were particularly critical of the ease and luxury of commercial society that privileged accumulation and consumption over "masculine" martial vales. "If the love of mere glory is selfish," wrote Mahan, "it is not quite as low as the love of mere comfort. To the latter the so-called respectable and intellectual class have unfortunately made themselves the mouthpiece."[14]

As Lears argues in *No Place of Grace*, Adams's and Roosevelt's "warrior critique" of business civilization did not mean a total hostility to capitalism. Indeed, their critique of the bourgeois type and the glorification of the martial type was not meant to completely eliminate the former. The problem with modern society, according to the warrior-critics, was not that there was such a creature as the bourgeois type or the Economic Man but that the bourgeois psyche and way of life dominated the nation's consciousness, its direction, and its reason for being.[15]

Roosevelt and Adams did not want to replace capitalism with an alternative economic system. They opposed egalitarianism and socialism. Nor did they seek to decentralize economic enterprises in accordance with a Jeffersonian republican political economy. Instead, they attempted to construct a paternalist imperial state administered by a public-spirited elite legitimized by a plebiscite and empowered to regulate corporate capitalism and direct it toward national aims. Admittedly, Roosevelt and Adams were not typical conservatives.[16] They welcomed business centralization as an invaluable component of America's strength on the world stage. But they believed that corporate capitalism needed to be controlled and regulated by the federal government in the interest of the Anglo-American nation. For Adams and Roosevelt, political centralization, economic regulation, and imperial expansion were not a choice but a necessity for America's economic and geopolitical competition with Russia, Japan, and the European powers as well as its concerns in suppressing labor and radical movements that were challenging capitalist hierarchical relations at home. Going backward by decentralizing business, or doing nothing and letting the laissez-faire market take over, was, for both Adams and Roosevelt, akin to national suicide.

BROOKS ADAMS'S LAW OF HISTORY

Both Brooks Adams and Theodore Roosevelt saw social development as having a competitive evolutionary nature. But they did not believe, as did the social Darwinists, that social classes owed nothing to one another.[17] For Adams and Roosevelt, national unity and strength were needed for the American republic to triumph in the struggle with other nations for survival and supremacy, and to reach this goal, the state had to play a major role. In *The Law of Civilization and Decay* (1896), his most influential work, Adams offered a cyclical theory of history based on the scientific laws of mass, energy, and acceleration. According to historian Charles Beard, Adams's *Law* was the "first attempt by an American thinker to reduce universal history to a single formula conceived in the spirit of modern science."[18] In his book, Adams explained the rise and fall of all past civilizations, arguing that the Anglo-American civilization was already in decline.

Adams explained that societies oscillate between barbarism and civilization in a cyclical manner. According to this theory, each

historical stage produces its own character type that becomes dominant until the conditions change and this character type fades away.
In earlier stages of society when economic activity was widely dis-
persed and there was little economic competition, human energy
was animated by fear, expressed in martial and imaginative, or war-
like and priestly, ways. The martial mentality—composed of physical
strength, virility, bravery, skill in combat, and sacrifice for one's nation
and people—received the highest esteem and was a source of security
and economic well-being. As a result, the martial class was the dominant ruling class in society. As civilization progressed, economic concentration and competition advanced. This ruling class remained as
long as it had an outlet for the marital spirit in the form of territorial
expansion and conquest. Once territorial expansion reached its most
distant boundaries, however, human energy turned inward, and a
new spirit was manifested among the people.

This new spirit was an economic spirit animated by greed. Accordingly, as economic thinking became dominant, civilization's focus
turned to the pursuit of self-interest, profit, and material consumption and luxury, which led to decadence. The martial and imaginative
spirit became obsolete. Then, once there were no new markets to pursue and the existing ones were saturated, economic concentration
intensified, leading to economic crisis and greater competition among
fewer and fewer individuals and businesses. Adams believed that this
competition existed not only among businesses but also between the
wealthy-owner class and the laboring class, which led to social strife
that further weakened society from within. Eventually, the society suc-
cumbed to war from within or was conquered by a more martial and
united people. Adams extrapolated his theory for nineteenth- and
twentieth-century America, pointing to its impending decay as a result
of economic competition and concentration and the devastating
social consequences when economic expansion reached its limits.
Adams worried that at the turn of the twentieth century, the United
States would have reached the condition of stagnation and decay outlined in the *Law*. The American frontier had been conquered.[19] The
nation's borders had reached the Pacific Ocean. Industrial production
was already outstripping the ability of the domestic market to consume,[20] and economic crises were a regular occurrence. Indeed, the

United States had never experienced the intensity, pervasiveness, and violence of class conflict as it did in the fifty years after the Civil War. Adams's theoretical conclusions in *The Law*, combined with the social, political, and economic upheavals of the late nineteenth century, filled him with foreboding regarding the future of the nation and of Western civilization. In a letter to his more famous brother, Henry, Brooks Adams's hopelessness was apparent:[21]

> [F]or the first time in human history there is not one ennobling instinct. There is not a barbarian anywhere sighing a chant of war and faith, there is not a soldier to sacrifice himself for an ideal. How can we hope to see a new world, a new civilization, or a new life? To my mind we are at the end; and the one thing I thank God for is that we have no children.[22]

Adams grounded his pessimism in his reading of history. "The presence and the absence of a supply of barbaric life" are key. The mentality of the Economic Man has taken over in modern society. The principal source of modern nations' weakness is the lack of the barbaric life's vitality.[23] In the conclusion to *The Law*, Adams mourned the passing of the martial elite in the modern Western world:

> The ideal statesman had been one who, like Cromwell, Frederic the Great, Henry IV, William III, and Washington, could lead his men in battle . . . the aristocracy had professedly been a military caste. Only after 1871 [in France] came the new era, an era marked by many social changes. For the first time in their history the ruler of the French people passed admittedly from the martial to the monied type, and everywhere the same phenomenon appeared; the whole administration of society fell into the hands of the economic man.[24]

In many ways, Roosevelt agreed with Adams's theory of history and endorsed his veneration of the martial spirit. Roosevelt reviewed Adams's *Law*, calling it a "brilliant book" and a "distinct contribution to the philosophy of history."[25] Yet he thought Adams's conclusion about America's inevitable decline was far too pessimistic. As William Appleman Williams noted, Adams himself soon did, too. For the next two decades, he worked tirelessly, through Roosevelt's political leadership, to implement a political program to delay the decay of the Anglo-American civilization.[26] For Adams, Theodore Roosevelt personified the hope that the martial man was not extinct in a society governed by the imperatives and values of a modern laissez-faire capitalism. Adams poured all his trust and optimism for the regeneration of a martial virtuous elite into the person of Roosevelt. Indeed, Adams urged him to lead "some great outburst of the emotional classes which should at least temporarily crush the Economic Man."[27] When Roosevelt assumed the presidency, Adams could not disguise his anticipation of his leadership:

> "Thou hast it now: king, Cawdor, Glamis, all—" The world can give no more. You hold a place greater than Trajan's, for you are the embodiment of a power not only vaster than the power of the Empire, but vaster than men have ever known. You have too the last and rarest prize, for you have an opportunity. You will always stand as the President who began the contest for supremacy of America against the eastern continent.[28]

THE CRITIQUE OF ECONOMIC MAN
AND THE CAPITALIST RULING CLASS

Adams's and Roosevelt's criticisms of capitalism flowed from their disgust with the Economic Man under capitalism, believing that he was a product of historical evolutionary development. He was an innovator and engineer of prosperity and material plenty. Thus, for both thinkers there was an important place for the capitalist in their alternative to laissez-faire. But as Adams wrote, capital was an "irresponsible sovereign."[29] For Adams, Benjamin Franklin was the best exponent of the capitalist mentality, and he derided Franklin's commonplace virtues as suitable for "counter jumpers."

> I know that George Washington would never have indulged in such calculation nor yet would have been proud to become the preacher

of such small ware if he had. I never said Franklin wasn't useful—so is the constable and so are your account books—but you don't see the constable by the side of your God nor make a bible of your ledger— though many folks have no other.[30]

Roosevelt and Adams contended that the government of a modern society with a corporate, industrial, capitalist economy required the leadership of skilled public administrators who governed in the interest of the nation as a whole, that the capitalist character was incapable of putting the national interest, the common weal, or any great noble endeavor ahead of his own monetary self-interest. This shortcoming made the capitalist unqualified to govern a modern state. In the *Theory of Social Revolutions*, Adams stated that the development of a capitalist environment "demanded excessive specialization in the direction of a genius adapted to money-making under highly complex industrial conditions."[31] In such an environment, Adams observed, the characteristic that is most highly privileged is "money-making," an attribute to which "all else has been sacrificed, and the modern capitalist not only thinks in terms of money, but he thinks in terms of money more exclusively than the French aristocrat or lawyer ever thought in terms of caste."[32] Even though Roosevelt was not as critical of modern life as Adams was, he nevertheless agreed with some of his criticisms.[33] In his "Strenuous Life" speech delivered in 1899, Roosevelt warned the Hamilton Club audience against becoming "content to rot by inches in ignoble ease within our borders, taking no interest in what goes on beyond them, sunk in a scrabbling commercialism."[34]

Adams and Roosevelt were not alone in their assessment of the capitalist or the values that capitalism engendered. In *The Theory of the Leisure Class*, Thorstein Veblen noted that the virtues and accomplishments valued most in capitalist society were those that generated wealth and displayed one's success at doing so through conspicuous consumption. Much like the liberal Veblen, Roosevelt and Adams despised the new rich. Unlike Veblen, Adams and Roosevelt mourned the disappearance of the old elite, those who were drawn to public life less by the pursuit of wealth than by a commitment to duty, public service, and the national interest, and the noblesse oblige expected of their class. The generation of the nation's founders and leaders such as John C. Calhoun, Henry Clay, Daniel Webster, and Abraham Lincoln personified the closest the United States came to this kind of public-spirited aristocracy.

It was this irresponsible ruling class of the capitalist new rich, who shirked their social responsibilities, that Roosevelt labeled the "malefactors of great wealth." He especially disliked corporations and their leaders who broke the law, corrupted political affairs, and made excessive profits by exploiting their workforce with low wages and miserable working conditions.[35] To Roosevelt, it was clear that at least some of the responsibility for the era's social upheavals rested with the capitalist elite, who did nothing but aggravate class antagonisms through their greed and self-interest.

Roosevelt's 1902 mediation of the anthracite strike is an instructive example.[36] The intransigence of the coal mine owners in their standoff with the striking workers forced Roosevelt's intervention and convinced him of the inability of the capitalist ruling class to protect their own interests, much less the general social and economic order. Years later, Roosevelt recalled his role in the 1902 strike, in which he betrayed his class affinities and his essential conservatism together with his belief in capitalists' shortsightedness. "I was anxious to save the great coal operators and all of the class of big propertied men, of which they were members, from the dreadful punishment which their own folly would have brought on them if I had not acted."[37] It was capitalists' greed and narrow-mindedness that produced the miserable wages and working and living conditions that led to the socially volatile condition in which labor unrest frequently turned violent and radical economic and political doctrines became appealing to the masses.

The virtues that Adams and Roosevelt counterpoised with those dominant under capitalism were virtues embodied by the aristocrat-warrior of antiquity, the Middle Ages, or the American frontier. The virtues that Adams and Roosevelt esteemed most were a masculine and virile character, physical strength, courage, valor, honor, and self-sacrifice earned in physical confrontation. It was a strength of will that Roosevelt described as "an indomitable will of power to do without shrinking the rough work that must always be done, and to preserve through the long days of slow progress or of seeming failure which always come before any final triumph."[38] These were not the characteristics of the Economic Man whom Adams personified in the form of the banker, the gold bug, the plutocrat, and the Jew.[39] The characteristics most esteemed by these thinkers were not those requisite for success in a capitalist economy. The attributes prized by the capitalist type, such as calculation, self-interest, narrow specialization, and moneymaking, were those associated with the head. For Adams and Roosevelt, however, the most highly esteemed character virtues were those synonymous with emotions, or the heart. In an address to a group of veterans in Burlington, Vermont, in 1901 Roosevelt stated:

> All great and extraordinary actions come from the heart. There are seasons in human affairs when qualities, fit enough to conduct the common business of life, are feeble and useless, when men must trust to emotion for that safety which reason at such times can never give. These are the feelings which led the ten thousand over the Carduchian mountains; these are the feelings by which a handful of Greeks broke in pieces the power of Persia; and in the fens of the Dutch and in the mountains of the Swiss these feelings defended happiness and revenged the oppression of man! God calls all the passions out in their keenness and vigor for the present safety of mankind, anger and revenge and the heroic mind, and a readiness to suffer—all the secret strength, all the invisible array of the feelings— all that nature has reserved for the great scenes of the world. When the usual hopes and the common aids of man are all gone, nothing remains under God but those passions which have often proved the best ministers of His purpose and the surest protectors of the world.[40]

To Adams and Roosevelt, the historical figures of ancient and medieval Europe exemplified character types that the American nation— and Western civilization—most urgently needed. According to Roosevelt, "military preparedness taught young men that there were ideals other than money making."[41] For the warrior-aristocrats, the loss of heroic virtues and martial and imaginative character types would lead to the decline of the nation and Western civilization. "If we ever grow to feel that we can afford to let the keen, fearless, virile qualities of heart and mind and body be lost," Roosevelt warned, "then we will prepare the way for inevitable and shameful disaster in the future."[42]

With only a slight modification, these attacks on the capitalist mentality and the failure of the ruling class were a theme for the majority of conservatives in this tradition. Where Adams and Roosevelt do differ is in their view of barbarism. Most conservatives, even those critical of capitalism, regarded barbarism as diametrically opposed to civilization and the values and institutions of conservatism. The threat of a return to barbarism is, in fact, a perennial shibboleth in the conservative discourse. For Adams and Roosevelt, however, barbarism, at least when exhibited by white Anglo-Saxons, reflected the martial spirit and had an ennobling and regenerative capability, and they mourned its extinction among the American population. Although they did not want to return to the primordial age, they did believe that a healthy dose of the barbaric, or martial, spirit would be a desirable antidote to materialism and decadence and necessary for the nation's health.

Recall that in *The Law*, Adams argued that the decline in a civilization begins when the spirit of the Economic Man becomes dominant and the martial spirit no longer animates human energy. The "savage" or "barbarian" immigrants from southern and eastern Europe, Native Americans, African Americans, Chinese, Filipinos, and Puerto Ricans required the direction and education provided by civilized white Americans, so the martial character of people fighting for their independence against American imperialism needed to be repressed and their "barbarianism" forcibly eliminated. Roosevelt's and Adams's conception of the ruling class's character type was specific to white men. Indeed, the frontier, for which Roosevelt was the superior character type, was exclusively male.[43] Women also had a role in Roosevelt's vision, but it was largely as mothers devoted to their family, nation, and race.[44] Likewise, Adams glorified maternity as a woman's highest achievement.[45] Clearly, if the training ground for public leadership took place on Roosevelt's American frontier or San Juan Hill, from which nonwhites and women were excluded, then their role in the regenerative project was clearly subordinate to that of white men.

To preserve Anglo-American civilization, Roosevelt and Adams sought the regeneration of the martial spirit embodied in an American "warrior-aristocracy" that could guide the capitalists' economic power for the nation's interest and benefit. For both men, the radical individualism and anti-statism of William Graham Sumner and Herbert Spencer were unappealing. Roosevelt drew on republican individualism, which held that an individual could reach his maximum potential only through being a member of and serving the interests of a larger community.[46] An emphasis on character, particularly on duty and the nation, was part of his belief that one cannot attain the fullest development of personhood through purely self-interested individualism. Besides, as both Adams and Roosevelt pointed out, the individualism of laissez-faire capitalism was an anachronism in a modern economy characterized by the concentration of business, labor, and other elements of modern industrial life. According to Adams,

> The Anglo-Saxon has been the most individual of races, and it reached high fortune under conditions which fostered individuality to a supreme degree. Such conditions prevail when the world was vacant and steam began to make rapid movement possible; but all must perceive that, as masses, solidify, the qualities of the pioneer will cease to be those that command success.[47]

In an age of concentration and economic competition, the lone economic individual of laissez-faire lore was incapable of guarding and guiding the evolutionary progress of the nation. The complexity and the interrelationship of the many, often conflicting, interests required administration and generalization. The faculty to administer and to generalize, or plan, wrote Adams, "is the faculty upon which social stability rests and is possible the greatest faculty of the human mind."[48] It is this faculty in which the modern capitalist class is weak because capitalism "demanded excessive specialization in the direction of a genius adopted to money-making." For Adams and Roosevelt, the modern economic environment made the capitalist way of thinking obsolete. The fact that they had held on as a ruling class had only intensified class antagonism. The resistance of a dying ruling class, which Adams believed capitalists to be, aggravated revolutions and makes them worse.[49] Laissez-faire capitalism, and the individualistic and self-interested mentality that it fostered, effectively became an evolutionary liability that handicapped the nation in its struggle for survival and, according to *The Law*, put it on a course toward decay.

Frederick Jackson Turner's thesis—that by the 1890s, the great and expansive America frontier had been tamed, settled, and therefore closed—had a profound influence on Roosevelt, for whom the frontier had a tremendous impact on American economic, social, political, and cultural life. The frontier symbolized the American ideal of social mobility and the opportunity to start over again, and it was an indispensable safety valve for averting class conflict.[50] Just as important, however, the frontier was a wild uninhibited space where the martial spirit could be developed, unleashed, and respected socially, and so the close of the frontier confined men to the decadent egotism and "soft-living" of bourgeois life and socially disintegrating class war.[51] It was this sense of stifled will that led Roosevelt to seek out "manly" adventures on the ranches of South Dakota, hunt wild game in Africa, and explore the Amazon River. Each adventure was about as far removed as possible from the urban, calculating life of business civilization. Although these adventures were for his own personal regeneration, the question remained: With the close of the frontier, where would the nation, and particularly the males of the Anglo-American race, find their regenerative adventure and, in the process, avert the decay of the civilization foretold by *The Law*? For Roosevelt and Adams, there was only one option: an American empire.

REGENERATING THE MARTIAL SPIRIT THROUGH AN AMERICAN EMPIRE

To Brooks Adams and Theodore Roosevelt, an American empire would serve social, cultural, political and economic purposes. Among the most important, it would provide access to new markets for American manufactured goods, which, they believed, would temper the antagonism between capital and labor and unite the two classes behind a national project of mutual class interest. Together, these features made empire the means by which America's inevitable decline, as suggested by the law of history, might be delayed or even averted. As Lears has contended, "The roots of the modern American empire were intertwined in economic interest and cultural crisis: the desire for foreign markets drew strength from elite fears that America was becoming sterile, stagnant. The effects of imperialism, too, were at once cultural and economic."[52] Adams's and Roosevelt's imperialism was intimately bound to their critique of laissez-faire capitalism and the modern life that it produced. They believed that empire provided the forum, or the alternative universe, in which capitalist calculation and self-interest were secondary to the heroic virtues, national glory, and preservation of Western civilization. Perhaps more important, empire offered economic growth, market expansion, capital accumulation, and the productive employment of America's large industrial working class. For Roosevelt and Adams, American imperial expansion was a social, cultural, economic, and political necessity that required a restructuring of American capitalism from chaotic laissez-faire competition into a state-regulated corporate capitalism efficiently administered and enlisted to both serve and profit from American empire.

Both Adams and Roosevelt operated under the assumptions of what today might be called the "realist school of international relations." They argued that nations were in constant struggle with one another over land, resources, labor, and markets and that imperialism was not a choice but was necessary for national survival. As Adams stated in *The Law*, America either had to expand or face degeneration and decay. "There is nothing stationary in the universe. Not to advance is to go backward," he declared.[53] He was very much an economic determinist. In *America's Economic Supremacy* and later in *The New Empire*, he maintained that international competition and the struggle for imperial supremacy were in fact struggles for economic supremacy.[54] For Adams, American imperialism in the Caribbean, the Philippines, and, most important, China, was essential to America's survival because it opened markets where American goods could be sold.[55] Adams saw China, in particular, as a market to absorb American manufacturing surplus, and he saw Russia and Japan as America's chief rivals in the region. Imperial expansion was an attempt to solve the problem of overproduction and the class conflict it produced in highly developed economies like the United States, where business and industry were consolidated and centralized.[56] An American empire was an outlet through which corporate capital could expand and sell its wares to new markets rather than compete into extinction at home.

According to Adams, for more than a thousand years, the "social center of civilization," that is, the economic and imperial center, had progressively moved westward.[57] The Dutch and then the British were the last great economic and imperial powerhouses, who spread development and civilization to all their colonies. The British, Adams believed, were in decline and it was America's turn to carry the torch for Western civilization. History had designated America to become the standard-bearer of Western civilization if, and only if, it chose to rise to the challenge. Roosevelt agreed and pointed to the subjection of the Native Americans and the white settlement of the western United States as one of the greatest civilizing events the world had ever known. In *The Winning of the West*, Roosevelt justified, in overtly racist terms, the white settlement of the American frontier and the destruction of the Native Americans who inhabited the land. His conclusions regarding the justification of the whites' conquest of the frontier remained unchanged throughout his life and informed his aggressive imperialism in the Caribbean and the Philippines. "During the past three centuries," he wrote, "the spread of English speaking peoples over the world's waste spaces has been not only the most striking feature in the world's history but also the event of all others most far-reaching in its effects and its importance."[58] For him, the conquest of the western frontier and the "inferior peoples" that inhabited it was fundamentally a project "in the interest of mankind and civilization."[59]

Roosevelt viewed the American colonial subjugation of the Philippines in the same way as he did the conquest of the American West. Anglo-Americans were not only justified in exploiting the markets of their imperial possessions but also historically obligated by the "white man's burden" to "improve" subjugated people. This improvement project, according to Roosevelt, involved making the colonized people "fit for self-government" by training them in the art of "obedience to law," which is the "first essential of civilization."[60] So long as the Filipinos failed to demonstrate otherwise, Roosevelt endorsed American imperial paternalism there. It was the duty of the Anglo-American imperialists to be the stewards of the Filipinos for the purpose of teaching them the republican virtues necessary for self-government.[61]

> Only the exceptional people have ever succeeded in the experiment of self-government because its needs, its interest, and its successful working imply the existence within the heart of the average citizen of certain high qualities. There must be control. There must be mastery, somewhere, and if there is no self-control and self-mastery, the control and mastery will ultimately be imposed from without.[62]

Influenced by Adams, Roosevelt was convinced that at some point in their existence, all nations become weak and stationary and must die. They both believed that the United States had an opportunity to join the pantheon of nations whose triumphs future generations would always remember:

> [T]he nation that has dared to be great, that has had the will and the power to change the destiny of the ages, in the end must die, yet no less surely the nation that has played the part of the weakling must also die; and whereas the nation that has done nothing leaves nothing behind it, the nation that has done a great work really continues, through in changed form, to live forevermore. The Roman has passed away exactly as all the nations of antiquity which did not expand when he expanded have passed away; but their very memory has vanished, while he himself is still a living force throughout the wide world in our entire civilization of today, and will so continue through countless generations, through untold ages.[63]

The Spanish-American War of 1898 afforded the United States the opportunity to travel the heroic road of the Romans. Adams and Roosevelt recognized the United States' national and economic interests in acquiring Puerto Rico, Cuba, and the Philippines. In fact, this point should not be underestimated, since both men highlighted the importance of imperial expansion and its economic benefits as a source of power, vis-à-vis other nations, particularly Russia and Japan, and also as a necessity resulting from competition and concentration in the U.S. domestic economy.

THE CONSERVATISM OF ROOSEVELT'S STATIST REFORM

An American empire required significant reforms on the home front in order for it to succeed. Roosevelt and Adams recognized that the United States was fundamentally different at the turn of the twentieth century from what it had been one hundred years earlier when economic laissez-faire seemed more compatible with the nation's economic development, which constituted primarily of slave plantations, small family farms, artisan workshops, and small manufacturing operations. The current era of Big Business, industry, and international finance, however, made the laissez-faire ideology of limited government antiquated and even dangerous to the nation's order, stability, survival, and imperial ambition. The consolidation and centralization that were evident everywhere in the world of business required the state to have an administrative capability of regulating business concerns in the interest of the nation. Therefore, out of the conservative principles that placed the highest value on maintaining class hierarchy, domestic stability, and an imperialist foreign policy, Roosevelt and Adams advocated reform.[64]

The problem with the concentration of economic power and the proper course of public policy in regard to the concentration of business was perhaps the central economic question of Roosevelt's presidential and postpresidential years. Lawyer and Supreme Court Justice Louis D. Brandeis, among other Progressives, argued that the best remedy against plutocracy, corporate power, and class conflict was a policy of economic decentralization.[65] Unlike Brandeis, Roosevelt did not believe that the problem with Big Business was size. Instead, for Roosevelt, the problem with Big Business was that government had minimal influence over their activities. As Michael Sandel has observed, Roosevelt broke with the republican tradition by embracing consolidated political power in the form of the federal government in order to counter and control the consolidated power of Big Business by using the language of republicanism.[66] In Sandel's estimation, Roosevelt "sought to cultivate in citizens the qualities of character essential to self-government."[67] However, Roosevelt's republicanism was not of the Jeffersonian sort. An essential precondition for a Jeffersonian republican citizenship is economic independence, as advocated by Brandeis. Brandeis's vision consisted of instituting industrial democracy in which workers, through their labor unions, would share decision-making power with the firm's owner, for whom they worked. In addition, Brandeis called for those companies that were too large and economically powerful to be broken up into smaller, more manageable firms. In Brandeis's view, Big Business wielded so much economic power that it threatened political democracy.

Brandeis's modern Jeffersonian republicanism implied a greater level of economic equality and a significant level of political initiative on the part of ordinary citizens that was lacking in Roosevelt's vision. Roosevelt's republicanism was concerned with such republican issues as the fear of corruption and luxury and the cultivation of civic virtue among citizens, but his conception of civic virtue was more narrowly defined. He placed the capability for political initiative with virtuous governing elites rather than with the average citizen. In addition, Roosevelt's republican vision lacked a critique of economic inequality and, by extension, an emphasis on greater economic equality as a necessary condition for republican self-government.

Roosevelt saw the capitalist, and in particular the capitalist elite, through a republican lens, which located a tension between commerce and civic virtue. According to republican theory, the stability and well-being of the republic and the liberty of its people depended on a high level of civic virtue among its citizens. Without this, the polity would gradually rot from within as citizens neglected the public sphere in favor of tending to their private affairs. With their liberty sacrificed to a corrupt political class, the republic would soon succumb to internal discord, decline, and despotism.[68]

Even though Roosevelt often made these republican arguments, his republicanism was not inclusive and participatory. Rather, to him the ideal republican citizen was one "willing and able to take arms for the defense of the flag" and father "many healthy children."[69] The gender exclusion of this definition of republican citizenship notwithstanding, it is nevertheless a very limited way of defining the duties of citizens. In particular, it lacks the core of republicanism, which is a politically active public. Roosevelt embraced the referendum during his Bull Moose insurgency campaign against the political establishment and often told audiences that republican citizenship required more than periodic voting. Yet throughout his political career, he dismissed popular protest as the work of demagogues, socialists, muckrakers, and other radicals. His faith in the wisdom of the public was further shaken when they did not give him their support. An instructive example is his disillusionment with the public following Woodrow Wilson's election. Roosevelt declared, "I despise Wilson, but I despise still more our foolish, foolish people who, partly from ignorance and partly from sheer timidity and partly from lack of imagination and of sensitive national feeling, support him."[70] Such statements suggest that Roosevelt's faith in the political wisdom of the average citizen was tenuous at best and that the republican renewal he envisioned was of an elite variety. Considering Roosevelt's ambivalence toward the common citizen, he may have expected the public to defer to the officials of the federal government, like himself, who possessed a strong sense of civic virtue to safeguard the public interest. Instead of a new republican political economy, then, Roosevelt embodied a state paternalism like that of the British prime minister, Benjamin Disraeli, and the German chancellor, Otto von Bismarck. Indeed, as historian Richard Hofstadter pointed out, Roosevelt saw himself and the virtuous elite like himself to stand above class and "special interests" and to govern in the interest of the nation.[71]

Roosevelt recognized the corrupting effects that large corporations and monopolies had on the body politic. But instead of breaking up large business concerns, he sought to control them "in order to protect the people" through the consolidated power of the federal government.[72] Departing from traditional republican political economy, Roosevelt, together with Adams and many influential Progressives including Herbert Croly, whose *The Promise of American Life* offered the theoretical justification for Roosevelt's "New Nationalism," saw consolidated political power in the national government as the most able defender of the republican nation. That is, the officials of the federal government were the guardians of the public interest, holding corporations accountable to the national interest.

Roosevelt believed that public officials needed to act as stewards of the public interest. In the economic domain, this meant that the state must intervene in the economy to ensure fair competition and to channel corporate interests toward the national interest. He knew that leaving regulation to the individual states would be ineffective, as many of the largest corporations were national in scope. For Roosevelt, the centralization of business was an inevitable product of the evolution and development of the economy. In addition, a modern nation with imperial ambitions required goods that could be efficiently produced by large corporations. "Either we must modify our present obsolete laws regarding concentration and co-operation," he declared, "so as to conform with the world movement, or else fall behind in the race for the world's markets."[73] Concentration was a "world-wide movement." To resist or ignore it was akin to national suicide.

As a reformer, Roosevelt sought to centralize power in the federal government as a counter to the power of Big Business and Big Labor. In his first annual message to Congress in 1901, Roosevelt stated:

> The tremendous and highly complex industrial development which went on with ever-accelerated rapidity during the latter half of the nineteenth century brings us face to face, at the beginning of the twentieth, with very serious social problems. The old laws, and the old customs which had almost the binding force of law, were once quite sufficient to regulate the accumulation and distribution of wealth. Since the industrial changes which have so enormously increased the productive power of mankind, they are no longer sufficient.[74]

Roosevelt became a reformer out of the fear that if capitalism was not regulated and capitalist greed continued unabated, the imperial panacea to America's moral and economic crises would be futile. Thus, over the course of his presidency and after, he endorsed measures like the regulation of railroad rates; legislation banning sweatshops; corporate transparency legislation; workers' compensation; child labor legislation; the eight-hour workday; workplace safety regulations; the right of unions to organize, strike, and bargain collectively; free schools; housing regulation; an inheritance tax; and an income tax. At the time, other conservatives and business interests charged that these policy positions were nothing short of socialistic.

But Roosevelt never meant to upend the social order, redistribute wealth, or replace capitalism. Although conservative reformers like him agreed with some of the grievances of workers, farmers, and poor people, Roosevelt detested socialists, radical labor leaders, Populists, and radical reformers who organized political movements around these grievances. He saw them as dangerous, and his reforms were meant to protect the established order from more radical demands for systemic change. Roosevelt derided those journalists as "muck-rakers" who wrote about the abuse, corruption, and injustice of corporate America, accusing them of insincerity and incitement of social unrest. In an 1896 campaign speech entitled "The Menace of the Demagogue," he equated William Jennings Bryan, Eugene Debs, Jacob Coxey, and others with the Reign of Terror of Jean-Paul Marat, Bertrand Barère, and Maximilien Robespierre.[75] In apocalyptical fashion, Roosevelt argued that Bryan, then the Democratic and Populist candidate for president, was "against morality and ability," aiming to "tear down the men of means, virtue, and talent," and, if elected would "substitute a government of a mob, by the demagogue, for the shiftless and disorderly and the criminal and the semi-criminal."[76] At one point, Roosevelt advocated "taking ten or a dozen of [the Populist] leaders out . . . standing them against a wall and shooting them dead."[77] The belief that politics was a life-or-death struggle permeated Roosevelt's career. In 1909, he concluded that socialism was "hostile to the intellectual, the religious, the domestic and moral life; it is a form of communism with no moral foundation, but essentially based on the immediate annihilation of personal ownership of capital, and, in the near future, the annihilation of the family, and ultimately the annihilation of civilization."[78] For Roosevelt and Adams, then, the social order, civilization, and America's supremacy were threatened not only by the irresponsible rule of the capitalist elite but, perhaps more important, by radicals from below. While the warrior-aristocrats' vision departed from the status quo rule of the capitalist elite and was hostile to the alternatives offered by Populists, agrarians, and social-ists, it was effectively meant to solidify the hierarchical social relations of the corporate capitalist economy and an expanding empire.

Roosevelt and Adams never tired of reminding their conservative colleagues that reform was a means to conserve. In the final annual message to Congress of his presidency, Roosevelt insisted that

> a blind and ignorant resistance to every effort for the reform of abuses and for the readjustment of society to modern conditions rep-resents not true conservatism but an incitement to the wildest radi-calism; for wise radicalism and wise conservatism go hand in hand, one bent on progress, the other bent on seeing that no change is made unless in the right direction.[79]

Betraying his class sentiments and the conservative assumptions behind his most progressive policy prescriptions, Roosevelt continued to justify the necessity of reform as a means to "save . . . the class of big propertied men" and to dodge the explosion of revolutionary fer-ment, which, he believed, was just below the surface.[80] In a 1910 speech in Denver to the Colorado Live Stock Association, Roosevelt main-tained that "true conservatism is that conservatism which is also the embodiment of the wise spirit of progress. It is that conservatism which acts conservatively before that has happened which will inflame men to madness."[81]

Adams and Roosevelt, atypical even among conservatives of their own era, worried about the danger to domestic stability posed by an uncontrolled capitalism. Thus their statist and imperialistic alterna-tive to laissez-faire came out of their conservative commitment to avert revolution and to save modern capitalism from its worst enemy, its own unrestrained self.[82] Through political centralization and a policy of corporate regulation, Roosevelt and Adams hoped to save the capi-talist elite from its own mistakes by ameliorating some of the most galling misery and exploitation produced by laissez-faire capitalism.

The enormous economic, social, cultural, and political transforma-tions that occurred during the decades between the end of the Civil War and the beginning of World War I produced Brooks Adams's and Theodore Roosevelt's distinct conservative critique of capitalism. It was the first American conservative critique of laissez-faire capitalism without the benefit of a conservative alternative material reality. Accordingly, Adams, Roosevelt, and other American warrior-critics of business civilization were forced to create a conservative alternative of empire and a regulated capitalism on which capitalism could be secured.

After the Civil War, there was a pervasive sense in the United States—a sentiment shared by Adams and Roosevelt—that the American republic and Western civilization were at a crossroads. The rule of the Economic Man had brought innovation, prosperity, and economic progress. Nonetheless, this was an era plagued by political corruption and class conflict, which Roosevelt and Adams worried would inevitably lead to revolution, foreign conquest, and national decay. Brooks Adams's and Theodore Roosevelt's indictment of laissez-faire capitalism marked a distinct chapter in the conservative intellectual tradition. They indicted capitalism for a number of reasons, some of which are consistent throughout the critical tradition, including its threat to stability and social hierarchy, the materialistic and self-interested virtues it cultivates, its destruction of a virtuous ruling class, and its failure to generate a responsible ruling class of its own. A recurring theme in the American conservative tradition critical of capitalism is the idea that the capitalist elite is, in various ways, an ineffective ruling class.[83] In this narrative, it is the ruling class that prioritizes class rule and private profit over the interests of the nation. Roosevelt's and Adams's elevation of the strenuous life, the martial and imaginative character type, and their depreciation of the capitalist life as preoccupied with moneymaking is part of this broader critical current of thought in the conservative intellectual tradition. The aim of Adams's and Roosevelt's alternative was to resurrect a passion to counterbalance a nation, its culture, and, in particular, its ruling class, which was animated exclusively by self-interested commercial considerations.[84] The two men, though, did more than merely update old critiques. They made an important contribution to the American conservative discourse on capitalism by bringing in the state and adding the imperial dimension to their alternative to laissez-faire.

Unlike the defenders of slavery before them and many of the twentieth-century critics after them, Adams and Roosevelt embraced the economic concentration and centralization of American business, industry, and finance. The warrior-critics at the turn of the century believed that America's prosperity and national strength were bound to the success of corporate capitalism, and, perhaps even more important, so were the class relations of hierarchy and power that conservatives had always defended. At the same time, however, corporate capitalism depended on a strong, active state both at home and abroad. For the warrior-aristocrats, the regulatory state and American empire were necessary to save capitalism materially, as it was a forum for civic renewal on which, at least in their minds, the progress of civilization depended. Roosevelt's and Adams's concerns about America's, and Western civilization's, impending decline may have been overstated. However, the warrior-critics' imprint on the trajectory that the United States would take in both domestic and foreign policy is evident. The horrors of World War I soon dispelled the illusion of adventure, heroism, and grandeur underlying Adams's and Roosevelt's regenerative vision. But the statist alternative to laissez-faire, together with the domestic benefits of empire in the form of U.S. economic supremacy, became the pillars of U.S. political economy and foreign policy continuing to the present.[85]

3

THE AGRARIAN CRITIQUE OF CAPITALISM

The amenities of life also suffer under the curse of a strictly-business or industrial civilization. They consist in such practices as manners, conversation, hospitality, sympathy, family life, romantic love—in the social exchanges which reveal and develop sensibility in human affairs. If religion and the arts are founded on the right relations of man-to-nature, these are founded on right relations of man-to-man.

Introduction: A Statement of Principles, *I'll Take My Stand*

There was a Southern civilization whose course was halted with those conventions of 1867 by which the negro suffrage in the South—not in the North—was planned, and the pillaging began. But that does not imply that this Southern civilization, once the fine flower of men's lives, is wholly dead; for the core of our humanity lies in the belief that the essence of the soul is its mockery of death.

Stark Young, "Not in Memoriam, but in Defense," *I'll Take My Stand*

n the 1920s, the United States found itself in a new position. The yearning of Brooks Adams, Theodore Roosevelt, and the warrior-aristocrats for American unity, will to power, and empire had been achieved only partially. The United States' imperial reach now extended beyond the continent to Puerto Rico, the Philippines, and elsewhere, and along with the European powers, U.S. businesses had penetrated the long sought after market of mainland China.[1] By the end of World War I, the United States had become the preeminent economic power in the world. It was the largest producer of goods and the world's foremost creditor nation. New York City had supplanted London as the leading financial center of international capitalism.[2] As one of the victors in the Great War, President Woodrow Wilson occupied a prominent seat at the Paris Peace Conference, indicating America's status and joining Great Britain and France as one of the great powers on the world stage. But if Adams and Roosevelt found solace in America's military triumph, their political project of restoring a virtuous ruling class of statesmen proved to be a failure. During the prosperity of the 1920s, wealthy capitalists—particularly industrialists, financiers, and bankers—continued to assert political, social, and ideological dominance. President Calvin Coolidge spoke in the spirit of the era when he declared, "The man who builds a factory builds a temple. The man who works there worships there."[3] In a clear repudiation of the martial spirit advocated by Adams and Roosevelt and a far cry from their call for Americans to do something worthy of historical memory, President Warren G. Harding promised the public "not heroics but healing, not nostrums but normalcy."[4]

Normalcy had wide-ranging economic, political, social, and cultural effects. The 1920s witnessed the greatest number of corporate mergers and consolidations since the 1880s and 1890s.[5] Corporate oligopolies, rather than monopolies, dominated entire industries, from banking to steel making, and their growth allowed them to expand to new markets, both domestic and abroad.[6] Aided by a business-friendly Supreme Court and the three pro-business presidents Harding, Coolidge, and Herbert Hoover, American manufacturers produced goods for a domestic consumer market that grew with the advent of Fordism and the expansion of consumer credit.[7] American consumers largely bought on margin and on the installment plan, which became widely used for buying everything from automobiles, radios, and refrigerators to stocks on the New York Stock Exchange.[8] Indeed, the shift in the 1920s was from an economy driven primarily by old industries like oil, steel, railroads, and textiles to one based on the manufacture of consumer goods such as processed foods, automobiles, and home appliances. Indicative of this trend, the Ford Motor Company opened the largest factory in the world in River Rouge, Michigan, which employed more than 75,000 workers to produce 10,000 cars per day. In addition, General Motors, Ford's rival, produced a full line of cars that were updated annually, offered in different colors, and priced for nearly every budget. This shift in the economy also fostered the growth of service industries such as finance, insurance, and clerical work.[9] The prosperity of the 1920s proved to be temporary, however.

The severe but relatively brief recession of 1920 was particularly hard on American farmers. As crop prices dropped and foreclosures mounted, 500,000 people—primarily small farmers, sharecroppers, and tenant farmers—and other people in rural areas migrated in droves to the cities in search of jobs.[10] In fact, in 1920, for the first time in U.S. history, more people lived in cities than in rural areas.[11] In the meantime, after the strikes in 1919—in which labor unsuccessfully fought wage cuts and layoffs resulting from the reconversion of industry from war production to consumer goods—the number of unions dropped throughout the decade. Aided by the government dragnet of radicals in the Palmer Raids, business and industry aggressively resisted unionization. Nonetheless, throughout the 1920s, business profits continued to rise as productivity continued to surge. But with the exception of a few industries, such as steel, in which labor saw notable wage hikes, the vast majority of workers received only marginal wage increases, contributing to the enormous wealth inequality on the eve of the Great Depression.[12] As economic historian Richard B. DuBoff argues, a major crisis was in the making by the middle of the decade, caused by an overcapacity of production and a decline in residential investment, both due to a lack of demand (at prevailing prices). Overcapacity and overproduction then led industries to reduce their workforces, which further undermined demand. Heavily indebted holding companies, insurance firms, and banks soon folded as their investors called in their debts, which led to the stock market crash on October 29, 1929.[13]

In the 1930s, the pervasive misery and suffering of the economic depression produced a plethora of social, political, and economic critiques and alternatives to the prevailing way. To be sure, there were influential defenders of laissez-faire capitalism who insisted that despite the mass unemployment, eviction, hunger, and poverty, the market would soon right itself and that no structural reform of the nation's political economy was necessary. Of this persuasion were the U.S. Chamber of Commerce, the National Association of Manufacturers, the Liberty League, and corporate executives such as Alfred P. Sloan of General Motors, Secretary of the Treasury Andrew Mellon, and President Herbert Hoover.[14] These individuals' and organizations' defense of laissez-faire was attacked by both the political mainstream and those on the margins of American politics. Many of these critics became New Dealers, some more progressive than others, but all believed that the Depression required government action in order to save capitalism. President Franklin Delano Roosevelt criticized big business as "economic royalists" and openly taunted the Liberty League but resisted the more radical measures advocated by those on the left and right, including some members of his cabinet, such as Secretary of Labor Frances Perkins, Secretary of the Interior Harold Ickes, and Secretary of Agriculture Henry Wallace; socialists and communists; the Congress of Industrial Organizations (CIO); Huey Long's "Share Our Wealth Plan"; and the fascist alternative offered by Father Charles E. Coughlin.

Among the most interesting and penetrating conservative critics of America's political economy in the 1920s and 1930s were the Southern Agrarians, who included John Crowe Ransom, Donald Davidson, Frank Lawrence Owsley, John Gould Fletcher, Lyle H. Lanier, Allen Tate, Herman Clarence Nixon, Andrew Nelson Lytle, Robert Penn Warren, John Donald Wade, Henry Blue Kline, and Stark Young. Some of the Agrarians are better known than others. Moreover, their renown stems not from their work on agrarianism but from their literary projects. Ransom, Tate, and Davidson, who spearheaded the group, were associated with the *Fugitive*, a short-lived but well-received journal of modernist poetry. Ransom was a well-regarded poet and later became the founder of the *Kenyon Review*, an influential literary journal of New Criticism, a text-centered theoretical approach to literary analysis that emphasizes a close reading of the text. Along with Ransom, Tate was a leading figure in New Criticism as well as an influential poet, novelist, journal editor, and literary critic in his own right. Davidson was a poet and essayist as well. In addition to his literary work, he continued to write political tracts long after the group had broken up. His *Attack on Leviathan* and other essays are ardent defenses of the South, including racial segregation, which he defended well into the civil rights era. Warren was a Pulitzer Prize–winning poet, novelist, and author of the classic *All the King's Men* (1946). The exceptions to the men of letters were Lanier, who was a psychologist, and Owsley and Nixon, who were historians. Owsley wrote neo-Confederate, racist histories. His "The Pillars of Agrarianism" is crucial to *Conservatives Against Capitalism* because it is the clearest expression of the Southern Agrarians' economic program. All the Agrarians except for Fletcher and Young were either faculty or students at Vanderbilt University. Of this group, Ransom, Tate, Owsley, and Davidson were the most overtly critical of corporate industrial capitalism, and their ideas were at the heart of the Agrarians' programmatic writings. Their manifesto, entitled *I'll Take My Stand: The South and the Agrarian Tradition*, first published in 1930, was a collection of essays that made the defense of the South and, to a lesser extent, agrarianism its centerpiece. Broadly, their manifesto was an indictment of industrial capitalism and consumerism, which they contrasted with the humanism of the agrarian rural South.[15] *I'll Take My Stand* and *Who Owns America?*, an overtly political and programmatic tract published in 1936 with contributions from Northern Distributists, were the most radical indictments of capitalism offered by twentieth-century conservatives.

Upon the publication of *I'll Take My Stand*, the Southern Agrarians were roundly criticized as antimodern, reactionary, and ignorant of history, as their tract romanticized and distorted the Southern past and ignored, even celebrated, the region's poverty.[16] Until the mid-1930s, the Southern Agrarians, or at least those among the original twelve who still subscribed to agrarianism, wrote their most political and programmatic works, which were a departure from the conservative thinking at the time and from much of twentieth-century conservatism. In the wake of *I'll Take My Stand*, the Agrarians tried to build a following through speaking tours, published rebuttals to their critics, and a failed attempt to found an agrarian journal, but they were unable to create much popular interest. Although their traditionalism influenced Richard Weaver, Russell Kirk, and M. E. Bradford, among others, their radical agrarianism—from which all the Agrarians except Davidson defected—never materialized into a political movement beyond a small group of intellectuals and social critics.[17] Indeed, Tate himself later admitted that Southern Agrarianism never intended to establish a political program, that it was merely an "reaffirmation of the humane tradition."[18]

THE SOUTHERN AGRARIANS' CRITIQUE OF LAISSEZ-FAIRE CORPORATE AND INDUSTRIAL CAPITALISM

Southern Agrarian thought was at the core of the tension in conservative thinking between free-market capitalism and a conservative social, political, and cultural order. The Southern Agrarians confronted this tension openly, arguing that a conservative culture and polity could not be based on the current capitalist model, which they viewed as destructive of the economic foundation of the Southern way of life. "We are on the side of those who know that the common enemy of the people, of their government, their liberty, and their property, must be abated," wrote Frank Owsley. "This enemy is a system which allows a relatively few men to control most of the nation's wealth and to regiment virtually the whole population under their anonymous holding companies and corporations, and to control government by bribery or intimidation."[19] The Southern Agrarians rejected capitalism in its corporate and laissez-faire forms, as well as socialism and communism, fascism, and much, but not all, of the New Deal. For them, a return to a traditional social order was a panacea for the ills of modern life that required a radical change in the nation's political economy. More specifically, they called for agrarianism based on a redistribution of rural private property. Their vision was to recover the individualism of a nation of yeoman farmers, whom, they believed, were the social and economic foundation of the South. To do this, the

Southern Agrarians called for the state to help preserve and expand a polity made up of small farmers and based on landed private property, religion, community, and the traditions and heritage of the South.

These cornerstones of Southern Agrarianism were threatened by plutocratic laissez-faire corporate capitalism, on the one hand, and movements for equality and empowerment by labor and civil rights groups, on the other, all of which threatened to destroy the traditional conservative order of the South. The Southern Agrarians' vision was premised on social hierarchy. Initially, some of the Agrarians esteemed the European feudal order and the planter elite of the Old South, but they soon recognized that there was no going back. Most of the Southern Agrarians were conservative populists, whose populism rejected corporate wealth but retained a faith in the racial and class hierarchies of traditional Southern society. Their conservative populist project made space for planters and large landowners, as well as white yeoman farmers, while subordinating poor whites and African Americans. Their vision, according to Owsley, meant that "the agrarian population and the people of the agricultural market towns must dominate the social, cultural, economic, and political life of the state and give tone to it."[20] The Southern way of life that the Southern Agrarians so esteemed was based on class and racial domination enforced by a regime of political disenfranchisement, white terror, and racial apartheid, none of which their alternative challenged. Indeed, several historians have pointed out that the Southern Agrarians were "unhistorical" and "utopian" for attempting to recover a political economy based on the family farm at a time when it was in a decades-long decline.[21] Thus, in many ways, the Southern Agrarians were the last gasp of a radically conservative critique of capitalism offered in American political thought.[22]

The Southern Agrarians believed that the small farmer was the repository of virtues such as self-reliance and moral integrity as well as the bedrock of a conservative, stable, republican society. For them, such a society was based on decentralized rural private property. Their defense of the yeoman farmer was, in large part, a reaction to the corporatization of Southern agriculture as holding companies, banks, insurance firms and other absentee landlords became owners of vast tracts of rural land.[23]

The Southern Agrarians—particularly Tate, Ransom, and Owsley—felt that a property system based on corporate industrial and financial capitalism was alienating and economically exploitative of laborers and farmers. The use of technology displaced laborers and robbed their work of its enjoyment. Similar to critiques by socialists and the defenders of slavery nearly a century before, the Southern Agrarians believed that industrial capitalism transformed labor from "one of the happy functions of human life" into an activity "evidently brutalizing."[24] "Labor is made hard, its tempo fierce, and employment is insecure," wrote John Crowe Ransom.[25] The Southern Agrarians viewed the work of farmers as more enjoyable because it was not as hurried or monotonous as that of an assembly-line employee. The agrarian way of life offered a natural, organic work routine fixed by the changing seasons and the unpredictable wonder of nature rather than the drudgery of industrial capitalism.[26] This critique of industrial capitalism made by John Crowe Ransom and Frank Owsley was similar to that made by the defenders of slavery. Perhaps not surprising, the Southern Agrarians were fond of comparing the humanism of farm life and the farmer's relationship to his land with the alienation of corporate industrial and finance capitalism. In "The South Defends Its Heritage," Ransom wrote:

A man can contemplate and explore, respect and love an object as substantial as a farm or a native province. But he cannot contemplate nor explore, respect nor love a mere turnover, such as an assemblage of "natural resources," a pile of money, a volume of produce, a market, or a credit system. It is into precisely these intangibles that industrialism would translate the farmer's farm. It means the dehumanization of his life.[27]

The agrarian way of life offered the individual an opportunity to develop a whole host of abilities beyond tending to the crops, including the building of his home and barn, metal working in the repair of his tools, cloth work in the sewing of his clothes, and cooking in the preparation of food. The Southern Agrarian Andrew Nelson Lytle described the variety offered by farm labor in the following idealized terms:

Each morning the farmer wakes to some new action. There is the time for breaking the ground, the time for planting, the exciting moment when the crops begin to show themselves, palely green, upon the surface of the earth, the steady progress toward the ripe harvest, or it may be a barren harvest.[28]

Industrial work, the Southern Agrarians argued, subjugated laborers to the tempo of the machines, the tyranny of the shop foreman, layers of corporate managers, and the artificial totalitarianism of the time clock, conditions that made workers little more than industrial slaves.[29] Corporate property relations gave the corporation immense power over the individual worker, who was ruled by a daily routine not of his making and made him dependent on the firm and the market for his survival.

Similar humanistic critiques made by the Southern Agrarians were made by other thinkers across the political spectrum, but the Southern Agrarians' central critique of capitalism came from a distinctively conservative orientation. They contended that capitalism and traditionalism were opposing tendencies and could not be reconciled. Corporate industrial capitalism was incompatible with time-honored traditions and customs and therefore was infertile ground for a conservative culture and social order. Indeed, other conservative critics, including Russell Kirk and Samuel Francis, came to a similar conclusion, but the Southern Agrarians, alone among twentieth-century conservatives, located the focus of reform in the economic base rather than in cultural reform, where present-day conservatives contend it should be. For the Southern Agrarians, culture had a material base:

The higher myth of religion, the lower myth of history, even ordinary codes of conduct, cannot preserve themselves; indeed they do not exist apart from our experience. Since the most significant feature of our experience is the way we make our living, the economic basis of life is the soil out of which all the forms, good or bad, of our experience must come.[30]

The agrarian way of life and labor was, in many ways, shaped by the farmer's dependence on nature, especially on the quality of the soil, the rain, the wind, the rising and setting sun, the heat and the cold, and the changing seasons, which dictated to him the work that had to be done. It humbled the farmer in ways that the industrial laborer, surrounded by gigantic and technologically advanced man-made tools, machinery, buildings, infrastructure, and organization, could not be. The contingency of an unexpected drought or an extended cold spell, natural forces that humans cannot control, did not affect the daily productive life of the industrial laborer in the metropolis in the way it affected the rural farmer. In fact, the farmer's work, his survival, depended on the forces of nature. Through his work, he had an intimate relationship with the power and unpredictability of natural forces. His own smallness and helplessness in the face of nature always were apparent to him. Through such a close and dependent relationship with the natural world and its forces, the Southern Agrarians contended, the farmer tended to be more superstitious and religious. As Lytle wrote in "The Small Farm Secures the State," the Southern Agrarians believed that religious belief had its basis in a particular mode of production, that without the yeoman homestead, religiosity would be threatened and the American republic imperiled:

> [T]he genuine farmer (and it takes a proper society to make a genuine farmer) never loses his belief in God. . . . When religion grows formless and weak, it is because man in his right role as the protagonist in the great conflict is forgotten or disbelieved. He becomes vainglorious and thinks he may conquer nature. This the good farmer knows to be nonsense. He is faced constantly and immediately with a mysterious and powerful presence, which he may use but which he may never reduce entirely to his will and desires. He knows of minor successes; he remembers defeats; but he is so involved in the tremendously complex ritual of the seasonal drama that he never thinks about idle or dangerous speculations.[31]

The Southern Agrarians recognized, as did the defenders of slavery, the intimate connection between religiosity and property relations. They believed that the source of moral behavior was found in religion, which required that market relations of exchange value, calculation, and buying and selling be circumscribed, even within the arena of production, to ensure that they did not impinge on the other spheres of social life. Ransom called for a return to the hard religion of the Old Testament, while Allen Tate suggested that a new popular religion was necessary to combat the hollow religiosity of contemporary America. But both thinkers were convinced that this cultural project required radical changes in the political economy.[32]

Another important conservative element in the Southern Agrarians' critique of corporate capitalism was that it divided owners of property from social community, customs, traditions, and local hierarchies. Corporate private property, albeit hierarchical, replaced an older pattern of relations that the Southern Agrarians believed were more personal, community oriented, and socially stable. Agriculture in the era of corporate capitalism was controlled by owners who were concerned only about whether the enterprise was profitable from year to year. Corporate managers were hired by the absentee owners to run the daily operation of the enterprise, to keep the workers in line, and to ensure that the enterprise produced more profits every year. Under such a system, the productive enterprise and the personal relations between owners and workers, each with obligations toward the other, that had been the hallmark of the Southern economic and social order, eroded. Owners were divorced from the management of the enterprise, the production process, workplace relations, and the community where the enterprise was located. Owners of corporate capital lost their sense of noblesse oblige and the deference from their social inferiors that their position merited. For the Southern Agrarians, the Economic Man of Big Business, who dominated American economic and political life, operated under social imperatives and ethical principles alien to the gentleman farmer of the Old South or the Southern Agrarians' yeoman farmer. As Ransom and the Southern Agrarians saw it, the moral and ethical obligations of a capitalist elite and those of a more responsible ruling class were worlds apart. Indeed, as with conservative critics of capitalism before them, a key aspect of the Southern Agrarian critique concerned the degradation of the ruling class under capitalism:

> The true economic man is the corporation, whose multitude of owners enjoy limited liability and leave the business to agents to run

with maximum efficiency. Under big business and limited liability the spirit of *noblesse oblige* has disappeared from the working habits of the rulers of society. If it remains somewhere within consciousness, it ceases to apply at the place where it would do the most good, for in the economic world a technique has been devised which will prevent it from having any effect.[33]

As a consequence of this change in the productive relationship, every social relation was transformed into a commodity relation in which isolated individuals exchanged quantifiable values in an open market. Unlike conservative New Humanists like Irving Babbitt and Paul Elmer More and other postwar conservative cultural critics, the Southern Agrarians believed "that the economic base of society affects the cultural superstructure," according to historian Patrick Allitt.[34] Specifically, they argued that a conservative culture and community were possible only in a predominantly agrarian economic system of yeoman farmers:

> [R]eal association exists, for the generality of people, only in the agrarian community and in the villages and towns which are its adjuncts. It depends upon a stable population, upon long acquaintances . . . the city necessarily means a diminution of these associations; the casual, fleeting, formal contacts with great numbers of people only enhance a sense of isolation.[35]

Private property in the form of land on which one lives and works was the foundation through which moral obligations are cultivated and traditions are transmitted across generations. The yeoman farmer who owned, worked, and lived on his own land established roots in the community, along with its traditions, culture, and heritage. He was intimately acquainted with the natural environment, the lay of the land, and the small town where he sought community and went to market. Its traditions, customs, and heritage, little changed over time, defined his identity and the identity of his ancestors. This rootedness gave him a sense of responsibility for the well-being of his family, his plot of land, and the community to which he belonged. The Southern Agrarians argued that these sensibilities that traditionalist conservatives prized were grounded in a distinct economic structure that nurtured these behaviors and sentiments. The Southern Agrarians understood—in ways that many more recent conservatives have not—that attempts to create the "right relations" between man and nature, man and God, and man and man required a critical exploration of the mode of production that sustained human life. Accordingly, the Southern Agrarians urged conservative humanists, traditionalists, and defenders of Southern culture not to ignore the economic base, as the New Humanists had done. Babbitt and More were conservative political thinkers and men of letters deeply critical of modern culture and art and its values, including individualism, equality, economic redistribution, and democracy as a danger to civilization. They sought to revive the notion of a natural aristocracy on whose leadership, according to Babbitt, "may depend the very survival of Western civilization."[36] Although the Southern Agrarians shared some of the New Humanists' concerns about contemporary society. they believed that Babbitt's and More's criticism, lacking an analysis of economic life, was abstract and, therefore, inadequate. Writing in the "Statement of Principles" of I'll Take My Stand, to which all twelve of the Southern Agrarians subscribed, Ransom repudiated the abstract speculation of the New Humanists: "We cannot recover our native humanism by adopting some standard of taste that is critical enough to question the contemporary arts but not critical enough to question *the social and economic life which is their ground.*"[37]

The agrarian way of life of the yeoman South was the economic basis of these "right relations," just as much as it was a bulwark against the incursions of corporate capitalism, its culture of consumerism and plutocratic elite, the centralized political state, and the socialist menace.[38] The Southern Agrarians' political economic program, which was formulated after the publication of I'll Take My Stand, consisted of radical measures in an effort to establish the economic basis for a conservative agrarian society.[39] According to Donald Davidson, under a system of industrialism, the actions of individuals are transformed from moral actions into economic transactions. Davidson explained that the development of the economic system into the modern industrial system transformed all actions into actions of distant consequences, in which everything was produced for, and dictated by, an abstract market. In this scenario, individuals produced for an abstraction, and in many ways, they became abstractions themselves. Such a productive relation robbed the individual of moral impulse, social will, and moral choice, Davidson contended. Everything was transformed into a money relation, and "eventually men become callous even to near consequences."[40] These impersonal relationships eradicated the will for benevolence and empathy that paternalistic relationships of control and deference made possible. Lyle H.Lanier captured the Southern Agrarians' indictment of the level of human alienation that corporate capitalism engendered:

> Systems of slavery or domination in some form constitute one of the outstanding facts of history. Our contemporary variety is perhaps as complete and vicious as any form of outright ownership, for there is no feeling of responsibility even for the physical welfare of individuals dependent for a living upon the caprice of modern industry.[41]

In this way, the Southern Agrarians restated one of the most powerful critiques made by John C. Calhoun, James Henry Hammond, George Fitzhugh, and the defenders of slavery. They argued that without an economy founded on private property and personal relations, social superiors' moral sense of obligation to be benevolent and social inferiors to obey, or, in the Southern Agrarians' terms, the "right relations of man to man," was lost. For the defenders of slavery, these "right relations" were rooted and embodied in the slave economy. While they were not defenders of slavery, the Southern Agrarians saw value in the paternalistic relations of the antebellum South. "For a society as a whole," wrote Tate, "the modern system is probably inferior to that of slavery; the classes are not so closely knit; and the employer feels responsible to no law but his own desire."[42] Even though the Southern Agrarians may have been nostalgic for an Old South, they had enough sense to know that its restoration was neither possible or desirable:

> If anything is clear, it is that we can never go back, and neither this essay nor any intelligent person that I know in the South desires a

literal restoration of the old Southern life, even if that were possible; dead days are gone, and if by some chance they should return, we should find them intolerable. But out of any epoch in civilization there may arise things worthwhile, that are the flowers of it. To abandon these, when another epoch arrives, is only stupid, so long as there is still in them the breath and flux of life. . . . It would be childish and dangerous for the South to be stampeded and betrayed out of its own character by the noise, force, and glittering narrowness of the industrialism and progress spreading everywhere, with varying degrees, from one region to another.[43]

The Southern Agrarians agreed with the defenders of slavery that the economic base was the foundation of morality and that the capitalist economic system was opposed to a system of Christian or moral conduct. According to the Southern Agrarians, the morality of traditional society required a certain set of property relations that bound ownership and control in the same person. This property relation, according to Tate, constituted "not only economic privilege but moral obligation; not only rights but duties; not only material welfare but moral standards."[44] Tate and the Southern Agrarians called such a social and economic arrangement the "traditional society." Corporate industrial capitalism divorced economic conduct or "making a living" from moral conduct or the "way of life."[45] The Southern Agrarian ideal was what Richard Weaver, a prominent conservative thinker who was influenced by the Southern Agrarians, later pronounced "social-bond individualism" to be a product of a social and economic system in which each person had a place in the family, community, and political order as well as in the grander scheme of nature and the divine order. It was, in Davidson's words, an "integrated life" in which the economic, social, political, and cultural were interdependent. Tate, Davidson, and the rest of the Southern Agrarians wanted a political economy in which the demands of economic life and moral life were consistent and mutually reinforcing. To recover a morally integrated life required a radical reorganization of property relations. As Tate understood it, "property is the concrete medium by which tradition is passed on."[46] The radical redistribution of agrarian property that the Southern Agrarians advocated was a return to the correct economic relationship that conservative morality and tradition could renew and pass on to future generations. In this, the Southern Agrarians charted a new conservative discourse that rejected the elitism of the defenders of slavery and the corporatism of the warrior-aristocrats and pegged the yeoman farmer as the social agent of regeneration and the bulwark against plutocrats and the totalitarianism of the left and right.

CONSERVATIVE HIERARCHY: SOUTHERN AGRARIANS, POPULIST-STYLE

The Southern Agrarian vision was an attempt to restore a noncapitalist economic class to economic, political, social, and cultural prominence. The yeoman farmer was a noncapitalist economic class because of the Southern Agrarians' emphasis on production for subsistence instead of the production of cash crops.[47] According to the Southern Agrarians, production for the market required the American farmer to depend on a one-crop system, which led to overproduction, the collapse of the price of agricultural goods, and his own bankruptcy. Indeed, the agricultural crisis in 1920, from which American farmers did not recover until World War II, was caused by the decline in the price of corn and cotton following the recovery of the European agricultural sector after World War I, as well as by the flood of Canadian, Australian, Argentine, and Brazilian agricultural goods on the international market.[48] In an effort to repay their mortgages and loans, American small farmers planted more crops, thereby saturating the market and causing agricultural prices to plummet throughout the 1920s and 1930s. In essence, the American farmer was subjected to the imperatives of the market, whose vicissitudes could not guarantee his economic security. The Southern Agrarian yeoman republic depended on the stable and economically independent class of farmers to which the fluctuations of such a market was antithetical. The Southern Agrarians thus endorsed a departure from capitalist economic thinking that emphasized production for the capitalist international market and instead advocated production whose limits were set by the consumption needs of the family farm and local community. The Agrarians' yeoman ideal posited contracting the sphere of market relations in both the exchange of commodities in the market and the sense of daily existence in the world of commodities.

As conservatives and defenders of the South, the Southern Agrarians feared the proletariatization of the lower classes and the Communist ideology taking hold among Americans, as exemplified by radicals in the labor movement and the Popular Front and by the legal defense of the Scottsboro boys in the early 1930s by a group associated with the Communist Party.[49] Although the Southern Agrarians feared political concentration as a precursor to Communism, they were not libertarian anti-statists regarding property and economics. In the 1920s and 1930s, the U.S. economy was dominated by large corporations, which the Southern Agrarians saw, together with the state, as a threat to private property. The dispossession of the yeoman farmer and the concentration of economic power in corporate enterprises resulted in the concentration of political power in the hands of a plutocratic corporate capitalist class that Tate described as "the 2000 corporate heads who rule America."[50] In *Who Owns America?*, a collection of essays published by eight of the Southern Agrarians— Herbert Agar, English Distributists, and Catholic Agrarians—Lyle Lanier wrote that corporations are the "instruments of economic fascism threatening American democracy" and "inevitably leading to Communism or Fascism," both of which the Southern Agrarians sought to avoid.[51] For the Agrarians, private property was essential to free citizens. As Frank Owsley stated in "The Foundations of Democracy," "the ownership and control of productive property sufficient for a livelihood gave a man and his family a sense of economic security; it made him independent; he was a real citizen, for he could cast his franchise without fear and could protect the basic principles of his government."[52] But the Agrarians did not believe that all private property was beyond the regulatory reach of the government. In fact, the yeoman ideal was premised on a significant role for government to ensure the permanence of private property.

The Southern Agrarians argued that the South and its people were exploited and oppressed by Northern finance and corporate capitalism, aided by their Southern surrogates who propagated the "New South" doctrine. "New South" ideas had been current since the 1870s. Following Reconstruction, some Southern elites tried to withdraw from the region's traditional economic underdevelopment, based on its agricultural plantation economy, by instituting an alternative development model, similar to that of the North, based on capitalist industrial development, urbanization, and thorough integration into the national market. This meant not only creating the economic conditions to create Southern business firms but also welcoming the Northern businesses' penetration of the South as agents of economic modernization.[53]

Even though the South remained the most impoverished and economically underdeveloped region in the United States well into the twentieth century, it was becoming more urban and gradually less dependent on agriculture. Banks and insurance firms bought up small plots of agricultural land, combined them into large farms, and operated them as giant agribusinesses from their corporate headquarters in cities in the North. From the Southern Agrarians' perspective, it was this reality of the corporate capitalist system that created the capitalist plutocratic elite and destroyed the economic foundation of a conservative republic.[54] By offering concrete steps for reform, they were determined to change this state of affairs and halt the transformation of the region according to "New South" thinking. The Southern Agrarians' political and economic program was a departure from conservative economic laissez-faire, as it called for encroaching on the rights of private property. Their program received its clearest expression in Owsley's "Pillars of Agrarianism," published in 1935, in which he argued that these "twentieth century robber-barons" would have to be "reduced and civilized."[55] He called on government to break up big businesses and to buy the land of absentee landlords, including banks, insurance companies, and landowners who had more land than they could put into productive use. Once bought by government, Owsley suggested that the property be immediately redistributed and each qualified person be given eighty acres, along with "a substantial hewn log house and barn . . . twenty acres for a pasture . . . two mules and two milk cows, and . . . $300 for his living expenses for one year."[56]

Their plan to appropriate land owned by corporations and to redistribute may seem radical, but the Southern Agrarians were certainly not radical egalitarians. In fact, the Agrarians' plan had several features that betrayed its conservative nature. It was not meant to challenge class hierarchy or racial relations in the South. Owsley assured planters and large farmers that they would keep their land and that because not all people would be entitled to a parcel of their own, planters and large farmers would "still have an abundance of tenants who work well under supervision."[57] Among those who would be excluded from the benefits of land redistribution were the black sharecroppers and agricultural wage laborers who, the Southern Agrarians believed (as was typical in the Jim Crow South), failed to demonstrate that they were "the really responsible farmers among them who know how to take care of the soil and who own their own stock and cattle." Likewise, the lower class of white tenants who "own no stock, plant no gardens, raise no chickens, who are frequently and perhaps accurately described as po' white trash" would also be excluded. Consequently, the primary beneficiaries of the Southern Agrarians' program would be the "higher-class white tenants" whom Owsley considered to be the majority in the South: "those who own their stock and cattle and have their gardens and truck patches" and who were "once a part of the Southern yeomanry."[58]

The class-based limit of the Agrarians' land redistribution scheme is evident in their making their agrarian brand of populism eminently conservative. Their scheme was definitely not an egalitarian program, nor was it intended to disrupt the South's racial and class status quo. This was crucial, since by the mid-1930s even though mechanization had begun to penetrate Southern agriculture, much agricultural work continued to be carried out by human laborers because they were so abundant and inexpensive. In fact, as Jonathan Wiener observes, Southern agriculture remained dependent on the coerced labor of African Americans and poor whites until World War II, when high agricultural wages persuaded landlords to invest in tractors and other agricultural machines. Until then, what Wiener calls "the system of labor-repressive agriculture" defined the rural South by which agricultural laborers were tied to landowners by economics and by legislation, which included sharecropping and the debt peonage that resulted; convict labor by which the state leased laborers to local land-lords; various statutes, including vagrancy laws; enticement laws that made it a crime for an employer to offer work to a worker already under contract with another employer; emigrant agent laws, which discouraged out-of-state labor recruiters; and contract enforcement laws that made it a crime for a laborer to break a labor contract.[59]

In addition to the reappropriation of absentee-owned property and its redistribution by the state, Owsley argued that in order to safeguard the yeoman property, the government had to be entrusted with ensuring that the land would be protected for future generations, keeping it out of the hands of both agribusinesses and the landless poor. Accordingly, the Southern Agrarians advocated for significant restrictions on the use and transfer of property, especially agricultural property. As Owsley suggested, the Southern Agrarians endorsed a number of regulatory measures prohibiting the mortgaging of land, the speculative sale of land, and the sale of land to real estate, insurance companies, or banks.[60] Furthermore, if a landowner failed to take proper care of his land—leaving it "un-drained, un-terraced, single-cropped land, and lack of deforestation"—with proper warning, the land could be expropriated and returned to the state to be given to another "worthy family."[61] Presumably, this condition would have adversely affected the poorest landowners, who might soon see their land expropriated and transferred to wealthier and more "worthy," albeit still yeoman, owners. As Owsley himself wrote, this program implied a "modified form of feudal tenure where, in theory, the King or state has a paramount interest in the land."[62]

As the Southern Agrarians' thinking evolved and became more specific regarding economic and social policy, fissures within the group emerged. In the 1932 and 1936 presidential elections, most of the Southern Agrarians supported the Democrat, Franklin Delano Roosevelt, over the Republican, Alfred M. Landon. Tate captured the Agrarians' sentiment in a *New Republic* article:

I shall vote for Roosevelt. . . . [T]here are very few of the President's policies that I like, but he has been aware that a crisis exists, and there is at least a strong probability that he will take firmer and more coherent ground, in his second administration, against privilege and

Big Business. Should Landon be elected he would certainly bring on a revolution of violence in his efforts to restore the good old days of finance-capitalism. If I were a Communist, I think I should vote for Landon.[63]

The Agrarians' tenuous support of Roosevelt soon wavered when it became clear that his vision of reform did not include breaking up Big Business, decentralizing government, or restoring the family farm to the yeoman farmer. But the Agrarians were not anti-statists. In addition to the measures just discussed, the Southern Agrarians supported public ownership of utilities, high taxes on corporations, government regulation of business, and the end to the legal protection provided to corporations by the Fourteenth Amendment.[64] When Roosevelt's policies had the result of decentralizing economic power, the Southern Agrarians were supportive. But when the intention and the effect of his policies were to concentrate power, especially where business was concerned, the Southern Agrarians remained formidable critics.

They opposed the progressive tax reforms of the Wealth Tax Act, not because they opposed a graduate tax structure, but because the tax reform did not graduate taxes enough.[65] Some of the Southern Agrarians supported ventures like the Tennessee Valley Authority (TVA), rural electrification, and public works initiatives such as road and school construction.[66] Granted, the Agrarians' support for these measures was not universal. When they did oppose them, it was not because they feared an oppressive state, as more contemporary conservatives might argue. Instead, their opposition was based on sectional fears that the Northeast would subjugate the South. More important, their opposition was rooted in their concern that corporate capitalism would use the state to become even more powerful. "Centralization of political power and government regulation of industrial processes—far from being tendencies toward any real socialism—offer even greater possibilities of economic domination, because of the comparative ease with which control of government agencies is secured by industrial interests," declared Lanier in a typical Agrarian criticism of the New Deal.[67]

The Southern Agrarians opposed Roosevelt's signature farm bill, the Agricultural Adjustment Act (AAA, 1933), which sought to address the crisis in agriculture and the poverty among America's rural population by raising the prices of agricultural goods by restricting production. But large landowners and agribusinesses ended up benefiting much more from the program than did small farmers, tenant farmers, and sharecroppers, because these large entities could make the greatest reductions in their crops and thus receive larger payments. In theory, the landowners were supposed to share the AAA payments with the sharecroppers according to their share of the crop. In practice, though, the landowners refused to sign contracts with their sharecroppers, evicted them from the farms, and freed themselves from sharing their payments. Instead, the landowners hired their former sharecroppers when needed, as wage laborers. Thus, as Wiener notes, between 1935 and 1940, the number of Southern sharecroppers fell by 20 percent while the number of wage workers rose by 50 percent.[68] As Frances Fox-Piven pointed out, the modernization of Southern agriculture also had wide-ranging economic, demographic, and political ramifications for the South's racial caste system.[69] With agricultural employment opportunities dwindling, African Americans began migrating to Southern cities and, particularly during and after World War II, to work in the war industries in the North, where even though Jim Crow and racial discrimination persisted, more social, economic, and political opportunities were available. The agents of the civil rights movement—the urban black middle class from which many of the civil rights movement's leaders emerged—were often a generation removed from the displaced sharecroppers and other rural workers.[70]

The Southern Agrarians' defense of the Southern way of life and their opposition to economic modernization, whether driven by capital, the state, or both, forced them to confront the issue of racism and segregation. Race permeated every institution and relation in the South and thus could not be ignored by thinkers who were self-conscious proponents of the South. This was a society of racial apartheid that disenfranchised, harassed, lynched, and otherwise terrorized the African American population. It kept many black sharecroppers in quasi slavery and perpetuated the poverty of blacks and many poor whites in the South overall. The Southern Agrarians' alternative did nothing to challenge that; in fact, the details of their alternative, as discussed earlier, make clear that it was meant to preserve and reinforce class hierarchy and the system of racial apartheid in America. As Davidson stated, "The Southern view of the Negro question . . . means segregation, no social equality, probably economic subjugation for a long time to come."[71] Whatever Davidson's and other Southern Agrarians' agrarianism may have meant for the economic status quo in the United States at that time, it did not mean altering the racial status quo. In fact, the Southern Agrarians' agrarian vision was meant to solidify it.

The Southern Agrarians' views of race and segregation varied, but most ranged from a moderate defense of segregation to outright racism. Ransom maintained that slavery was monstrous in theory but not in practice, going so far as to defend the institution as more humane and less exploitative of labor, much as the defenders of slavery had done.[72] Tate and Owsley believed that blacks were treated rather well under slavery.[73] Among the more moderate voices was that of Robert Penn Warren, who parted from the Southern Agrarians early on and never wrote anything on agrarianism and who called for equal protection of the law for blacks but agreed that segregation was the best remedy for avoiding racial conflict between whites and blacks. In his contribution to *I'll Take My Stand*, entitled "The Briar Patch," Warren, typically of moderate segregationists, contended that black advocacy for equal rights provoked racial conflict, which turned out to be a position that he regretted and from which he eventually retreated.

The racism of Tate, Davidson, and Owsley was much more overt, as they portrayed African Americans as being racially inferior, little more than cannibals, and fit only to be ruled. Social and political equality with whites was therefore out of the question and would lead only to a race war and social disorder.[74] Owsley even defended lynching as a necessary measure to control blacks,[75] and Davidson glorified the KKK and was a leading figure in the Tennessee White Citizens Council, tying the Southern identity to the maintenance of segregation and racial purity. The "race-question," as Davidson called racial apartheid in the South, was the defining feature of the South and the only issue on which the "southern people" were united.

The white South denies the Negro equal participation in white society, not only because it does not consider him entitled to equality, but because it is certain that social mingling would lead gradually to biological mingling, which it is determined to prevent, both for any given contemporary generation and for its posterity.[76]

The Southern Agrarians were defending a real historical community, the South, of which racism, segregation, and racial terror were defining characteristics. Thus for Davidson, in a biracial society, which the South was, democracy characterized by social, legal, and political equality—which was possible, in his view, only in a homogenous society—was not only undesirable but impossible.

Although most of the Southern Agrarians eventually retreated from this position on race and segregation, Davidson and Owsley remained committed racists and segregationists well into the 1960s. Both men viewed civil rights for blacks as a tyrannical imposition by the North on the South's internal affairs. Likewise, they believed, erroneously but not uncommonly, that because economic modernization had transformed the rural agricultural land tenure and labor discipline system that was both a function of racial oppression and its consequence, it would ultimately upend Jim Crow and the South's racial hierarchy.[77]

The Southern Agrarians should be understood as defenders of a racist hierarchical system that dehumanized and robbed an entire race of their liberty, property, and, in many cases, life, which in turn undermined the Southern Agrarians' yeoman vision. An agrarian scheme to redistribute land to small farmers would have been supported by African Americans because it would have fulfilled a long sought after goal, since at least Reconstruction, of black landownership. In the 1930s, before the Great Migration North began, most African Americans still lived in the rural areas of the South. In addition, as Davidson himself once confessed, rural blacks embodied the culture and traditionalism of the agrarians' vision. "The Negro," he wrote in 1949, "so far as he had not been corrupted into heresy by modern education was the most traditional of Southerners, the mirror which faithfully and lovingly reflected the traits that Southerners once all but unanimously professed."[78] As historians Emily S. Bingham and Thomas A. Underwood have pointed out, "Most in the group not only refused to consider blacks as full-fledged citizens of a republic but barely thought of them as sentient beings. Even when they made suggestions for improving the lot of black tenant farmers, they did so with the goal of preserving a segregated society."[79]

The growth of the federal government during the New Deal signaled to the Southern Agrarians the political establishment's endorsement of the economic modernization that was seen as a threat to the Southern racial hierarchy. The Agrarians, particularly Davidson and Owsley, thought at length about ways of structuring government to protect the "Southern way of life." Both were proponents of sectionalism and state's rights. Davidson argued that the current system of federalism was a failure because it concentrated too much power in the federal government. Furthermore, this power had been used by corporate capitalism and by race radicals in the North to subordinate the South. Owsley and Davidson pointed to the military occupation of the South following the Civil War and Reconstruction and to federal economic policy since then, including the tariff, as well as later modernization schemes by proponents of the "New South," that together, the two segregationists believed, would turn the South into little more than a colonial territory of northeastern capital and industry. For too long, they contended, northeastern capital's agents in Southern businesses and in the government had exploited, robbed, and oppressed the South and other regions. Both of them believed that the U.S. Constitution was partly to blame.

As an alternative to the current federal structure, Davidson and Owsley advocated for regionalism, citing inspiration from Calhoun's concurrent majority and Southern nullifiers in the antebellum era.[80] Owsley's and Davidson's regionalism included dividing the country into legislative and administrative regions and giving the regional governments many of the domestic powers of the federal government. These powers would include economic development, taxation, as well as the power of nullification over issues of trade, tariffs, and the like. The U.S. House of Representatives would be abolished, leaving only the U.S. Senate, with the senators representing and elected by regions rather than states. Justices of the U.S. Supreme Court would be appointed by the regional governments, and each region would be equally represented. In defense of this radical repudiation of the U.S. Constitution, Owsley and Davidson argued that since each region was culturally, socially, economically, and politically different from the others, a regional system was commensurate with maintaining the diversity of each region, as well as with preserving the democratic principle of self-government. But underneath the surface of calls for regional autonomy and self-government lay an undemocratic and inhumane system that more than anything made the South distinct: its system of racial apartheid and oppression.

The Southern Agrarians sought the regeneration of a yeoman tradition and culture, which, they believed, was more consistent with a humane and moral existence than laissez-faire and corporate capitalism were. They were defenders and promoters of Southern culture, tradition, and prejudices because they believed that the South embodied, more than any other region in the United States, the economic, social, political, and cultural elements of America's yeoman past.

In this spirit, the Southern Agrarians offered a prescient critique of corporate capitalism in the 1920s and 1930s. Their alternative of self-sufficient yeoman communities envisaged a major departure from capitalism as it then existed. Indeed, their alternative sought not only to halt the expansion of capitalism and the commodification of economic and social life but also to roll it back. Yet as radical as the Southern Agrarians' alternative may seem, it was meant to be conservative. It was highly provincial, hierarchical, and, ultimately, premised on a social basis that was rapidly disappearing from the American political landscape. Their vision of a humane, un-exploitative social system in which individuals might live in economic security, community, and with real political sovereignty was limited to the white rural middle class. In the end, their vision was meant to uphold a class structure that elevated white middle- and upper-class landowners and to protect the racist system that daily dehumanized and terrorized African Americans in the South.

In the conservative tradition that has been critical of capitalism, the Southern Agrarians mark the last radical indictment of, and alternative to, the capitalist system. Contrary to Brooks Adams and Theodore Roosevelt, who sought political regeneration in war and empire, the Southern Agrarians sought regeneration in the common, routine, everyday life of the yeoman farmer in the agrarian South. Like Adams and Roosevelt, the Southern Agrarians rejected laissez-faire capitalism and fascism, as well as socialism and Communism. They made it clear that their alternative was meant to preclude the others, especially the latter two. The Southern Agrarians, albeit not principled anti-statists, were repulsed by the concentration and centralization of political and economic power advocated by Adams and Roosevelt and preferred decentralized economic and political institutions.

Southern Agrarianism was never a popular political movement and was only a short-lived intellectual movement. By the late 1930s, the group had broken up. The Southern Agrarians' affiliation with the Seward Collins, an anti-Semite, fascist, and publisher of the *American Review*, an organ for which they wrote extensively, damaged their reputation and credibility.[81] Davidson, although not a fascist himself, did not distance himself from Collins, whereas Ransom and Tate repudiated Collins and fascism. By then, however, all but Davidson had rejected agrarianism as a political program. Dispirited by the turn that politics and economics had taken in the United States, they returned to writing poetry, literature, and literary criticism.[82]

Nevertheless, the Southern Agrarians had a significant influence on twentieth-century American conservative thought.[83] Their critique of capitalism, like that of the antebellum defenders of slavery before them, recognized that a social order characterized by religious faith and tradition required a radical restructuring of capitalism. The Southern Agrarians' emphasis on religion and their opposition to centralized political power, rootless individualism, consumerism, and materialism, together with their defense of Southern traditions, heritage, and culture—in other words, their unique strand of cultural critique of capitalism—has been a source of inspiration for many traditionalist conservatives, including Richard Weaver and Russell Kirk; neo-Agrarians like M. E. Bradford; and paleoconservatives like Thomas Fleming and Samuel Francis.[84] In the post–World War era, Kirk revived the Southern Agrarians' anti-industrialism, and echoes of their indictment of consumerism and commodification as the destroyer of Southern culture and heritage appeared in Francis's thought. As Paul V. Murphy demonstrated in *The Rebuke of History*, however, these later conservatives distorted the Southern Agrarians' views. In particular, Weaver and Davidson reconfigured the Southern Agrarians' thinking to conform to the traditionalist conservatism of the postwar era that privileged an anti-statist social-bond individualism rooted in private property, social hierarchy, traditional culture and values, religiosity, and anti-Communism as the operative elements of a conservative social order.[85] To be sure, the Southern Agrarians' critique of industrialism and, to a lesser extent, the critique of economic centralization continued to find a home in the postwar traditionalist conservative narrative. Typical of postwar traditionalists, Weaver was critical of industrialism, corporate capitalism, the plutocratic elite, and consumer culture. Well into the 1950s, he continued to espouse agrarianism as a conservative alternative to corporate industrial capitalism, but unlike the Southern Agrarians, he opposed any attempts at concrete economic reform.[86] Eventually, he came to terms with capitalism as "delivering the goods" of material abundance and comfort.[87]

With the exception of Weaver's ideas, missing from much of postwar conservative thought were core elements of the Agrarians' thought. Of notable absence was the Agrarians' critique of capitalism, which was the basis of their social and cultural conservatism, and their rather complex view of the state's role in economic life. To say that the Southern Agrarians were decentralists and, by implication, economic libertarians, distorts their thought. Rather, this reinterpretation transformed the Southern Agrarians' thought, which was based on a radical economic program, into a form of social and moral traditionalism that separated social and cultural critique from economic critique and its political consequences. This reinterpretation did, however, make the Southern Agrarians' ideas more palatable to the post–World War II conservative intellectual movement, whose political economy in the context of the Cold War had mostly come to terms with capitalism and had become, at least discursively, anti-interventionist.

The Southern Agrarians are not irrelevant. With the ascendance of conservatism since the 1970s and its rhetorical embrace of populism with its electoral strength located primarily in the South and the Midwest has come a renewed interest in conservative radicalism, which historically has had a Southern manifestation. Indeed, without the agrarianism, much of contemporary paleoconservatives' thought would parallel that of the Southern Agrarians. But as a group, the Southern Agrarians—alone among twentieth-century conservatives—confronted the central tension within American conservatism between capitalism and traditionalism. They resolved it with calls for significant restraints (including by the state) of the former. Between the Southern Agrarians and the postwar conservative critics of capitalism—Peter Viereck, Russell Kirk, and Robert Nisbet, whom I explore in the next chapter—there was a dramatic shift in tone as well as content. Two of these shifts are key: how conservatives framed the problem of modern society and who or what was the target of their criticism. First, the Southern Agrarians believed that in order to reform culture along traditional lines, society's economic base had to be changed. Second, the primary focus of the Southern Agrarians' critique was capitalism. Critiques of the state were secondary, and the context of most of their critique of the state was their fear of plutocracy and state-assisted economic modernization and centralization. Both these core elements in the Southern Agrarians' thought were marginalized in the postwar conservative intellectual discourse. In the postwar era, the New Deal and the Cold War undoubtedly affected how conservatives thought about capitalism, the state, and their relationship to American conservatism.

4

THE NEW CONSERVATIVES

The Cold War and the Making of Conservative Orthodoxy

> "Man was born free" (said Rousseau, with his faith in natural goodness of man) "but is everywhere in chains." In chains, and so he ought to be, replies the thoughtful conservative, defending the good and wise and necessary chains of rooted tradition and historic continuity, upon which depend the civil liberties. . . . Without the chaos-chaining, the Id-chaining heritage of rooted values, what is to keep man from becoming Eichmann or Nechayev—what is to save freedom from "freedom"?
>
> Peter Viereck, *Conservatism Revisited*

The post–World War II period was a pivotal moment for American conservatism. Before the war, twentieth-century conservatives such as the warrior-aristocrats and the Southern Agrarians offered various critiques of and alternatives to laissez-faire capitalism. In both alternatives, the state played an active role in economic life. Despite their differences, both the warrior-aristocrats' and the Southern Agrarians' variants of conservatism shared the view that their versions of conservatism were in tension with conservatives who advocated economic laissez-faire and anti-statism. Indeed, a conservatism that was critical of capitalism, such as that of the warrior-aristocrats and the Southern Agrarians, was a legitimate

"conservative" position and not uncommon in the conservative discourse before the Cold War.

The Cold War dramatically changed the way that conservatives
could talk about capitalism and still be called "conservative." Although
a conservative critique of capitalism remained in the post–World War
II conservative discourse, the critique was less about actually existing
capitalism than it was about laissez-faire capitalism as an ideological construction gaining currency on the political right. Postwar conservative critics of capitalism Peter Viereck, Russell Kirk, and Robert
Nisbet wanted to redefine conservatism away from the popularly held
notion that it prioritized economic freedom and unrestrained individualism and was merely an apology for the unbounded accumulation
of wealth at the expense of other values. Instead, for them, conservatism was based on a different set of principles, values, and traditions—
ones that might restrain the unfettered individualism that, they
believed, led to totalitarianism and the destruction of both liberty
and capitalism. They meant to recover the conservatism of Edmund
Burke and its emphasis on tradition, gradual change, prudence, experience, and religion, as distinct from the defenses of the laissez-faire
capitalism of Herbert Spencer and William Graham Sumner.[1] "The
apologetics of the William Graham Sumner school of capitalism,"
wrote Viereck, "are no old or deep-rooted part of the American tradition, being rather a product of the relatively recent, post–Civil War
Gilded Age."[2] As Kirk argued, traditional conservatives tried to disentangle themselves from "the impression [in America] that the new
industrial and acquisitive interests are the conservative interests, that
conservatism is simply a political argument in defense of large accu-
mulations of private property, that expansion, centralization, and
accumulation are the tenets of conservatism."[3] Moreover, Viereck
implored like-minded thinkers to "take conservatism away from the
wrong—the solely economics minded—conservatives."[4]

Postwar conservative critics combined Theodore Roosevelt's goal
of saving capitalism from the excesses of laissez-faire with the Southern Agrarians' concern for preserving the conservative civil society's
traditional institutions. Whereas there was significant disagreement
even among conservative critics with regard to the conservatism of
the New Deal—as Viereck pointed out—all of them—Kirk, Nisbet, and

Viereck—esteemed the authority and function of traditional institutions that imparted the values of and provided the necessary restraints on people's behavior that made capitalism and a free society possible. For postwar conservative critics of capitalism, the market needed to be subordinated to the family, the church, and the local community and its customs and mores rather than to the state or its own economic logic.

The postwar conservatives' emphasis on order and traditional values and institutions sounds like that of the Southern Agrarians, but there were significant differences. Among the most important was the Southern Agrarians' distinctively southern and decentralist economic program discussed in the preceding chapter. Postwar conservatives did not have a southern orientation, and they eschewed programs. Instead, they were more focused on the enunciation of conservative values and principles. Even Kirk's Program for Conservatives opts for a larger conservative vision and lacks specific political and economic policy prescriptions.[5] The Southern Agrarians' vision and the program required to implement it carved out a significant role for government intervention in the capitalist economy. Like the Southern Agrarians, the postwar conservatives believed that traditional institutions needed to be restored, a point on which they widely agreed. Where the postwar conservatives diverged not only from the Southern Agrarians but also from one another was over the role of the liberal welfare state in this restorative project.

The Cold War made the postwar conservative critics' overriding concern the spread of Communism, which prompted the reorientation of their thought away from capitalism and the capitalist and toward the state. The Cold War's anti-Communism structured much of American social, cultural, and political life. Indeed, the ideological impact of anti-Communism cannot be overestimated, as capitalism, or the free market, was ideologically wedded to freedom and democracy. The discursive space for critiques of capitalism was drastically narrowed as criticism of the economic system was often equated with un-Americanism or sympathy with Communism. As a result, anti-Communism and the coupling of capitalism with freedom and democracy came to define American conservatism in the postwar era.[6] In fact, twentieth-century liberalism, consisting of regulated welfare-state capitalism and concern with civil rights for racial and ethnic minorities, was equated with incipient Communism.[7]

In the Cold War context, the once vibrant critique of capitalism became mild and marginal as conservatives began to reconcile themselves to capitalism. To be sure, postwar conservatives continued to critique capitalism, but their criticism no longer questioned the inner working of the economic system. Rather, it de-politicized the capitalist as an agent of social change, thereby discarding the critique of plutocracy that was a key element of pre–Cold War conservative critiques. In addition, by reorienting their focus on the American political economy almost exclusively on the liberal welfare state, they marginalized the conservative defense of economic statism that had been prescribed by Theodore Roosevelt and continued by Viereck's conservative defense of the New Deal.[8] In this transition in the discourse, conservatives laid the theoretical foundation for a "conservative" alternative to both economic laissez-faire and the liberal welfare state that was to emerge in the thought of the neoconservatives and among the New Right. This paradigmatic shift in the conservative narrative about the American political economy, which took place in the first two decades after World War II, transformed conservative thinking about the complex link among the state, the economy, and civil society for decades to come.

Soon after the conclusion of World War II, the Soviet-American alliance that defeated the Axis powers crumbled as both the Soviet Union and the United States began to carve out spheres of influence in which their respective economic and political systems would be adopted. It did not take long before Eastern Europe came under Soviet influence and Communists threatened to take power in Italy, France, and Greece. In less than five years after the war, Chinese Communist Mao Zedong had expelled the American allied-right nationalists to Taiwan under the leadership of Chiang Kai-shek, and the United States was in the midst of a bloody proxy war against the spread of Communism in Korea. Nationalist leaders in Asia and Africa—including India, Vietnam, Algeria, and Ghana—began national liberation struggles against the European imperial powers weakened by World War II. Nor was the United States' Cold War anti-Communist foreign policy purely defensive. The United States was committed to expanding the global capitalist market under its leadership, to which America's global military presence, the rebuilding of Europe through the Marshall Plan, the Bretton Woods monetary system, and the extension of foreign access to the large American consumer market were crucial.[9] Postwar U.S. politics linked American capitalists' concerns to increasing profits; domestic political leaders' concerns with unemployment and efforts to avoid the violent struggles of the past between capital and labor; and the foreign policy establishment's preoccupation with international anti-Communism.[10]

In the roughly five decades until the collapse of the Soviet Union in 1991, anti-Communism was a defining feature of American foreign and domestic politics. On the domestic front, especially in the first two decades after the war, the perceived threat of Communism was used to justify purges of accused radicals in labor unions, civil rights organizations, the entertainment industry, and government. The mere accusation of association with or sympathy for Communists destroyed many people's lives in the public show trials under the auspices of Senator Joseph McCarthy (R-Wis.) and the House Un-American Committee. The fear of Communism resulted in loyalty oaths and public rituals like the nuclear bomb drills in which schoolchildren practiced crouching under their desks during a nuclear attack, as well as massive public spending on the defense industry, the interstate highway system, the space program, and public higher education.

For postwar intellectuals, both liberal and conservative, the market had been subordinated to the liberal welfare state and the managerial revolution became the structuring force of society.[11] A regulated corporate capitalist economy combined with the New Deal welfare state provided the nation, or so it was thought, with rising standards of living and relative domestic peace and stability. Whereas liberals saw the postwar order largely as a positive development, conservatives worried about the growth of a federal government "leviathan."

Before the war, President Franklin Roosevelt had created important social and economic programs under the New Deal, including Social Security, unemployment compensation, Aid to Families with Dependent Children, rural electrification and infrastructure, and a plethora of corporate public subsidies, together with regulations for agriculture, banking, and industrial production. The Wagner Act gave workers the right to organize into labor unions and to bargain collectively, which created a legal environment conducive to the growth in union membership. But by 1938, further reforms were stymied by an anti–New Deal coalition of Republicans and southern Democrats, and the country plunged back into depression. Then mobilization for the war quickly solved the unemployment problem, led by an unprecedented expansion of government geared toward winning the war. Liberals and progressives were confident that after the war and demobilization, the federal government would address poverty, unemployment, and economic inequality. In fact, President Roosevelt offered this hope in his 1944 State of the Union address, in which he outlined a "second Bill of Rights" guaranteeing a right to employment, a decent wage, a decent home, adequate medical care, and a good education for all, regardless of social station, race, or creed.[12] But his death in 1945 and the increasing conservatism at all levels of government in the postwar period kept his promises unfulfilled.

Until the mid-1960s, when President Lyndon B. Johnson embarked on his "Great Society," the federal government refrained from any major new non-defense-related programs, including the GI Bill, which subsidized the growth of suburbanization and higher education. Nonetheless, military spending gained bipartisan approval throughout the postwar period,[13] as it was a boon for the South and the West, where it was responsible for much direct and indirect employment.[14] As economic historian Richard B. DuBoff suggests, military Keynesianism, or defense-related government spending that was intended to spur demand, was the politically expedient means of maintaining full employment and averting economic stagnation after the demobilizations at the end of World War II, the Korean War, and for decades afterward.[15] Owing to the massive government spending, the power of organized labor to collectively bargain for increasing wages and, crucially, the competitive advantage enjoyed by the United States as the only major economy to escape the war's devastation, the fabled American middle class grew exponentially. Between 1945 and the mid-1970s, a period sometimes considered the "golden age" of American capitalism, poverty declined, working people's incomes rose, and economic inequality was greatly reduced.[16] This postwar framework was largely accepted by both political parties. Even a Republican-controlled

Congress under the leadership of Robert A. Taft and eight years of a Republican president, Dwight D. Eisenhower, did not reverse the major achievements of the New Deal.

In the context of the Cold War, conservatives became more concerned with the growth of the state and the power of organized labor than with the concentration of great wealth or the threat of capitalism to a conservative social order. Previously, this had been a marginal view even among conservatives, but by the 1950s, many postwar conservatives believed there was "common cause" between New Deal liberalism and Communism.[17] Even though the conservative electoral movement that would upend the postwar liberal order was still a few decades away, the conservative ideas that would inform that movement took shape in the late 1940s and 1950s among Viereck, Kirk, Nisbet, and others.[18]

Despite their differences, which I will discuss later, the crux of the conservatives' criticism of contemporary society was their belief that the liberal ideas undergirding the welfare state, especially the belief in the innate goodness of humans and in human progress, led to totalitarianism because it challenged the existence of a transcendental order of values, classes, and social hierarchies manifested in traditional cultures and institutions. Moreover, in the conservative tradition, postwar thinkers subscribed to the belief in "original sin"; that inequality and hierarchy were natural, justified, and necessary; and that traditional institutions were the means by which human's "irredeemably flawed" nature was restrained, making it possible to live in society with others. Kirk and Nisbet argued that the New Deal was a revolution because it undermined the authority and function of local hierarchies and shifted the loci of power to the centralized state, which, in the postwar era, seemed more amenable to the demands of workers and, later, racial minorities who challenged the traditional hierarchies of domination and control. Politically, the clearest manifestation of the weakening of traditional hierarchies was the struggle over civil rights and states' rights. Conservative thinkers believed that this massive reorientation in the relationship between the federal government and local hierarchies in civil society concentrated too much power in the centralized state and freed individuals from the bonds of local culture, tradition, and hierarchies of local control, a process that postwar conservatives linked directly to the twentieth-century totalitarianisms that had produced the Holocaust and the Soviet gulag.

But not all postwar conservatives viewed the New Deal as the destructive totalitarian force of what would become the conservative mainstream as did Frank Meyer, the originator of conservative "fusion," and William F. Buckley Jr., the founder and editor of the conservative periodical the *National Review*.[19] In conservative intellectual circles, August Heckscher, Clinton Rossiter, and, especially, Peter Viereck resisted their colleagues' apocalyptical prophecies of a too-powerful state. For nearly two decades after the end of World War II, Viereck and Rossiter retained a critical orientation to economic laissez-faire and defended the inherent conservatism of the New Deal.[20] Writing in *Conservatism Revisited*, Viereck exemplified this sentiment when he declared that "conservatism fights on two fronts," against "the atomistic disunity of unregulated capitalism and the bureaucratic mechanical unity of modern socialism."[21] As I will explain later, Viereck's conservatism soon diverged from the ideological orientation of the movement conservatism that was beginning to form around the editors of the *National Review* in the 1950s. Subsequently, for his "heretical" positions, Frank Meyer banished Viereck from the conservative movement.[22]

Peter Viereck (1916–2006) was a Pulitzer Prize–winning poet, a specialist in Russian history, an emeritus professor at Mount Holyoke College, and a political thinker whose book *Conservatism Revisited* "created the new conservatism as a self-conscious intellectual force."[23] Indeed, George Nash credited Viereck for "labeling" and "popularizing" a revived conservative movement. Shortly before Viereck's death in 2006, Tom Reiss, himself a Pulitzer Prize–winning author and contributor to the *New Yorker* magazine, noted that Viereck had both "inspired and lost" a nascent "new conservative" movement that sought to distinguish itself from the backward-looking Southern Agrarians and the economic libertarianism of the Liberty League.[24] His conservatism emphasized the conservative aristocratic nature of the American conservative-liberal synthesis that allowed for reform but tempered democratic excesses. Viereck's *Conservatism Revisited*

(1949) was one of the first statements of postwar conservatism. It was welcomed as a sensible conservative position distinct from both twentieth-century welfare-state liberalism and twentieth-century conservatism, which were little more than classical liberalism. By the mid-1950s, however, in part because of Viereck's critiques of McCarthyism and his support for the conservatism of the New Deal, the gulf between Viereck and other postwar conservatives had widened. Russell Kirk criticized Viereck for "McCarthyism against McCarthy," and conservative political philosopher Willmoore Kendall questioned whether Viereck could be a conservative if he "agreed with Liberals about Everything."[25] In addition to *Conservatism Revisited*, Viereck's most important political tracts are *Metapolitics* (1941), *Shame and Glory of the Intellectuals* (1953), *The Unadjusted Man* (1956), and a history of conservatism entitled *Conservatism: From John Adams to Churchill* (1953). In addition, many of Viereck's essays can be found in these books.

Russell Kirk (1918–1994) studied at the University of St. Andrews in Scotland where he immersed himself in the thought of Edmund Burke. He founded the *National Review* (1955) and the traditionalist journal *Modern Age* (1957), served as a Distinguished Fellow at the Heritage Foundation, supported Barry Goldwater for president in 1964, and sparred with Meyer over fusionism. Like many other conservatives at that time, he became a "movement" conservative but always believed that beyond conservatives' and libertarians' mutual opposition to Communism and the totalizing state, traditional conservatives, of whom he was the most important exponent, had nothing in common with libertarians. In a pointedly critical article, Kirk wrote:

> So in the nature of things conservatives and libertarians can conclude no friendly pact. Conservatives have no intention of compromising with socialists; but even such an alliance, ridiculous though it would be, is more nearly conceivable than the coalition of conservatives and libertarians. The socialists at least declare the existence of some sort of moral order; the libertarians are quite bottomless. It is of high importance, indeed, that American conservatives dissociate themselves altogether from the little sour remnant called libertarians.[26]

Along with Viereck, Kirk attempted to distance the "real" conservatism of tradition from the conservatism that prioritized economic laissez-faire. Kirk's *The Conservative Mind*, originally published in 1953, is considered one of the most influential books of twentieth-century conservatism. In Kirk's obituary, the *New York Times* called it the "intellectual bible for the conservative movement,"[27] in which Kirk sought to establish a conservative Anglo-American intellectual tradition that led from Burke through John Adams, Samuel Taylor Coleridge, John Randolph, John C. Calhoun, Benjamin Disraeli, Brooks Adams, and Paul Elmer Moore, among others. In Kirk's telling, conservatism is defined by a set of principles, including a belief in a transcendent order; faith in custom and prescription; and a belief in the necessity of orders and classes, private property, prudence, and in the "variety and mystery" of the human world. These principles ought to convince conservatives that liberals' and radicals' attempts to "improve" the world through "social planning" or "social engineering" were a deeply suspicious endeavor.

Despite these defining conservative principles, Kirk's exemplars of the conservative tradition were diverse. As Kevin Mattson observes, Kirk's conservative tradition included an amalgamation of thinkers and statesmen who were animated by a variety of principles and policy prescriptions. Kirk's tradition, Mattson wrote, "included Federalists who championed national unity over decentralization and southerners who championed states' rights and local government over national unity."[28] Indeed, Kirk even wrote favorably of Woodrow Wilson, who had long been detested by conservatives for beginning the process of government centralization that led to the New Deal.[29] Notably absent from the conservative tradition of *The Conservative Mind* were those in the pantheon of economic laissez-faire thinkers, including social Darwinists Herbert Spencer and William Graham Sumner.[30]

Kirk was a prolific author, writing thirty books and thousands of articles of political and social commentary. Besides *The Conservative Mind*, his other important political works include *A Program for Conservatives* (1954), *Academic Freedom: An Essay in Definition* (1955), *Beyond the Dreams of Avarice* (1956), *The American Cause* (1957), and the *Politics of Prudence* (1993). But it was *The Conservative Mind* for which he is rightfully remembered for inspiring many conservatives, not the least of whom were Barry Goldwater and Ronald Reagan. Reagan even called Kirk an "intellectual leader" who "shaped so much [sic] of our thoughts."[31]

Robert A. Nisbet (1913–1996) was a conservative sociologist heavily influenced by Edmund Burke, Alexis de Tocqueville, and Emile Durkheim. He taught at the University of California at Berkeley and Columbia University and was a resident scholar at the American Enterprise Institute and a fellow at the Hoover Institution in Stanford, California. Nisbet, too, was a prolific writer, publishing many articles and more than a dozen books, including *Tradition and Revolt: Historical and Sociological Essays* (1968), *The Social Philosophers: Community and Conflict in Western Thought* (1973), *History of the Idea of Progress* (1980), *Prejudices: A Philosophical Dictionary* (1983), and *Conservatism: Dream and Reality* (1986). His first and most influential book, published in 1953, was *The Quest for Community*, reissued in 1962 under the title *Community & Power*. His lifelong scholarly work, first undertaken in *The Quest for Community*, focused on the human need for community and the importance of traditional "intermediary" institutions. Like Viereck and Kirk and conservatives generally, Nisbet was an anti-egalitarian who believed that equality was the greatest threat to liberty and social initiatives. Natural inequalities, he believed, produced inequalities of result.[32] Accordingly, he was deeply skeptical of liberals' and radicals' faith in human progress and social planning and posited the state as the greatest threat to traditional institutions and thus to individual liberty. Anti-statism and the nurturing of intermediate institutions are the pillars of Nisbet's thought, on which his reputation as a "communitarian traditionalist" is based.[33] Nisbet was deeply influenced by Kirk's *The Conservative Mind*, and both authors admired and recommended each other's work.[34] In his obituary, the *New York Times* stated that "he was hailed as an intellectual mentor of the American right."[35] As Brad Lowell Stone, who wrote a biography of Nisbet, pointed out, his thought proved influential, having "contributed greatly to salutary changes over the last several decades in the way Americans conceive and speak about social issues and their solutions." His influence, Stone continued, may have informed public policy, as in the transformation of "welfare" from the New Deal's Aid to Families with Dependent Children to President Bill Clinton's decentralized Temporary Assistance for Needy Families (1996), which granted states and localities much discretion over the program and its recipients.[36]

PETER VIERECK: NEW DEAL CONSERVATISM

As was the case of much political writing across the American political spectrum in the 1940s and 1950s, Peter Viereck's political writings focused on explaining how totalitarianism arose in Europe and how to prevent it from taking root in the United States. With some differences, Viereck, Kirk, Nisbet, and other postwar conservatives also explained the rise of Soviet Communism and the temporary triumph of Nazism. They located the source of totalitarianism not in people's material conditions, their economy, or politics, as writers on the left tended to do, but in the realm of ideas and ideology. For these conservatives, the liberal thinkers of the Enlightenment—Thomas Hobbes, John Locke, and, in particular, Jean-Jacques Rousseau—were most to blame.[37] According to Viereck, Kirk, and Nisbet, liberal thinkers placed rational, free, equal, and self-interested individuals at the center of the social and political universe, where their freedom was everywhere hindered by various social, cultural, political, and institutional arrangements that placed them in a religion-based cosmic order. As ideas of liberal individual freedom took hold, these various social, political, and economic restraints were undermined, freeing individuals but at the same time alienating them from their social nature and the social institutions to which they belonged. Without these social institutions, individuals were free to pursue their egoistic interest in their social and economic relations with others. Laissez-faire capitalism, conservatives argued, was the product of the ideological triumph of liberalism over conservative traditional institutions.

In the conservatives' view, liberal social contract theory is unsatisfactory because humans have a social nature; that is, they need to belong to something larger than themselves, to be rooted in morality and ethics, which need to be socially enforced. Individuals also need to be protected, especially from the self-interested but potentially socially damaging economic pursuits of others. In search of belonging and without the authority and function of traditional institutions that liberal individualism has undermined, atomized individuals turn to radical doctrines, whether socialism and Communism on the left, or fascism and Nazism on the right, each of which saw the state as a collective salvation. Thus postwar conservatives hold liberalism in special disregard because they see it as opening the door to totalitarianism. Indeed, the extent to which each conservative was willing to condemn twentieth-century liberalism was the litmus test of what it meant to be a conservative.

Viereck's conservatism was based on the belief in gradual reform informed by the ethics and values of America's Judeo-Christian heritage. He argued that America's traditions, which dated back to the Founding Fathers, were both liberal and conservative. In the postwar era he urged conservatives to synthesize moderate liberalism and moderate conservatism as a bulwark against totalitarianism. Although credited with inspiring the postwar conservative movement, Viereck remained independent of it. Over the years, he became disillusioned with the conservatism of Russell Kirk, William F. Buckley Jr., and Frank Meyer for their support of Joseph McCarthy and their failure to build on America's established traditions, which, Viereck believed, were partially liberal. Liberals viewed Viereck as a spokesman for the "new" conservatism, and by the mid-1950s, he was scorned by many conservatives for his accommodation to liberalism and the New Deal.[38]

Viereck and other postwar conservative thinkers, particularly Clinton Rossiter and August Heckscher, were theoretical Burkeans. They believed that a conservative polity cannot be constructed by abstract theories or imported ideas, but must be grown organically and developed over time in the existing traditions, cultures, and institutions. In the American context, this premise led to many problems for conservatives defining American conservatism as well as struggling over what the conservative vision for postwar America should be. Was the vision to conserve what currently existed? Should postwar conservatives work to preserve the status quo of large corporations, powerful labor unions, and the liberal welfare state? Or should the conservative vision repudiate American liberalism and reconstruct the foundations for a conservative polity? And if it were to reconstruct or reclaim a polity based on "tradition," what tradition would be reclaimed? After all, as some of the most influential political thinkers at the time contended, American traditions, and even their more conservative elements, were liberal at their core.[39] As the dispute between Viereck and Rossiter, on the one hand, and Kirk and Nisbet, on the other hand, demonstrated, even Burkean conservatives could not agree on the meaning of American conservatism, much less on the path forward that it should take.

Surveying postwar America, Viereck believed there was much to conserve.[40] He saw corporate capitalism as a "justified necessity" and wrote that capitalists were "morally entitled to derive material profits" for their "service to freedom" that emanated from their role in producing "higher living-standards at home and defense against aggressors abroad."[41] But he believed that utility should not be the only criterion by which an economic system, or anything else, ought to be judged, and he remained unconvinced of the "mystical, self-regulating perfection" of Adam Smith's invisible hand.[42] Reform of unfettered capitalism was both necessary and inevitable in order to fend off social revolution, as, Viereck believed, the New Deal had done. Along with only a few postwar conservatives, Viereck was sensitive to the destructive potential of laissez-faire capitalism and the inability of capitalists to guarantee social order and stability. Similar to the arguments made by Theodore Roosevelt and Brooks Adams nearly a half century earlier, Viereck suggested that by "thrusting off the old guard businessmen," President Franklin Roosevelt had saved the country from class war, had saved the capitalists from themselves, and, in the process, had doubled their dividends.[43] Viereck believed, as did the warrior-aristocrats, that when the reins of government are in the hands of an aristocratic spirited elite, the state can be entrusted to act responsibly to ameliorate the destructive effects of capitalism and to aid in the creation of the kind of community that laissez-faire had destroyed. Viereck's conservatism did not stubbornly resist change; he rejected William F. Buckley Jr.'s conservatism, which propounded to "stand athwart history, yelling Stop."[44] Instead, in Viereck's view, conservatism's proper task was to conserve, through gradual reform, those traditions and institutions, including the traditional family, the church, labor union, mutual aid society, and the local community, that had living historical roots in the contemporary world. For Viereck, the New Deal and its effort to save American capitalism embodied this kind of conservative reform.

Viereck distinguished his conservatism from the "pseudo-conservatism" of the Manchester Liberals, advocates of laissez-faire capitalism whose philosophy was "hostile to a decent compassion for child labor and slum conditions," and the antimodern agrarianism of the Southern Agrarians.[45] He recoiled from American capitalists who had an "almost corybantic devotion to economic production figures."[46] For Viereck, capitalist materialism had too much in common with Marxist materialism in their rejection of transcendent values and the divine, albeit fallen, nature of man. But he also criticized conservatives like Frank Meyer, whose unequivocal support for laissez-faire capitalism pointed to "a return to that Sahara of inhuman aridity: the belief in Economic Man, a return to the incomplete liberties—merely top of the iceberg—of private economic liberty. It ignores the nine-tenths of human liberties beneath the top of the brain: the nine-tenths of imagination and art and religion."[47] The problem with American capitalists and those who defended laissez-faire capitalism is that they prioritized economic freedom above all other values, and by doing so, they "give us only the negative liberty to starve and be unemployed."[48] Defenders of laissez-faire "overlook[ed] those psychological, moral, and traditionalist shields of freedom against tyranny."[49] Capitalism needed cultural and traditional supports that were not primarily economic, yet it was precisely these cultural values and institutional supports that laissez-faire capitalism destroyed.

Viereck was critical of laissez-faire, but he was equally impatient with the conservatism that ignored the Burkean tenet to "build on the concrete existing historical base." Viereck identified himself as an "evolutionary conservative" descended from Burke, Samuel Taylor Coleridge, and Benjamin Disraeli. For him, the Southern Agrarians' conservatism was little more than a "utopian dream," an abstract conservatism "of yearning, contrasting the cultivated human values of a lost aristocratic agrarianism with northern commercialism and liberal materialism, but lacking the living roots of genuine conservatism and has only lifeless ones . . . contrived by romantic nostalgia."[50] The Southern Agrarians, Viereck argued, sought to re-create the traditions, values, and institutions of an era long ago eclipsed by the developments of the modern state and the Industrial Revolution. Their conservatism ignored the Burkean dictate to conserve and build on the roots that were "really there." It was the kind of conservatism that Viereck attributed to some of his contemporaries, especially Russell Kirk, whose conservatism Viereck called "rootless and abstract . . . unhistorical appeal to history, and tradition-less worship of tradition."[51]

Viereck's support for the New Deal flowed from a belief that unregulated laissez-faire capitalism created suffering and misery, which could lead to social upheaval. He viewed the New Deal legislation that created the Federal Deposit Insurance Corporation (FDIC), the Securities and Exchange Commission (SEC), and Social Security, and, later, President John F. Kennedy's New Frontier programs as remedies for the atomization that resulted from "excessive laissez-faire economics and greedy profiteering."[52] According to Viereck, the Great Depression was a "revolutionary powder keg, needing only a spark,"[53] and the New Deal took revolution in America off the table. It saved not only American political institutions but also capitalism and class hierarchy from socialism and class war.[54] The New Deal and the expansionary fiscal policy during World War II gave the potentially revolutionary American working class a "real stake in the status quo" of American capitalism.[55] It drained the working class's zeal for thoroughgoing changes to the capitalism system. Indeed, Viereck endorsed the expanded role of the federal government in regulating the economy because it solidified the established social order. The reforms rerouted workers' grievances into legitimate channels and minimized the violent confrontations that had so often typified labor relations in the United States.[56] Much like Theodore Roosevelt, Viereck believed that capitalist intransigence vis-à-vis workers' legitimate grievances was a recipe for revolution.

For Viereck, the postwar reality was complex. Although he warned against centralized government as a threat to freedom, he believed that this threat was manifest in both political and economic sources. Indeed, without proper constitutional checks (meaning not only some abstract scrap of paper about liberal Rights of Man but the proper traditions to make those rights concrete) the worker will get crushed not only by the social indifference of King Log (his employer) but by the social progress of King Stork (his own government).[57]

To check the power of the state and economic actors, Viereck endorsed strengthening the institutions of civil society, including labor unions, by means of government legislation as the model conservative social policy. Such legislation "encourage[d] voluntary participation" and not "reckless spending and enlargement of the federal bureaucracy." It also fortified the function, community, and authority of an important intermediate institution, the labor union.[58] For Viereck, labor unions were a conservative force in society because they diffused power, a necessary component of a pluralist society. But more important, they "restored to [the] atomized proletariat an organic unity."[59] They offered their members a sense of belonging and solidarity and meaning and purpose outside the state, conditions that transformed workers from masses into individuals.[60] Modern history was plagued by the weakening and collapse of one intermediate institution after another, beginning with feudal institutions based on an ascribed status, religious institutions, and the nuclear family. The trade union, he suggested, was the only "true society" that industrialism had fostered.[61] The labor union was an institution with real authority, a defined purpose, and existing roots, and it embodied "the possibility of both freedom and the security essential to human dignity."[62] It was this sort of institution that conservatives like Viereck hailed as the greatest protection against the excessive individualism of laissez-faire capitalism and the mass totalitarianism of the state. For Viereck, New Deal liberalism had preserved the order and capitalist economic liberty and had rescued America from the revolutions animated by dangerous ideologies such as classical liberalism, in which the individual is everything and the "whole" is nothing, or by ideologies of left and right, totalitarianisms in which the "whole" is everything and the individual is nothing.

Other conservatives shared some of Viereck's views regarding the importance and promotion of social bonds as a way to prevent revolution, yet they remained staunch opponents of the New Deal. Viereck, however, defended the New Deal as prudent reforms that built on America's "concrete existing historical base" in liberalism.[63] To the dismay of many of his contemporaries on both the left and the right, Viereck argued that the American heritage rested on a synthesis of Lockean liberalism and Burkean conservativism.[64] "American conservatism," he wrote, "in absence of feudal relics, must admit it has little to conserve except liberalism, which turns out to be relatively conservative liberalism."[65] Based on this insight and the Burkean belief in prudential reform, Viereck argued that the New Deal was a natural product of America's liberal, aristocratic heritage. Besides, by the 1950s it had become a "conservative and rooted tradition here to stay."[66] He scolded fellow traditionalist conservatives for repudiating America's liberal heritage:

> [I]t is imprecise to call conservative those counter-revolutionary ideologues of the right who defy the conservative principles of continuity with the past by trying to wrench American life out of its liberal and New Deal past. Such a violent wrench, such a combination of utopianism and coercion, based on abstract a-priori blueprints rather than a concrete historical experience, is what caused the French Revolution to degenerate from wholesale reform into murderous despotism. That is why *Shame and Glory of the Intellectuals* defined Old Guard Republicans and their intellectual apologists as "Jacobin endimanches" . . . What I meant and mean is: the abstract doctrinaire leaders of Republicanism and of a capitalist Adam Smith a-priorism in the north—and analogously the more doctrinaire aristocratic southerners—are applying the same violent wrench, the same discontinuity with the past, the same combination of utopian blueprints with coercive conformity which characterized the French Revolution and which, in Burke's analysis, doomed it to inevitable disaster.[67]

Viereck was bewildered by contemporary conservatives who ignored the teachings of Burke concerning the proper role of conservatism. For Viereck, "in a liberal state," the contemporary conservatism of the "fusion" variety "is the destroyer rather than the conserver."[68]

A final important theme in Viereck's thinking about the relationship between capitalism and the state was his belief in the need for a class of aristocratic leaders to resist the demands of both the plutocrats and the egalitarian masses. Viereck was no egalitarian, nor was he a democrat. In fact, he firmly believed, as all conservatives do, in order, classes, and social hierarchies, without which there would be no distinction and everyone would sink to a leveling mediocrity. He believed that the brilliance of the Federalists was in the aristocratic, conservative structure of the Constitution, which placed limits on the power of democratic majorities. "Democracy," Viereck wrote in *Shame and Glory of the Intellectuals*, "is housebroken, is tolerant, humane, civil-libertarian, only after being filtered, traditionalized, constitutionalized through indirect representation."[69] He believed that such a constitutional system allowed for modern-day aristocrats, such as Franklin Roosevelt and Adlai Stevenson, to rule and filter the potentially radical demands of the masses. "The aristocratic spirit sustaining our democracy," Viereck wrote, "is whatever conserves not real-estate values but real values, not gold standards but cultural standards."[70] This aristocratic spirit he characterized as "dutiful public service, insistence on quality and standards, and the decorum and ethical inner check of noblesse oblige."[71] The recovery of ethics and values rooted in the Judeo-Christian heritage that was taught in the family and the church and was practiced in the close personal relations experienced in a corporate body such as a local community was the medium by which the aristocratic spirit might be diffused to make "all men aristocrats."[72] The way to do this was to "subordinate economics to cultural values and to subordinate external coercion to internal self-discipline" and to strengthen the intermediate institutions in which this spirit and compassionate traditional Christian ethical values necessary for social reform were cultivated. To be sure, others advocated for the state to legislate culture, but what makes Viereck's thought distinct is that unlike the vast majority of conservatives, he saw active state intervention in the economy as essential to strengthening these institutions.[73] He did not view the relationship between the state and institutions of civil society as engaged in a zero-sum battle for authority and function but instead as both sustaining and reinforcing the social order.

For Viereck, when the state was administered by the likes of Prince von Metternich, Benjamin Disraeli, Winston Churchill, or Franklin Roosevelt, it served as a valuable partner of traditional institutions. It strengthened the Burkean "little platoons," such as the family, the local community, and the intermediary associations that Viereck, Kirk, and Nisbet all agreed were of the utmost social value. But Viereck's analysis also pointed to using the state to restrain capital, to mitigate its most destructive effects, and to force capitalists to meet their obligations to their workers and society at large. Although it was crucial to Viereck that intermediate institutions be strengthened, he did not think that they alone could restrain the power of corporate capital. He recognized the instability and suffering unleashed by laissez-faire corporate capitalism, and he believed that the restraints on it must come from moral instruction, the authority of traditional and intermediate association, and, just as important, the selective use of the power of the state.

By the mid-1950s, Viereck's interpretation of America's liberal-conservative tradition and his "vital center" conservatism became an outlier in the conservative movement. Because of his defense of labor unions, Adlai Stevenson, and the New Deal, along with his opposition to Joseph McCarthy, Viereck no longer represented what Frank Meyer called the "conservative mainstream." Meyer's conservative fusionism, which blended laissez-faire capitalism with traditionalism, was the dominant ideological position of the most influential conservative publication at the time, the *National Review*, and thus was the triumphant interpretation of conservatism in postwar America. Despite the inherent tension between libertarians and traditionalists, the conservative mainstream's aversion to Viereck's accommodation to the New Deal was enough to make him persona non grata. Criticized by Russell Kirk, Willmoore Kendall, and other conservatives, Peter Viereck was informally excommunicated from the conservative movement by Meyer in a stinging article he wrote in the *National Review*. "In an age in which grammar, rhetoric, and logic are no longer taught, the mass production of counterfeits is likely to continue apace. Viereck is not the first, nor will he be the last, to succeed in passing off his unexceptionably Liberal sentiments as conservatism."[74] Viereck's excommunication was an attempt to establish a postwar conservative orthodoxy. But this was not an orthodoxy that defined what conservatism is, but what it is not. It was not, at least in the first two decades of the postwar period, an orthodoxy that saw anything worth conserving in the New Deal.

RUSSELL KIRK: DE-RADICALIZING ROMANTIC ANTICAPITALISM

Peter Viereck was not the only conservative in the postwar era to critique laissez-faire capitalism and attempt to redefine conservatism on traditionalist lines. But whereas Viereck accepted corporate capitalism regulated by the welfare state as part of his "evolutionary conservatism," Russell Kirk repudiated both.

Much like the Southern Agrarians, Kirk detested the Big City, Big Government, Big Labor, and Big Business. Instead, he endorsed a decentralized economy and called for a greater "regard for the claims of rural life."[75] He rejected televisions as "electronic computers" and refused to drive an automobile, calling cars "mechanical Jacobins." Kirk was a bitter critic of industrialism, as were the Southern Agrarians, yet his critique of capitalism was much more limited than the Southern Agrarians' had been.[76]

Much like the Southern Agrarians, Kirk romanticized the preindustrial past of small, self-sufficient family farms and shops. Similarly, Kirk was no egalitarian and regarded inequality as essential to preserving society. "There ought to be inequality of condition in the world. For without inequality, there is no class; without class, no manners and no beauty; and then a people sink into public and private ugliness."[77] In Kirk's view, as is standard among conservatives, inequality is both necessary and a precondition for excellence and distinction. For him, the artisans and small businessmen were where "traditional human nature still has its healthiest roots," and they were the core of his scheme for a decentralized economy rooted in transcendental myths.[78]

The basis of Kirk's critique of capitalism was cultural. According to him, capital was short-sighted to assume that it could maintain allegiance without the ideological supports of tradition and religion.[79] Capitalism is not a religion, a moral philosophy, or a body of moral habits, he argued. "Fidelity to the dogmas of capitalism will not in and of itself make us all good, happy, and rich."[80] In *A Program for Conservatives*, Kirk argued that capitalism was supported not only by reason and economic arguments about utility or by levels of material consumption but by "myths" of divine intent, tradition, and natural law. These myths, according to Kirk, provide the measure of social conduct that make it possible for people to interact with one another in a peaceable and mutually beneficial way. Capitalism essentially rests on these myths because they teach individuals to respect the ideas at the root of the economic system, including private property, private rights, and order.[81] These myths were taught and embodied in the traditional institutions that were under attack by rationalism, liberalism, the centralized state, and industrial capitalism. As the centralized political state undermined these myths and institutions, it eroded the moral and institutional foundations of capitalism.[82] "Once supernatural and traditional sanctions are dissolved," Kirk explained, "economic self-interest is ridiculously inadequate to hold an economic system together and even less adequate to preserve order."[83]

But it was not only the centralized state that undermined the foundations of capitalism. Advocates of laissez-faire capitalism, like Ludwig von Mises, who focused solely on pure rationalism in their defense of the economic system and ignored the importance of community as a basic human need, contributed to the heartless individualism that threatened capitalism. Kirk contended that those who conceived of capitalism as an absolute good ignored "the genuine cause of dissatisfaction" when they failed to recognize "the ugliness, monotony, the ennui of modern industrial existence" and dismissed the traditional ideological and institutional foundations on which capitalism rested. The rationalist and utilitarian arguments of political economists could not persuade the working class to accept their subordinate position in the established order. This was because the working class was inherently conservative, Kirk believed, but their conservatism was "weakened by dislocations and destruction of community by industrialism."[84] In *The Conservative Mind*, Kirk wrote:

[T]his network of personal relationships and local decencies was brushed aside by steam, coal, the spinning jenny, the cotton gin, speedy transportation, and other item in the catalogue of progress . . . capitalism turned the world inside out . . . personal loyalties gave way to financial relationships . . . the wealthy man ceased to be magistrate and patron; he ceased to be neighbor to the poor man; he became a mass-man, very often, with no purpose in life but aggrandizement.[85]

Statements like this indicate Kirk's awareness of the revolutionary character of capitalism and echo criticisms made by defenders of slavery, the warrior-aristocrats, and the Southern Agrarians. Industrial capitalism had transformed social relationships by setting them on the ground of utility. It also had transformed labor from an activity of personal meaning and fulfillment into a monotonous exercise of social boredom. But in Kirk's view, capitalism need not take this form. "We can humanize the industrial system," he proposed, "against monotony (sacrificing efficiency, if necessary) to a variety of tasks and pride in workmanship, by standing guard against over-industrialization, by bringing back to the industrial laborer the reality of community and a taste of things beyond the pay-check."[86] Kirk believed that the best way to "humanize" capitalism and restore individual liberty was to promote economic independence in a society in which the "masters" are peasants, artisans, small traders, and small and medium-size businessmen.[87] To do this, Kirk suggested looking to a "third way" out of the "dilemma of capitalism and collectivism."[88] He endorsed Robert Nisbet's idea of the laissez-faire of autonomous groups and Wilhelm Röpke's economic decentralizing scheme.[89] Kirk wanted to order economic life away from the centralized and industrialized form it had taken and to move it toward an arrangement he called "local paternalism."[90] In regard to securing people from the vicissitudes of the market, Kirk observed, reminiscent of the Southern Agrarians, people do not become wholly dependent on the market for their income and sustenance but supplement their market activity with nonmarket productive activity. Citing Röpke, Kirk counseled that "people get their sustenance from outside the immediate realm of financial disturbances so find lunch in the garden, supper in the lake, and earn his potato supply in the fall by helping his brother clear his land."[91] Compared with Viereck and Nisbet, Kirk was the closest intellectual heir of the Southern Agrarians, although his critiques of capitalism were much less forceful and direct. Kirk's vision may have been similar—if not agrarian, then decentralist—to that of the Southern Agrarians, but whereas the Southern Agrarians critiqued capitalist profits and the plutocratic political system, Kirk did not. He seldom linked the economic wealth and power of corporations and elites with their political power. Furthermore, he was critical of the inhumanity of businesses' preoccupation with "efficiency," which, he observed, resulted in all kinds of negative social consequences, such as social disorder and the ruin of Detroit. But Kirk said very little about profits, which is the end in a capitalist economy, with efficiency as the means.

Russell Kirk's vision of a "restored," decentralized, petit-bourgeois economy was perhaps more reactionary than that expounded by the Southern Agrarians thirty years earlier. By 1962, the year that Kirk wrote *The Program for Conservatives*, his primer for a conservative movement, the American economy was dominated by large corporations like General Motors, General Electric, Westinghouse, DuPont, Ford, and J.P. Morgan. In addition, the highway system had made the automobile a necessity for many Americans and had fixed it in the American culture and psyche. The population of the nation's urban centers now dwarfed the rural population.[92] Clearly, Kirk's economic vision was not a practical political program for a modern nation, but it had much cultural appeal then, just as it continues to have among conservatives today. While Kirk rejected the language of "efficiency" and "economic growth" that is central to conservative discussions about capitalism today, his vision of petit-bourgeois capitalism continues to be the principal narrative about capitalism in the conservative discourse. Kirk's and others' depiction of capitalism as hermetically sealed petit-bourgeois relations marked a significant turn in how conservatives thought about it. This reinterpretation conceived of capitalism as a benign force in which power relations were absent and freedom would be allowed to flourish, were it not for the domineering and intrusive state. When this narrative came to dominate the conservative discourse, it buried the whole tradition of a conservative critique of capitalism, from the defenders of slavery through the warrior-aristocrats, the Southern Agrarians, and some of the "new" conservatives. Kirk, for all his ambivalence about capitalism, helped popularize a fictional notion of it.[93]

ROBERT NISBET: THE VANISHING CAPITALIST REVOLUTIONARY

Robert Nisbet was a harsh critic of the New Deal and, along with Kirk, endorsed political and economic decentralization.[94] In his influential *The Quest for Community*, Nisbet outlined the importance of traditional institutions as checks on economic laissez-faire and especially on the power of the state. Like many postwar conservatives, his thought was prompted by the rise of totalitarianism. Along with other conservative critics of the state, Nisbet believed that the triumph of totalitarianism in Europe was the "offspring of liberalism and the result of its failure."[95] Following the influence of Burke, he pointed to the French Revolution, which he saw as inspired by the liberalism of Rousseau and as the precursor to twentieth-century totalitarianism.[96] Under the pretext of freeing individuals from traditional fetters, the liberal democratic state has destroyed the intermediate institutions that stood between it and the individual. Without the community offered by traditional institutions, Nisbet argued, individuals found community in the state, which resulted in totalitarianism. For him, the surest bulwark against totalitarianism was what he called "a conservative pluralism of intermediate institutions."

Inspired by Enlightenment liberal thinkers and legitimated by popular support, the power of the state grew exponentially in the nineteenth and twentieth centuries. As Nisbet theorized, the state used its power to curtail and destroy the authority and function of traditional institutions.[97] As the power of the state grew, the authority of the institutions of civil society declined. And as the individual was freed from traditional institutions, the capitalist economic system was transformed from one restrained by obligations to the family, community, and church into an economic system in which the individual was free but uprooted and alone. This left the human passion for self-interested maximization of profit and the freedom to accumulate to rise to the top of the hierarchy of social values. No longer bound by the values, customs, and traditions of organic social units, capital grew bigger, more concentrated, and more industrialized and driven solely by the profit motive. As capitalist enterprises grew and property increasingly took the form of stocks, dividends, and faceless corporate behemoths rather than material property in farms, factories and buildings, big capital completed the rout of traditional institutions by accelerating the misery, instability, and anomie of individuals. The social consequences of this state of economic affairs was that as economic competition intensified and economic crisis deepened, people seeking relief from material insecurity and hardship were left with no other recourse but to turn to the state. According to Nisbet, "Far from proving a check upon the growth of the omni-competent State, the old laissez-faire actually accelerated this growth. Its indifference to every form of community and association left the State as the sole area of reform and security."[98] The threat to capitalism and established class and racial hierarchies by the egalitarian demands of politicized masses, Nisbet believed, was the result of the destruction of traditional institutions by the three-headed monster of liberal dogma (primarily the belief in individualism and abstract liberty), the centralized political state, and laissez-faire capitalism.

Despite his criticism of centralized political power and his concern with the potential danger it posed to human freedom, Nisbet was also skeptical of economic laissez-faire. His critique of capitalism centered on the role of capitalism in undermining the institutional foundations of the economic system that were found in the institutions of civil society. According to Nisbet, the so-called free market never existed. That is, the notion of a true free market that proponents suggest existed in the nineteenth century was historically inaccurate. Instead, as Nisbet argued, the origin of the purported "natural economic order" could be traced to "a special set of political controls and immunities existing on the foundations of institutions, most notably the family and local community, which had nothing whatsoever to do with capitalism."[99] These "noncapitalist" political controls and institutions lent nineteenth-century capitalism a semblance of stability and created the conditions that allowed the mechanisms of capitalism such as "the freedom of contract, the fluidity of capital, the mobility of labor, and the whole factory system to thrive."[100] As the capitalist revolution became more "complete"—meaning that as capitalist market relations expanded and encompassed greater aspects of social relationships—the physical community, the sense of community, and individuals' allegiance to the social and economic system as a whole were destroyed.

The heart of postwar conservatives' critiques of capitalism was cultural, and Nisbet's work was no exception. Agreeing with Kirk and as the neoconservatives contended a decade later, Nisbet argued that capitalism could not sustain itself in the people's imagination merely on abstract odes to individualism, impersonal corporatization, and materialism. Rather, capitalism's symbolism and normative aspects had to have demonstrable meaning to people's lives for them to remain faithful to the system. "Not all the asserted advantages of mass production and corporate bigness will save capitalism if its purposes become impersonal and remote, separated from the symbols and relationships that have meaning in human lives."[101] To this end, Nisbet urged his conservative colleagues to support modern labor unions and cooperatives because they "actually reinforce capitalism." "In such associations, the goals of production, distribution, and consumption can be joined to the personal sense of belonging to a social order. For in such an association the individual can find a sense of relatedness to the entire culture and thus become its eager partisan."[102]

According to Nisbet, as the power of the centralized state grew by destroying the feudal arrangements that were already weakened by liberal ideas, the emerging bourgeoisie allied with the state against the feudal fetters. As a junior partner of the state, the bourgeoisie was granted legal concessions, subsidies, and aid, all of which allowed capital to industrialize, expand into new markets and territories, and grow bigger and more concentrated than ever before. Nisbet wrote:

> We should not suppose that the laissez-faire individualism of the middle nineteenth century was the simple heritage of nature, the mere untrammeled emergence of drives and motivations with which man is naturally endowed. Laissez-faire . . . was *brought* into

existence. It was brought into existence by the planned destruction of old customs, associations, villages, and other securities; by the force of the State throwing the weight of its fast-developing administrative system in favor of *new economic elements of the population.* And it was brought into existence, hardly less, by reigning systems of economic, political, and psychological thought, systems which neglected altogether the social and cultural unities and settled single-mindedly on the abstract individual as the proper unit of speculation and planning.[103]

The role of the state in the development of capitalism, markets, and wealth creation is very well established, as Karl Polyani thoroughly demonstrated. That is, capital could not have achieved its rise and triumph without the help of the state's legal and coercive power.[104] But when Nisbet concluded that "there is much to be said for regarding capitalism as *simply* the forced adjustment of economic life to the needs of the sovereign State," he was minimizing the decisive role of capitalists in shaping the economic environment of a market society.[105] This is another key turn in the conservative discourse that ignores the critique of plutocracy that was a major component of the conservative critique of capitalism before the Cold War found in the writings of Theodore Roosevelt, Brooks Adams, and Allen Tate. It depoliticizes capitalists and underestimates their role in Nisbet's own historical narrative and in the historical development of the nation's political, economic, and social institutions. The postwar conservatives' narrative diminishes the role of the capitalist class as powerful political agents and understates the coercive nature of capitalist economic relations and the inequalities produced by it. When these inequalities are acknowledged, they are often blamed on natural inequalities, about which nothing should be done, or on the state, especially on taxes and regulations rather than on the power and influence of the wealthy and corporations, in both the economic and the political arenas.

Postwar conservatives opposed the individualist laissez-faire capitalism of Herbert Spencer and William Graham Sumner, which offered intellectual justification for the ruthless exploitation of capital. The social Darwinists accepted—indeed, they saw it as a motor of progress—that in the competitive struggle of capitalism, some grew stronger, larger, and more concentrated while others failed, went bankrupt, and died. Nisbet and Kirk did not, however, view economic concentration as a natural consequence of a competitive market but as the work of a centralized political state. For them, capital seemingly played a mostly secondary role in this process, merely filling the void of hollowed-out traditional and intermediate institutions deprived of authority and function. When reading Nisbet's works, one gets the sense that the capitalist was merely on the sidelines cheering on the centralized state as it destroyed the traditional institutions that were assumed to restrain the expansion of both the state and capital.

Nisbet, Kirk, along with most of the other postwar conservatives, deprived capitalism of its revolutionary characteristics as an economic system that, by its nature, "can never be stationary," as economist Joseph Schumpeter put it. They minimized the capitalists' decisive role through the mechanism of the market, as well as through the medium of the state, against the fetters of tradition. Whereas the critique of capitalist plutocracy was a key component in the thought of George Fitzhugh, the warrior-aristocrats, and the Southern Agrarians, the postwar conservatives' indictment of the capitalist seems to have focused on his ignorance to realize that traditional institutions were his political allies and lay at the foundation of the capitalist mode of production. For conservatives like Kirk and Nisbet, the biggest sin of capitalists seems to be that they were too short-sighted and focused on profits and production figures to perceive that as the state challenged the relations of domination and control exerted by traditional institutions, it was also weakening the necessary noneconomic foundations of capitalism's own existence.

THE RUDIMENTS OF A CONSERVATIVE WELFARE STATE

For the postwar conservatives, the restoration of traditional institutions was an attempt to diffuse power away from the state and toward multiple centers of authority. But restoring the function of traditional and intermediate institutions was meant not only to check the power of the state but also to rescue individuals from their individualism and egoism and recover the centrality of traditional religious values. Like their predecessors in the conservative tradition, Viereck, Kirk, and Nisbet believed that traditional institutions ameliorated individualism because they inculcated the values and bonds of kinship, locality, and the Judeo-Christian religion, all of which prevented alienation and anomie. These institutions socialized individuals to value deference to social superiors, thus reinforcing the unequal, hierarchical, natural order and the resulting social stability. Whereas Viereck believed that the state could strengthen intermediate institutions through legislation like the Wagner Act and the Fair Labor Standards Acts, Kirk and Nisbet repudiated the New Deal in its entirety, with Kirk writing that "community cannot be restored through any vaunting program of positive legislation."[106] Despite Kirk's and Nisbet's opposition to the New Deal, they offered few concrete policy proposals about how their vision could be achieved or what such a society would look like in a modern context. Kirk proposed an antimodern romanticized inegalitarian petit-bourgeois economy. Nisbet idealized the days before World War I when there was an abundance of churches, voluntary associations, and mutual aid societies with "significant function and role in the larger society."[107]

Despite both Kirk's and Nisbet's hostility to the New Deal welfare state, neither believed that the authority of traditional institutions would be immediately restored when the state retreated from providing social welfare. Instead, they—and especially Nisbet—crafted the contours of a new relationship between intermediate institutions and the state. According to Nisbet:

> [T]he role of [the] political government becomes clear in the democracies. Not to sterilize the normal authorities of associations, as does the total State through a pre-emption of function, deprivation of authority, and a monopolization of allegiance, but to reinforce these associations, to provide, administratively, a means whereby the normal competition of group differences is held within bounds and an environment of law within which no single authority, religious or

economic, shall attain a repressive and monopolistic influence—this is the role of government in a democracy.[108]

The kind of social balance and pluralism that Nisbet and Kirk had in mind required an active government. In *The Quest for Community*, Nisbet approvingly quoted Frank Tannenbaum on the role of government to ensure "personal freedom and associative authority":

> The road to social peace [wrote Tannenbaum] is the balance of the social institutions, and a wise statesman would *strengthen* those institutions that seemed to be losing ground, even if he were not addicted to them; for the only way to peace in this world of fallible human nature is to keep all human institutions strong, but none too strong; relatively weak, but not so weak as to despair of their survival.[109]

While the role of a "statesman" in "strengthening of institutions that seem to be losing ground," need not point to support for the New Deal, it does suggests more than merely a policy of dismantling the liberal welfare state and letting intermediate associations fend for themselves. Rather, it suggests that government can maintain an environment of healthy competition among social groups by means of aid or regulation and keep social institutions afloat that no longer are the recipients of public allegiance. Nisbet's political project for American conservatism as strengthening intermediate institutions departed from the logic of laissez-faire and carved out an active role for the state in cooperation with the institutions of civil society. Moreover, it took the conservative discourse about the role of the state away from one with only two options: laissez-faire or totalitarianism. It also laid the theoretical foundation for what would become the conservative welfare state in which authority and function were devolved from the federal government to state and local governments, as with President Bill Clinton's Temporary Assistance for Needy Families in 1996 and President George W. Bush's faith-based initiative programs that transferred some social welfare programs to local religious organizations.

Whatever influence on public policy and on the Republican Party that Viereck, Kirk, and Nisbet may or may not have had, their importance is not in that they created a political program of conservative politics that the Republican Party, with varying degrees of success, implemented. Instead, their mark is in distinguishing conservatism from classical liberalism by legitimating an intellectual conservatism based on a tradition and a set of values distinct from the mere defense of wealth. To the point that they succeeded, it was a major intellectual triumph, as in the immediate postwar era to be called a conservative was generally a label of derision. Viereck, Kirk, and Nisbet saw themselves as thinkers who were informed by their conservative principles and thus held a deep distrust of social scientists and policy intellectuals enamored with "social planning" and the totalitarianism to which such hubris led.

The conservative critiques of capitalism changed dramatically in the postwar era from what it had been for a century before the Cold War. The pre–Cold War critique, which began with John C. Calhoun and George Fitzhugh and was given another dimension by Brooks Adams and Theodore Roosevelt, was reformulated by the Southern Agrarians. They all differed greatly but were united by their critique of laissez-faire capitalism and not just purely in theory. Specifically, prewar conservatives attributed the misery and exploitation of workers and their families to unrestrained capitalism much more so than to the state. They politicized the economy and the capitalist as revolutionary agents active in the nation's social, political, and economic transformation.

The thinking about capitalism among conservative critics evolved in the postwar era, and the change in the substance and the tone of criticism may be attributable to the ideological and political contexts of postwar America. First, postwar conservatives sought to define themselves ideologically, by recovering a conservative tradition and heritage of which Kirk's *The Conservative Mind* and Viereck's *Conservatism Revisited* are exemplars. In the process of defining what it meant to be a conservative, they distinguished conservatism from the defense of laissez-faire capitalism and its economic libertarian adherents. The source of much of the postwar conservatives' critiques of capitalism lay in their emphasis on their principled distinction from libertarians. The second context was the Cold War rivalry between two competing economic systems, of which conservatives found affinity with capitalism and the fact that the New Deal stabilized the United States' political and economic systems, thereby reducing the likelihood of revolution and class conflict. Their concern about revolution, in particular the violent confrontations between capital and labor, had always been important elements of conservatives' criticisms of capitalism. But owing to the relative economic stability in the postwar era, conservative critics of capitalism were less concerned about domestic revolution. Ironically, that may have been, as Viereck believed, because the New Deal had addressed the most exploitative and immiserating aspects of capitalism, thus providing American workers with unparalleled economic security and prosperity. Indeed, Viereck himself wrote that material and economic critiques of capitalism have become "archaic." Those that remained relevant were spiritual or cultural.[110] It is in these contexts in which postwar conservative critics' thinking about capitalism can explain the evolution of the critique. Viereck's, Kirk's, and Nisbet's critiques of capitalism were not intended to transform its operation, as earlier critics suggested. Rather, their goal was to strengthen capitalism by disentangling it from its laissez-faire variety and tying it symbiotically to the noneconomic values and institutions that served as its cultural and institutional supports.

Henceforth, conservatives would no longer seek to transcend capitalism or to reconcile it with conservatism by constructing alternatives to the prevailing political economy, as the defenders of slavery or the Southern Agrarians had done. Instead, the core of their critique of capitalism increasingly became cultural, to the nearly complete exclusion of it as a mechanism for allocating goods and services and structuring the relationships production, thereby leaving its material foundations and mechanisms intact.

Postwar conservatives broke with the robust critiques of capitalism offered before the Cold War and reformulated the discourse about capitalism in cultural terms that are still heard today on the right. This intellectual development indicates how far American conservatives have departed from earlier conservative thinkers and how American conservatism has made its peace with capitalism. It was in the early decades of the Cold War that the litmus test for conservatives became a principled anti-Communist and unwavering support of capitalism. A regulated capitalism that in one form or another was endorsed by the warrior-aristocrats and the Southern Agrarians became heretical among postwar conservatives, as illustrated by Viereck's expulsion from the movement. This continues to be the case today. In a *National Review* article written long after the acrimony of the 1950s that exiled Viereck from the conservative movement had ended, John J. Miller wrote, "Although Viereck was a strong critic of Communism . . . the fundamental weakness of his conservatism was [his] disdain of capitalism . . . he personally preferred a mixed economy to free markets."[111] Although a cultural critique of capitalism remains in the conservative discourse, American conservatism is fundamentally, more so now than ever before, about a defense of capitalism.

The 1960s and 1970s brought far-ranging transformations to America's politics, its economy, and its social and cultural fabric. The expansion of the welfare state by the Great Society expanded the role of the federal government in economic life while it brought millions of people out of poverty. Movements by racial minorities and women dealt significant blows to long-entrenched racial and gender hierarchies and the customs and institutions that sustained them. Yet despite the economic boom of the 1960s, which was largely the result of greater government spending on the Great Society and the war in Vietnam, American capitalism was structurally deeply flawed, as the stagflation crisis would soon reveal. Capitalism was in the midst of a crisis of legitimacy. The political and economic response to the crisis would result in paradigmatic shifts in the U.S. and global economies that would drastically alter class and power relations in the United States and pave the way for a greater crisis to come. Conservatives would be at the ideological forefront of this historic transformation. With a renewed focus and important contributions from neoconservatives, the right brought the capitalists back into the discourse, reformulated the conservative defense of capitalism, took aim at the liberal welfare state, and, in the process, created levels of economic inequality and class stratification that had not been seen in the United States since before the New Deal.

5

THE NEOCONSERVATIVE CRITIQUES OF AND RECONCILIATION WITH CAPITALISM

[M]ost Americans are now quick to believe that "big business" conspires secretly but most effectively to manipulate the economic and political system—an enterprise which, in prosaic fact, corporate executives are too distracted and too unimaginative even to contemplate.

Irving Kristol, *Two Cheers for Capitalism*

T he 1960s and early 1970s have rightly been called the zenith of twentieth-century liberalism and the beginnings of its collapse in the United States. The roughly decade and a half were years of prosperity, unprecedented gains by racial minorities and women, as well as the lowest levels of economic inequality in the twentieth century.[1] These years were also, however, the beginning of a sweeping backlash against the progressivism of the 1960s, particularly President Lyndon B. Johnson's Great Society and the gains toward inclusion and equality made by African Americans, Latinos, and women, which conservatives perceived as attacks on the nation's social, cultural, and political traditions and institutions. On the other end of the political spectrum, opposition to the war in Vietnam and the decolonization movements in Asia and Africa inspired radical activists at home to challenge the capitalist system. While these challenges to American capitalism in the 1960s and 1970s gained much more traction in theory than in practice, they made conservatives worry that the capitalist system was in jeopardy. In a report to the Chase Manhattan Bank, New York's governor, Nelson Rockefeller, wrote, "It is clear to me that the entire structure of our society is being challenged."[2] Lewis Powell, who was later appointed to the U.S. Supreme Court, urged the U.S. Chamber of Commerce and American businesses to "apply their great talents vigorously to the preservation of the system itself."[3] With the perception that the capitalist system itself was under attack, conservatives shed their ambivalence to capitalism and joined business interests on the ideological front lines to defend it.[4]

The 1970s was pivotal in conservative thought because the neoconservatives, arguably the most influential conservative thinkers of the last forty years, reconciled the American conservative mainstream with corporate capitalism and a reformed, but circumscribed, welfare state.[5] The neoconservatives' defense of corporate capitalism was a repudiation of the critique of the corporate model and of Big Business that had been central to earlier critics such as the Southern Agrarians and mid-twentieth-century thinkers Russell Kirk and Robert Nisbet. Although a critique of capitalism can be found in contemporary conservative thought, after the events of the 1970s it was only a shell of its former self, devoid of the core elements of the historical critique that stressed the exploitative and dehumanizing aspects of capitalism, along with its threat to community, that were once important components of the conservative critique. In the following decades, the neoconservatives' critique of capitalism was wholly cultural and was intended to strengthen capitalism's ideology and the economic system itself, not to weaken it.

The neoconservative critique of capitalism had two parts. The first was offered by Irving Kristol and Daniel Bell and centered on how capitalism undermined the "bourgeois virtues" of the hard work, thrift, and delayed gratification associated with the Protestant ethic.[6] As J. David Hoeveler Jr. pointed out, for first-generation neoconservatives, the central concern was the failure of capitalism to secure its cultural legitimacy in the world that it created.[7] For neoconservatives, "an effective defense of capitalism required a defense of the cultural assumptions on which a commercial civilization is based."[8] Its cultural foundation was rooted in the Judeo-Christian heritage that gave morality and meaning to life and also in the Protestant ethic, which legitimated capitalist society as just and rewarded hard work and virtuous living. As originally articulated by Bell and Kristol, capitalism needed to recover the lost values that once made it morally defensible and culturally legitimate.[9] Their critique of contemporary capitalism centered on its amoralism and how it contributed to a cultural nihilism perilous to the American economic and political system. They called for a cultural renaissance that repudiated the emphasis on self-absorbed consumerism and immediate gratification of contemporary capitalism in favor of a return to the moral foundations of the Protestant ethic, which justified capitalist accumulation and economic inequality. The key to the recovery of an ethics that legitimized capitalism, especially for Irving Kristol, was supply-side economics.[10] In his view, this offered a model in which the economy rewarded hard work, productivity, and saving, that is, the core bourgeois virtues and character traits that legitimized the economic system. Indeed, the neoconservatives were at the ideological forefront of the defense of capitalism and the retrenchment of economic inequality that began in the 1970s and that defines the American political economy today.

It did not take long for the second, more persistent, and culturally based critique of capitalism to emerge among the neoconservatives. The fall of the Soviet Union in 1991 resulted in a unipolar world in which the United States was the only superpower. The neoconservatives viewed this international landscape as an opportunity for the nation to fashion a new world order founded on democratic capitalism. In fact, neoconservatives were so convinced of the global appeal of such an order that some concluded that the "end of history" had arrived.[11] Because American political leaders were reluctant to engage in such a globally transformative project, some neoconservatives wondered whether the materialistic culture of capitalism was contributing to America's unwillingness to remake the world. For conservative thinkers and columnists such as William Kristol and David Brooks, late-twentieth-century capitalism had created a decadent populace that had become solely focused on its own personal material concerns.[12] Although necessary for capitalism, bourgeois virtues are "prosaic" and fail to inspire the courage, patriotism, and national sacrifice necessary for the United States to play a globally transformative role. America has attempted to fulfill its global hegemonic destiny only in fits and starts. Neoconservatives attributed this failure in part to the culture of capitalism, which prioritizes moneymaking, consumption, materialism, and personal satisfaction.

Contemporary neoconservatives look to the prospect of an American empire as the antidote to the malaise generated by welfare-state dependency and capitalist self-interested consumerism. Neoconservatives hope that an American imperial project will rescue American society, politics, and culture from its decadence, depravity, and egoism, by transforming the American consumer into a supportive citizen of what William Kristol called the "benevolent global hegemony."[13] This revolution in American political culture, neoconservatives argue, is the key to "shaping the contours of a world order that is conducive to our liberal democratic principles and our safety."[14]

Conservative thinking about capitalism and the welfare state had many ideological architects, among whom the most important were the neoconservatives. Barry Goldwater's unsuccessful 1964 presidential campaign revealed to movement conservatives that its ideological underpinnings, consisting of laissez-faire capitalism and a complete dismantling of the welfare state, lacked popular electoral appeal. Voters supported New Deal programs such as Social Security and unemployment compensation. Neoconservatives, particularly Irving Kristol, recognized that an ideology and a political movement bent on eviscerating the welfare state were an electoral dead end. Accordingly, in the decades since Goldwater's defeat, conservative intellectual and political leaders crafted an ideology and a political movement that gave conservatism a growing electoral following and intellectual rigor, especially in public policy. Moreover, it successfully challenged liberalism's ideological hegemony and the electoral power of the New Deal Democrats.[15]

Many scholars have written on the economic, cultural, and political transformation of the United States that took place in the 1970s.[16] Neoconservative thinking about capitalism helped propel these economic and political changes and altered the way in which Americans think about and discuss capitalism and the welfare state.[17] By 1980, assaults on the welfare state, the regulatory regime, and organized labor were the norm, and the New Deal Democratic electoral coalition was smashed to pieces. With the election of Ronald Reagan came the architects of a neoconservative ideology that redefined the relationship of the market, the citizen, and the state. Reagan's conservative policies, including tax cuts, aggressive anti-Communism, military Keynesianism, monetarism, assaults on organized labor, and government regulation redistributed income and wealth to the rich and corporations. Together, these policies, carried out by both Republican and Democratic administrations over four decades, have had a profound effect on American politics. They reoriented the welfare state toward conservative ends by slashing programs that assisted the poorest and most needy, increased economic inequality, restricted upward social mobility, and reestablished economic hierarchies of power to discipline and command labor in the interest of greater profits.[18]

Few conservative critics of capitalism have had as profound effect on public policy as the neoconservatives did. Their influential presence in the media, Washington think tanks, corporate boards of directors, NGOs, IGOs, and the federal government has been well established. Many neoconservatives have been intellectually and politically influential, such as Francis Fukuyama, Nathan Glazer, Gertrude Himmelfarb, Jeanne Kirkpatrick, Seymour Martin Lipset, Daniel Patrick Moynihan, Norman Podhoretz, James Q. Wilson, and Paul Wolfowitz. I will focus, however, on the thought of Daniel Bell, Irving Kristol, William Kristol, and David Brooks.

Daniel Bell (1919–2011) was a sociologist and a professor at Harvard University, and his book *The Cultural Contradictions of Capitalism* (1976) is the clearest and most thorough expression of the decline of bourgeois virtues. Bell wrote several other important books, particularly *The Coming of the Post-Industrial Society* (1973) and an edited book entitled *The End of Ideology* (1960). Along with Irving Kristol, Bell was the founder of the first neoconservative publication, the *Public Interest*.

Irving Kristol (1920–2009) is considered by many to be the founder of neoconservatism. In his obituary, the *New York Times* called him "a political commentator who as much as anyone, defined modern conservatism."[19] Kristol frequently wrote for conservative magazines, including the *Public Interest*, *Commentary*, and the *National Interest*, which he founded. His ideas reached the general public through his frequent contributions to the *Wall Street Journal*. He taught at New York University and was a senior fellow at the American Enterprise Institute, a conservative think tank. He influenced corporate business leaders and powerful Republican officials like Jack Kemp, Robert H. Bork, and William E. Simon. In 2002, President George W. Bush awarded him the Presidential Medal of Freedom.

As regular contributors to the opinion pages of the *Wall Street Journal* and the *New York Times*, William Kristol and David Brooks also became important figures in conservative policy circles. Arguably, the peak of their influence on policy was during the administration of George W. Bush and the "war on terror." In addition to his frequent opinion pieces in the *Wall Street Journal*, William Kristol, Irving's son, is a fixture on the Fox News channel and has written editorials for *Time* magazine and the *New York Times*.[20] He has advised a number of high-ranking Republican officials, including William Bennett, who was Ronald Reagan's secretary of education, former vice president Dan Quayle, and 2008 Republican presidential nominee John McCain. William Kristol also was the founder of the *Weekly Standard*, a neoconservative magazine, and is a member of several conservative think tanks, such as the Project for a New American Century and the Manhattan Institute.

While not as prominent in conservative circles, David Brooks (1961–) writes political commentary for the *New York Times*, and PBS and NPR have made him a well-known figure and a best-selling author of such books as *Bobos in Paradise: The New Upper Class and How They Got There* (2000) and *On Paradise Drive: How We Live Now (and Always Have) in the Future Tense* (2004).

CAPITALISM'S CRISIS OF LEGITIMACY

When they were writing in the 1960s and 1970s, neoconservatives were not avid free-market enthusiasts; rather, they operated under the premise that the socialist alternative to capitalism had been discredited by the failures of the Soviet experiment and that Friedrich Hayek's and Milton Friedman's laissez-faire alternative was equally problematic. For Daniel Bell and Irving Kristol, the main problem with capitalism—and the reason that it suffered from a crisis of legitimacy—was that it had been divorced from the cultural and moral precepts of the Protestant ethic.[21] Following Max Weber, Bell argued that capitalism had its origins in Protestant asceticism.[22] Irving Kristol saw the Protestant ethic as inculcating what he called "bourgeois virtues" such as thrift, self-reliance, industry, sobriety, and self-discipline, which were rooted in traditional structures of authority like family, church, neighborhood, and ethnicity. Furthermore, these bourgeois virtues linked capitalist accumulation to an ethic that justified inequality.[23] Those who worked hard, invested prudently, and had the personal fortitude to save rather than spend irresponsibly would not only be the most socioeconomically well-off but also receive God's highest grace of everlasting salvation. These virtues propelled individuals to pursue their economic self-interest within the confines of moral strictures. Again in keeping with Weber, Bell contended that the Protestant commitment to work, accumulation, and the belief in an occupation as a "calling" was not motivated primarily out of the desire to accumulate wealth but as a means to one's own salvation.[24] As long as capitalism was bound by these religious and ethical parameters, individuals' profligacy and acquisitiveness would be held in check, and the inequalities that resulted from capitalist accumulation would be largely accepted as deserved.

According to neoconservatives, by the 1970s these virtues could no longer be found among the highest socioeconomic classes. Writing in the epilogue of *Two Cheers for Capitalism* (1978), Kristol declared, "No one seriously claims that these traditional virtues will open the corridors of corporate power to anyone, or that those who now occupy the executive suites are—or even aspire to be—models of bourgeois virtues."[25] Although capitalism and big business brought material comforts and prosperity to more people than ever before, the popular perception of a successful corporate executive was one who was greedy, cutthroat, and solely concerned with profits. It was no wonder that the left's criticisms of economic inequality, capitalism, and big business were so appealing, Kristol believed. Who would want to defend a system like that, anyway?

The Protestant ethic was never the only validation for capitalism or the only justification for its inequalities. As Kristol pointed in his essay "Capitalism, Socialism, and Nihilism" (1973), the inequalities of capitalism were being defended from a number of different perspectives. Some thinkers justified accumulation and profit maximization as values in themselves. Others defended inequality from a social Darwinist perspective. These explanations for capitalism and inequality shifted away from the religiously inspired Protestant ethic. According to Kristol, they eclipsed the Protestant justification and created a crisis of legitimacy for capitalism:

> This definition [of distributive justice], propagated by Mandeville and Hume, is purely positive and secular rather than philosophical or religious. It says that, under capitalism, whatever is, is just—that all the inequalities of liberal-bourgeois society must be necessary, or else the free market would not have created them, and therefore they must be justified. This point of view makes no distinction between the speculator and the bourgeois-entrepreneur: Both are selfish creatures who, in the exercise of their private vices (greed, selfishness, avarice), end up creating public benefits.[26]

This reconceptualization of capitalism and its inequalities unfolded gradually and had both material and philosophical causes. As capitalism developed and became more industrial and concentrated, the Protestant justification began to lose ground. The enormous concentration of wealth in the hands of the robber barons and New York's banks and investment firms no longer reflected the personal traits of the God-fearing Protestant capitalist. Before long, the religious and moral justification for capitalism was replaced by utilitarianism, social Darwinism, and the young intellectuals of the early twentieth century, such as Walter Lippmann, Van Wyck Brooks, John Reed, and Harold Sterns. They argued that American cultural values, like the Protestant ethic and the romanticism of small-town life, did not represent reality. America had become much more religiously, ethnically, and racially diverse. As the nation became more cosmopolitan and urban populations were introduced to new ideas, Americans began to rebel against the restraints imposed on individual behavior by Protestant values.

As a result, the Protestant ethic's moral justification for accumulation and its restraints on consumption began to diminish.[27]

It was not only the intellectual attack on the Protestant ethic that undermined the religious foundation of capitalism. Capitalists also seized on this cultural shift and created a way in which it could increase their profits. For example, both Bell and Kristol highlighted the invention of the installment plan and consumer credit as essential tools by which capital could be made more profitable. In the process, these finance and credit instruments contributed to a culture that privileged instant gratification over the more moderating values of the bourgeois ethic.[28] According to Bell, the installment plan was "the most 'subversive' instrument that undercut the Protestant ethic."[29] In addition to the installment plan, capitalists further weakened American capitalism's cultural foundations by inventing an efficient and profitable advertising industry that extended the demand for immediate self-gratification.[30] Ultimately, Irving Kristol observed, as a result of the cultural and ideological shifts during the late-nineteenth- and early-twentieth centuries, together with changes in the way that capital operated, "capitalism outgrew its bourgeois origins and became a system for the impersonal liberation and satisfaction of appetites—an engine for the creation of affluence."[31]

Gradually divorced from its moral foundations, in both theory and practice, capitalism's legitimacy rested on its hedonistic and materialistic benefits of being able to confer a higher standard of living than any alternative could. Resting on such purely materialistic foundations, capitalism became a system in which, in Bell's words, "nothing is sacred."[32] According to Kristol, the economic defenders of capitalism had brought about the cultural crisis of capitalism. For him, post–Protestant ethic capitalism

> does provide more food, better housing, better health, to say nothing of all kinds of pleasant conveniences. . . . But anyone who naively believes that, in sum, that they suffice to legitimize a socioeconomic system knows little of the human heart and soul. People can learn to despise such a system even while enjoying its benefits.[33]

Hence, in Kristol's view, the social justice movements of the 1960s that demanded radical changes to the economic structure were not the

product of exploitation and an undemocratic structure of the capitalist economy but were a protest against capitalism's amorality. Kristol
dismissed the inequalities of capitalism as "trivial."[34] Instead, as he
saw it, the problem was that the basic social-moral idea of capitalism
in which the invisible hand of the free market transformed private
vices into social benefits was no longer effective in a modern liberal
capitalist society. It was a failure of "imagination when it came to vice
on the part of the secular libertarian tradition of capitalism."[35] Moreover, this was a failure, in Kristol's view, to which Ludwig von Mises,
Friedrich Hayek, Milton Friedman, and the libertarian conservatives
had no satisfactory answer. Kristol wrote:

> The intense focus on economics and economic growth that is so nat-
> ural to the heirs of Adam Smith has left them powerless against cap-
> italism's cultural critics, as distinct from its economic critics. Adam
> Smith himself, though a creative genius in economic thought, was
> something of a philistine, believing that cultural attitudes and opin-
> ions, like religious ones, were matters of personal taste about which
> reasonable men would not and should not get particularly excited.
> For two centuries now, Western civilization has been haunted by this
> stupendous error of judgment, with the result that today, even as a
> market economy is accepted as superior to any other, at least in prin-
> ciple, the bourgeois society on which the market economy is based
> is being challenged with unprecedented boldness and success.[36]

Capitalist freedom without moral restraints and a moral compass
allowed capitalists to invest in and peddle anything and everything
with the potential to realize profit. The problem for neoconservatives
was that this included the ideas of capitalism's ideological adversar-
ies. Capitalism's amoralism both contributed to and profited from a
dangerous cultural nihilism[37] that included pornography, obscenity,
and drugs that weakened the character of the citizens and threatened
the social, cultural, and political institutions of Western civilization
itself.[38]

In the late 1960s and 1970s, neoconservatives worried that capitalism's crisis of legitimacy had become critical. According to Kristol,
"the spiritually impoverished civilization that we have constructed
on what once seemed to be sturdy bourgeois foundations, is in

desperate need" of a moral vision. "Liberal capitalism," he declared, "has been living off the inherited cultural capital of the bourgeois era and has benefited from a moral sanction it no longer even claims. That legacy which stressed hard work, delayed gratification, and saving is now depleted, and the cultural environment has turned radically hostile."[39]

SUPPLY-SIDE ECONOMICS AND THE RECOVERY OF THE PROTESTANT ETHIC

For Kristol and the neoconservatives, the question then was how to relegitimize capitalism. The answer, for Kristol, was twofold: The American corporation must undergo a public relations makeover, and public policy needed to be altered to create incentives for the bourgeois virtues that legitimated capitalism. The American corporation, and particularly corporate elites, would have to present themselves in a new light and also develop new rationales for their authority and wealth.[40] For Kristol, the corporation was crucial to the future of liberal democracy because it diffused the economic and political power that was necessary for individual liberty, and he urged corporate elites to make themselves publicly visible by advertising their Horatio Alger origins and promoting their firms' public service. He stressed the task of relegitimizing the corporation and creating a political constituency to save themselves and to justify the hierarchical social order of the capitalist system.

Beyond the corporate public relations campaign, the motor for renewing bourgeois virtues was supply-side economics. Supply-side is an old idea of economic growth dating back to French economist Jean-Baptiste Say's *A Treatise on Political Economy* (1803). Supply-side economics holds that supply creates its own demand and results in economic growth.[41] Discredited in the 1930s by the Great Depression and Keynesian economics, the theory gained a new lease on life in the 1970s in the form of the "Laffer curve" when both unemployment and inflation soared, a scenario that Keynesian logic thought impossible and that government was seemingly unable to resolve. Supply-siders held that lower taxes on business would expand private-sector employment and greater revenues for the state. As a result, it would both stimulate investment and economic growth and maintain those government revenues needed to fund and administer a modern state. The theory gained an influential following among conservatives, especially Ronald Reagan, who chose a number of supply-side economists, including Arthur Laffer, to serve on his Economic Advisory Policy Board. Then in 1981 Reagan pushed through one of the largest tax cuts in the nation's history, which disproportionately benefited the wealthy and business.[42]

For neoconservatives like Kristol, supply-side was more important for its ideology than for its potential economic benefits. Supply-side economics met his challenge to return to a fusion of capitalism and the Protestant ethic of diligence, honesty, and hard work that was being lost in America's consumer capitalism.[43] Kristol favored supply-side economics because he believed that it provided the correct set of incentives needed to recover the character attributes of the bourgeois ethic. Supply-side rewarded the innovation and production that encouraged an entrepreneurial spirit. According to the theory, taxing higher incomes at higher rates discourages people from working harder and earning more income. Instead, taxes on the wealthy should be lower to inspire them to work harder and invest more, knowing that their work and additional investments will not be taxed away by the government. This tax policy, argue the purveyors of supply-side, offers a number of benefits, including greater private investment in an economy that creates jobs, increases in the number of tax-paying citizens, and greater taxation revenues. Most important for Kristol, supply-side rewarded the values of hard work and prudent investments, offering a mechanism for cultural transformation.

Supply-side economics was a key turning point in how conservatives reconciled conservative values with capitalism in the late twentieth century. Past reconciliations with capitalism by conservatives had emphasized the tension between capitalism and conservative values and traditions. They stressed strengthening traditional institutions such as the family and the church, which teach values that serve as counterweights to the selfish values inculcated by the market.[44] For Kristol and other neoconservative thinkers such as George Gilder and

Michael Novak, supply-side capitalism created an arena in which conservative values were taught and rewarded through participation in the market. In their analysis, although traditional institutions remained important, they were no longer the "values" counterweight to American capitalism's excesses. Neoconservatives fashioned the capitalist market and traditional institutions as domains with shared values and thus fused capitalism with conservative values, eliminating, in their view, the ideological tension in the conservative discourse. This was a major rethinking of capitalism and has informed conservative thought up to the present.

Supply-side became the official tax and regulatory policy of the Republican Party and was central to Reagan's policies of deregulation and massive tax cuts for the wealthy. Neoconservatives were satisfied that capitalism finally had a mechanism to regenerate the character type that was at the foundation of the economic system. Certainly, the cultural recovery of the bourgeois ethic would not take place overnight, but through supply-side, an enormous step had been taken in that direction.

TOWARD A CONSERVATIVE WELFARE STATE: THE DESERVING AND THE UNDESERVING POOR

If reforming the culture of capitalism was one pillar on which America's social, cultural, economic, and political regeneration stood, reform of the welfare state was the other. But for neoconservatives, jettisoning President Johnson's Great Society did not mean repudiating the idea of a welfare state. Instead, in their criticisms of the latent consequences of the Great Society, neoconservatives formulated a vision of a conservative welfare state that has had great influence on American politics on such figures as President George W. Bush. This vision entailed the erosion of the welfare state from one of entitlements to one that prioritized self-reliance and that restored the power of corporate economic elites.

Many of the first-generation neoconservatives, such as Irving Kristol, Daniel Bell, and Norman Podhoretz, were former leftists who became New Deal liberals, but as the New Deal changed into the Great

Society, they became the Great Society's most formidable critics. They argued that the Great Society's welfare state had too many unintended consequences and that it was counterproductive because it perpetuated what President Johnson's assistant secretary of labor, David Patrick Moynihan, called "the cycle of poverty."[45] Programs like Aid to Families with Dependent Children (AFDC), Medicaid, food stamps, subsidized housing, and other means-tested programs undermined such traditional institutions as the two-parent family by tying eligibility to poverty-level income.[46] Faced with the prospect of losing all public assistance if employed and earning an amount just above the poverty line, public assistance created a disincentive to work, the neoconservatives insisted. These programs and policies degraded character by encouraging dependency; were harmful to the family structure by encouraging out-of-wedlock births and female-headed households; and reinforced a culture of poverty that created disincentives for personal responsibility (that is, those attributes of the Protestant ethic or bourgeois virtues).

Despite their opposition to the Great Society, neoconservatives did not advocate for the immediate and total destruction of the welfare state. Although they opposed the concentration of services in government and endorsed welfare state reform by eliminating most of the Great Society programs, they differed from their more conventional conservative colleagues. Neoconservatives believed that the welfare state grew out of a sense of insecurity felt by a public that had struggled through economic depression. The welfare state, especially the New Deal, was a response to the desire of citizens and the government to mitigate the negative effects of the capitalist economic cycle. For Irving Kristol, policy measures like Social Security and unemployment compensation were political expedients by which "a liberal capitalist society inoculate[s] itself against a resurgence of anti-capitalist dissent."[47] In "A Conservative Welfare State," he wrote, "If the American people want to be generous to their elderly, even to the point of some extravagance, I think it is very nice of them. . . . So, in my welfare state, we leave social security alone—except for being a bit more generous, perhaps."[48]

The polarity for first-generation neoconservatives was not between the free market and the welfare state. Instead, it was between two versions of the welfare state. The first version was the "older, masculine, paternalistic version of the welfare state" associated with Theodore Roosevelt's Fair Deal and Franklin D. Roosevelt's New Deal. The second was the "newer and firmly established feminine-maternal conception of the welfare state" associated with Johnson's Great Society.[49] In Kristol's view, programs like Social Security and unemployment compensation were social safety nets for the "productive" members of society. The limited welfare state of the New Deal distinguished between the deserving and the undeserving poor. Widowed mothers and the disabled who were unable to work were the deserving poor and therefore were entitled to public assistance. Likewise, seniors were entitled to assistance, as were the temporarily unemployed. Kristol sought to re-create this older, more limited version of the welfare state because it fostered self-reliance and a sense of "sympathy" rather than "compassion." According to him, sympathy is a male quality, directed at people "who want to help themselves and need a helping hand."[50]

In contrast, the Great Society, Kristol argued, was predicated on the feminine quality of compassion. The Great Society programs did not merely seek to help those who "needed a helping hand," as Kristol put it, but to aid everyone in need. Compassion, he felt, does not discriminate between deserving and undeserving and is potentially limitless because it esteems protection above all other values. This sentiment places demands on government to satisfy the public's infinite appeals for aid. Individuals then look to government to solve all their problems rather than trying to help themselves.

None of these criticisms of the welfare state in the 1970s was new. In fact, these ideas had been common among conservatives during economic booms and busts throughout the nineteenth and twentieth centuries, including during the Great Depression. Why then, did the conservatives' critique of the welfare state and their adoration of the potentialities of the market resonate with the American public as much as it did beginning in the 1970s?

The answer lay in the contemporary economic and political environment. As many historians and commentators of the period have written, 1973 marked the end of America's so-called postwar golden age.[51] This period, from 1945 to 1973, was one of unrivaled U.S. economic dominance. The era was characterized by domestic manufacturers' increasing productivity; low unemployment; rising wages to keep pace with rises in productivity; strong industrial unions; a social welfare state; subsidies for homeownership and education; public policies that mitigated the hardships of occasional and temporary unemployment; and a long period of economic growth sustained largely by Keynesian economic policies that obscured a long-brewing crisis in demand.[52] The combination of Keynesian economic policies, institutionalized industrial unions that guaranteed uninterrupted production in exchange for increased wages and/or benefits for workers, and an international market with few competitors created an environment of labor and management peace and broad economic prosperity. But the economic prosperity and the minimal welfare state of the New Deal excluded many poor Americans, disproportionally African Americans and Latinos.

By the mid-1960s, it had become apparent that things were changing. Long excluded from American prosperity and the opportunities it afforded, African Americans, Latinos, and women were finally beginning to be gradually incorporated into the political and economic system on an equal basis as white men. Meanwhile, the formerly decimated economies of Japan and Germany had recovered, and U.S. firms could no longer expect to dominate the international market as they had done for nearly two decades following the war. As U.S. firms faced stiffer competition abroad and at home, businesses invested heavily in machinery and technology and sought less costly labor markets. At first, U.S. companies shifted their business to nonunionized factories and shops in the U.S. South that were hostile to organized labor. Then these firms moved abroad, where labor costs were even lower. Private-sector union jobs continued their decline, and wages began to stagnate. As the U.S. economy deindustrialized, unemployment in the Northeast and the Midwest industrial belt, particularly in the cities, began to climb. Then when firms did not profit as expected from their investments in manufacturing plants and equipment, they began to shift to financials, stock buybacks, and corporate mergers, which helped drive up inflation and aggravated unemployment, a scenario that came to be known as *stagflation*.[53] Most important, this transformed the structure of American capitalism, as finance and associated sectors of the economy, collectively known by the acronym

FIRE (finance, insurance, and real estate), came to occupy a larger share of overall economic activity than ever before, thereby signaling the preeminence of finance, rather than manufacturing, in the American economy.

These changes in the American economy during the 1960s and 1970s and government spending on an increasingly costly and deadly war in Vietnam; the costs of expanding Johnson's War on Poverty; and the oil crisis in 1973 all combined to expose the structural weaknesses of the postwar economy. Spending on the Vietnam War ballooned the national debt and drained spending on domestic antipoverty programs. Despite the significant strides toward inclusion and equality, the 1964 Civil Rights Act and the 1965 Voting Rights Act by themselves could not deliver on the promise of racial equality, much less socioeconomic upward mobility. As Martin Luther King Jr. wrote in 1967, less than a year before his assassination,

> The practical cost of change for the nation up to this point has been cheap. The limited reforms have been obtained at bargain prices. There are no expenses, and no taxes are required, for Negroes to share lunch counters, libraries, parks, hotels, and other facilities with whites. Even the psychological adjustment is far from formidable. . . . Even the more significant changes involved in voter registration required neither large monetary nor psychological sacrifice. . . . The real cost lies ahead. The stiffening of white resistance is a recognition of that fact. The discount education given Negroes will in the future have to be purchased at full price if quality education is to be realized. Jobs are harder and costlier to create than voting rolls. The eradication of slums housing millions is complex far beyond integrating buses and lunch counters.[54]

Blacks, Hispanics, women, and welfare recipients began to make demands on the state beyond nondiscrimination or affirmative action. They began to demand substantive economic changes to address the dire economic plight of groups, particularly blacks previously excluded from the economic prosperity and the welfare state that had created the white middle class.[55]

As Jefferson Cowie explains in *Staying Alive*, the increased competition in the labor markets from groups previously excluded at a time of deindustrialization, coupled with the expansion of the welfare state in the form of the War on Poverty, resulted in resentment among working- and middle-class whites.[56] To many people, it looked like the state was serving the interests of nonwhites while ignoring the growing economic insecurity of working- and middle-class whites. The neoconservatives' and the paleoconservatives' (who will be discussed in greater detail in the next chapter) narrative of an overstretched welfare state coming to the aid of perennially underemployed and unemployed blacks and welfare mothers resonated with working- and middle-class whites' feelings of being passed over.[57] Social programs that aided the poor took on a racial character, even though more whites than blacks benefited from these programs.[58] Kristol's division of the welfare state into the masculine New Deal versus the feminine Great Society struck a chord among working-class whites. When seeking the Republican presidential nomination in 1976, Ronald Reagan seized on the caricature of the "welfare queen," female and black, as the embodiment of reckless, wasteful welfare programs that fed into white working-class males' resentment of rising taxes, government profligacy, dangerous inflation, deindustrialization, and the threat of unemployment.[59] Their perception was that the "nonworking" population—that is, blacks and welfare mothers—benefited most from the welfare state.

According to neoconservatives like Irving Kristol, the conservative opposition to a minimal welfare state was a political miscalculation because it failed to appreciate the essential conservatism and popularity of the New Deal. Indeed, while working- and middle-class whites felt their interests were, at best, ignored and, at worst, undercut by the War on Poverty's social programs, their hostility to aspects of the Great Society did not translate into opposition to the welfare state as a whole. "It has long been my opinion," wrote Irving Kristol, "that the conservative hostility to social security, derived from a traditional conservative fiscal monomania, leads to political impotence and a bankrupt social policy."[60]

Compassionate conservatism, which received national attention during the presidency of George W. Bush, was an alternative to both the liberal welfare state and the minimal "night watchman" state. It was conservatives' attempt to construct a welfare state premised on a conservative worldview informed by the melding of religious traditionalism and market triumphalism with the realization that dismantling the entirety of the welfare state was not politically or electorally feasible. For the then House Speaker Newt Gingrich, it was the "key to how to replace the welfare state."[61] President George W. Bush viewed compassionate conservatism as offering an approach to solving social problems different from "either big Government or indifferent Government. Government cannot solve every problem, but it can encourage people and communities to help themselves and to help one another."[62] Compassionate conservatism thus shifted the burden of solving social problems away from the state to individuals and civil society, but the state did not recede entirely.[63]

For conservatives, the problems of poverty, unemployment, crime, and substance abuse are largely cultural rather than economic. Recall that Irving Kristol believed that the economic inequalities created by capitalism were "trivial." That is, the problem of poverty is caused by individuals' lack of certain character traits such as personal responsibility, delayed gratification, hard work, sobriety, and abstinence. In other words, poverty is not an economic problem or a capitalist problem but is the result of poor people's lack of bourgeois virtues. For conservatives, compassionate conservatism is the vehicle for recovering the Protestant ethic. Accordingly, compassionate conservatism sought to strengthen the institutions and organizations of civil society responsible for transforming social and cultural values. In the words of President Bush, such organizations "inspire hope in a way that Government never can . . . and often, they inspire life-changing faith in a way that Government never should."[64]

The emphasis on culture and the strengthening of civil society did not imply, however, that is the state had no role in solving social problems. Indeed, even such firm believers in compassionate conservatism as Stephen Goldsmith, a former mayor of Indianapolis and Bush's adviser on faith-based issues, suggested that a lesser role for the state did not mean that the market ought to fill the void. While praising the virtues of the competitive economy in creating prosperity, Goldsmith conceded that "the prosperity created by the marketplace has left many Americans behind."[65] There is a role for government in the compassionate conservative vision in assisting those in need through programs that strengthen traditional civil society institutions like the family, the church, community groups, and charitable associations that might protect the victims of market competition:

> Compassionate conservatives acknowledge the role of government in helping those who need assistance; they do not believe that government itself needs to deliver those services. Small, local civic associations and religious organizations have the detailed knowledge and flexibility necessary to administer the proper combination of loving compassion and rigorous discipline appropriate for each citizen.[66]

Compassionate conservatism, as its advocates conceptualized it, did not reject the idea of helping the poor, but it sought to do so by outsourcing the administration of welfare from the federal government to states, localities, and private organizations.[67]

In practice, George W. Bush's faith-based initiatives did not radically transform the welfare state.[68] The reorientation of the conservative welfare state did not return authority to traditional associations, as postwar conservatives like Robert Nisbet had hoped. Instead, the conservative welfare state made only minimal efforts in that direction. The real reorientation was toward the private provision of social welfare through the corporate-dominated market. Bush's Medicare Modernization Act and President Barack Obama's Affordable Care Act are good examples of this approach, as both rely on the private market and place constraints on the state in the provision of health care, that is, through the absence of a public option and in the regulation of its cost.

Despite these changes in the ideological thinking about capitalism and the welfare state, tax policy and welfare policy can do only so much to alter the values of a society. For Irving Kristol, despite the renewal of the bourgeois ethic that a supply-side economy and a reformed welfare state offered, late-twentieth-century American capitalism was incapable of cultivating the virtues necessary for the polity's survival. While the bourgeois virtues made capitalism defensible as an economic system, they did not add up to a "complete moral code."[69] Those virtues that were missing included charity, physical courage, and patriotic self-sacrifice, and their regeneration required more than changes in economic policy and reform of the welfare state; it required a national political project. Neoconservatives thought that Reagan's apocalyptic view of the Soviet Union as the "evil empire" and, later, George W. Bush's "war on terror" provided for the opportunities for such a transformational project.

CAPITALIST CULTURE VERSUS *PAX AMERICANA*

The renewed cultural critique of capitalism offered by neoconservatives William Kristol and David Brooks rested on a value system radically different from that which concerned the first generation in the 1970s. Whereas Daniel Bell and Irving Kristol worried that the culture of capitalism was undermining the "prosaic values" associated with the Protestant ethic, contemporary neoconservative critics no longer consider these values to be casualties of capitalism. Writing about the eclipse of Bell's and the elder Kristol's critique, Tod Lindberg commented, "It became harder and harder to find evidence regarding the 'depleting of moral capital' of capitalism . . . the system's potential for self-perpetuation became more evident."[70] Instead, contemporary neoconservative indictments of capitalism emphasize its material decadence in creating a docile and spiritually weak public devoid of the heroic virtues and lacking in the political will to embark on a project of grand purpose.

Following the fall of the Berlin Wall in 1989, neoconservatives eagerly anticipated the rise of America as the next great empire in the tradition of Rome and Great Britain. These hopes were soon dashed. In the 1990s, an era when the United States was the lone superpower, neoconservatives saw elected officials as dithering in politically trivial matters and uninspiring, both internationally and at home. As David Brooks wrote,

America is a more dominant power in the world than Americans a century ago could ever have imagined. Yet we have almost none of the sense of global purpose that Americans had when they only dreamed of enjoying the stature we possess today. Domestically, we have a president and a Congress whose major common purpose is . . . balancing the budget.[71]

Just as Theodore Roosevelt, Brooks Adams, and other nineteenth-century warrior-aristocrats linked the culture of capitalism to the degenerating character of the body public and impending national decline, the 1990s neoconservatives were just as frustrated with America's lack of imperial will. To them, the 1990s was a time when the dominant ethos encouraged a "preoccupation with one's own petty affairs."[72] It was an era of docility, materialism, frivolity, and parochialism. "We've spent much of the past few decades building little private paradises for ourselves," Brooks complained. "We've renovated our kitchens, refurbished our home entertainment systems, invested in patio furniture, Jacuzzis and gas grills. We withdrew from public life, often not even bothering to vote."[73] The triumph of the mundane character combined with the self-indulgent material decadence that capitalist prosperity created were now the major obstacles preventing America from fulfilling its imperial destiny. Bourgeois society is "prosaic," as Irving Kristol suggested,

> not only in form but in essence. . . . It is a society organized for the convenience and comfort of common men and common women, not for the production of heroic, memorable figures. It is a society interested in making the best of this world, not in any kind of transfiguration, whether through tragedy or piety.[74]

This world of "convenience and comfort" in which capitalism thrives and is most profitable requires peace and stability. But the heroic virtues of self-sacrifice, martial strength, valor, and physical courage do not have a prominent cultural and practical place in a prosperous, peaceful, capitalist world.

Following Reagan's retirement from political life, the absence of political will for empire among the American political class and the citizenry was more than just a missed opportunity for America to play the role of a benign hegemon. For neoconservatives, it was also a question of renewing the domestic body politic, both politically and culturally, with a sense of common purpose. The imperial vision was about forging a unity of purpose that was more than a mere agglomeration of private interests. "To create a world," in the words of Corey Robin, writing in the *Boston Review*, "that is about something more than money and markets."[75] Neoconservatives believe, as did the warrior-aristocrats a century ago, that the international goals of American hegemony and domestic renewal are interdependent. In "Toward a Neo-Reaganite Foreign Policy"—widely considered to be the neoconservative manifesto on foreign policy and the outline for much of the Bush Doctrine—William Kristol and Robert Kagan declared, "It is foolish to imagine that the United States can lead the world effectively while the overwhelming majority of the population neither understands nor is involved, in any real way, with its international mission."[76] But in a world without a cosmic enemy like the Soviet Union, what might grasp the attention of a public distracted by and preoccupied with self-gratification and material comfort? Kristol and Kagan believed that American empire and a renewal of the martial spirit required a formidable adversary, and so one needed to be found.[77]

Just as Theodore Roosevelt mourned the closing of the American frontier, the neoconservatives mourned the end of the Soviet Union. Irving Kristol wrote,

> With the end of the Cold War, what we really need is an obvious ideological and threatening enemy: One worthy of our mettle, one that can unite us in opposition. Isn't that what the most successful movie of the year, *Independence Day* [1996], is telling us? Where are our aliens when we most need them?[78]

The neoconservatives missed the Soviet Union because it evoked fear (whether real or imagined) in the American public, and this fear translated into a heightened sense of patriotism and a commitment to a collective purpose—the defeat of Communism. Once the Soviet Union was gone, however, the new "monsters" on the block—Somalia, Iraq, Serbia, and North Korea—failed to inspire or justify any kind of grandiose ambition.

The attacks on September 11, 2001, afforded the opportunity to re-create a world of Manichean struggle that neoconservatives believed was necessary for persuading the American public to support the United States' hegemonic role in the world. "Conservatives thrive on a world of mysterious evil and unfathomable hatred," Robin argued, "where good is always on the defensive and time is a precious commodity in the race against corruption and decline."[79] As conservative political leaders never tire of reminding the public, the post–September 11 world is filled with evil and nebulous enemies.[80] In such a dangerous environment, the neoconservatives contend, the United States is justified in acting like an imperial power. It has a responsibility to protect itself and its interests and be the force behind a grander humanitarian commitment of spreading democratic governance to the Middle East and ensuring a world free from the threat of terror. As early as January 2002, William Kristol urged the Bush administration to invade and occupy Iraq and remove President Saddam Hussein. "At a more fundamental level," wrote Kristol and Kagan, "the failure to remove Saddam would mean that, despite all that happened on September 11, we as a nation are still unwilling to shoulder the responsibilities of global leadership, even to protect ourselves."[81] As Defense Secretary Donald Rumsfeld explained, in a world filled with "known knowns, the things we know we know . . . known unknowns, the things we know we do not know . . . and unknown unknowns, the ones we don't know we don't know," mystery, unpredictability, and adventure have once again returned to political life.[82] This is a geopolitical environment very different from that in the 1990s. It requires a character and a way of thinking that are not bourgeois. In a global environment that breeds anxiety and fear, the United States would not need to justify to its own public, much less the international community, when it "goes abroad looking for monsters to destroy."[83] In this new, dark, and mysterious global environment, the "monsters" or "evildoers" must be lurking somewhere in every metropolitan subway system, plotting in every desert, training in every arid mountain range, receiving assistance from a host of unfriendly political regimes, and ready to strike without a moment's notice.

Indeed, this altered environment made neoconservatives hopeful and enthusiastic. Neoconservatives saw September 11 as an opportunity that might result in a domestic cultural regeneration of the body politic and the long-frustrated realization of American global hegemony. As a result of the September 11 attacks, Tod Lindberg explained, "after a long absence, Americans returned to the public square they had left for their private gardens, and to make sure everyone knew, they draped it in red, white, and blue."[84] The changed global environment once again made the world an unconquered and unsolved frontier. The neoconservatives persuaded the Bush administration to seize the opportunity and wipe the slate clean of the principles, philosophies, and regulations that had governed the international arena since the end of World War II. In this way, they laid the groundwork for future leaders' disregard of diplomatic and international norms.[85] The Bush Doctrine's moralizing mission of spreading freedom and democracy and its privileging of preemptive war were a clear refutation of the postwar international consensus and a decisive embrace of the neoconservative imperial vision characterized by a moral unilateralism.

Even under President Barack Obama, U.S. foreign policy, despite its less bellicose rhetoric and some tactical shifts in the war on terror, has changed little from that of the previous administration. President Obama's request for the largest defense budget ever, the use of drones in extrajuridical killings (of noncitizens and U.S. citizens on foreign soil), his failure to close the Guantanamo Bay prison complex, his support of regime change (in Honduras, Libya, and Syria), together with his Nobel Peace Prize speech in which he declared, "Make no mistake: evil does exist in the world,"[86] suggests that the American political elites of both political parties have accepted the neoconservative view of the world and America's exceptional place in it.[87]

Under President Obama and also conservatives, the neoconservatives fell out of favor among Washington policymakers. However, neoconservatives' impact on contemporary public policy and political discourse has remained significant. Since the 1970s, the neoconservative narratives of capitalism, the welfare state, and foreign policy have dominated the political debate. The turn in neoconservative thinking about capitalism beginning in the late 1960s through the 1970s is central to understanding American ideology, public policy, and political economy in the twenty-first century. What started out as a poignant cultural critique of capitalism morphed into standard conservative policy prescriptions of low taxes, an eroded regulatory and welfare state, and a freer hand for the market cloaked in the garb of the Protestant ethic.

While supply-side is no longer a popular term and the September 11 attacks illustrated that war and imperialism as the antidote to public malaise and self-indulgent consumerism have limits, the neoconservatives' influence on public policy, both foreign and domestic, has been immense. The purportedly emasculating effects of capitalism have not undermined the American empire. There also may not have been a radical conversion in American political culture away from decadent consumer capitalism, as the 2008 financial meltdown and the global economic crisis that followed clearly illustrate, but economic inequality and the political and ideological power of corporate America is greater than ever.[88]

For nearly forty years, the legitimacy of capitalism was not in doubt. Neoconservatives believed that it had been restored on culturally and politically solid foundations. Perhaps, though, their optimism was somewhat premature. While elected officials were reluctant to expand the role of government in a New Deal for the twenty-first century, the public is very skeptical of capitalism. In a Pew Research Center survey of the public's perceptions of "capitalism" and "socialism" in December 2011, only 50 percent of Americans had a positive view of "capitalism," and 40 percent had a negative view of it. Among eighteen- to twenty-nine-year-olds, 47 percent had a positive view of "capitalism," and an equal number had a negative view. Most disturbingly of all for neoconservatives are the 39 percent of self-identified conservatives who reacted negatively to "capitalism."[89]

The "Great Recession" beginning in 2008 and the neoconservatives' critique of the welfare state may have created the conditions for a new crisis of legitimacy, in which in the public's mind, both capitalism and the state are suspect. Such a crisis of public confidence has a credible basis, as in recent decades the market has produced record economic inequality and a devastating financial crisis while the state's efforts to address both have proved anemic. These crises in the legitimacy of the institutions of capitalism and the state have weakened the ideological legitimacy of liberalism and neoconservatism. The popular electoral appeals of Senator Bernie Sanders's (D-Vt.) social-democratic message and the right-wing nationalist populism of the 2016 Republican president-elect Donald Trump indicate deep dissatisfaction among the American people with the direction that American economy and its politics have taken in the last forty years, a direction that the neoconservatives did so much to fashion. In the next chapter, I will turn to the strand of conservatism that has been most critical of neo-conservatism; that offers its own, distinct critique of contemporary capitalism; and, at present, that is ascendant in conservative electoral politics: white ethnic, populist nationalism.

THE PALEOCONSERVATIVE CRITIQUE OF
GLOBAL CAPITALISM

The global capitalist and the true conservative
are Cain and Abel.

Patrick Buchanan, *The Death of the West*

Every day I wake up determined to deliver for the people I have
met all across this nation that have been neglected, ignored and
abandoned. These are the forgotten men and women of our
country. People who work hard but no longer have a voice. I am
your voice.

Donald Trump, acceptance speech, Republican National Convention, 2016

As I pointed out in chapter 5, the 1960s and 1970s were water-
shed decades for American conservatism. The perceived
overexpansion of the liberal welfare state, the turmoil in
America's cities and on university campuses, the relative success of the civil rights movement, and the launch of the women's liberation and the gay rights movements had animated American
conservatism.[1] Beginning in the 1970s, conservative ideas gained a
currency in the American political discourse, and many were translated into public policy, especially economic and social welfare policy.
The neoliberal political and economic order driven by the interests

of capital, with support from both Republican and Democratic administrations in the White House, has produced a market triumphalism in the mainstream political discourse and a circumscribed belief in the ability of government to address the nation's most pressing challenges.

Despite these discursive and policy successes, however, some on the right worry that conservatism in America has been defeated because it has abandoned its principles and traditions.[2] In particular, paleoconservatives are among those most repelled by the state of contemporary conservatism and of America's economy, politics, and culture. Paleoconservatives purport to represent the values, heritage, interests, and concerns of the white middle and working classes— Richard Nixon's and now Donald Trump's "silent majority"—whose economic status and security have gradually been eroded over the past forty years by deindustrialization, stagnant wages, and other structural changes in the nation's political economy. Challenges to established racial and gender hierarchies, resulting from the civil rights and women's liberation movements have further been perceived as threats to the way of life of the white middle class and the working class.

Paleoconservatives are critical of both these movements and capitalism. Their critique is not, however, a refutation of capitalism as an economic system per se. Indeed, capitalism is "part of the genius of the American people," as paleoconservative founder Clyde Wilson pointed out, and the movement regards private enterprise as essential to individual freedom, political liberty, and the efficient distribution of goods and services.[3] Nor is the paleoconservatives' critique an indictment of exploitation or economic inequality. Instead, their critique focuses on global free-trade capitalism, driven by transnational corporations and their allies in government on both the Republican and the Democratic sides. Paleoconservatives' issue with capitalism, in its global "free-trade" variant, is that it is unmoored from and ultimately antagonistic to the nation's interests. At the core of their critique of global capitalism is that it is degrading American national identity by sacrificing its cultural and political traditions and its economic independence to the demands of the free-trade regime of transnational capital. Political commentators have noted that Donald Trump's political orientation does not fit neatly into left or right ideological categorizations or party labels. But as this chapter will show, Trump's politics closely approximates paleoconservatism, although he himself has never used that label. This is significant, because paleoconservative ideas have always been at the margins of the conservative intellectual tradition, but with Trump, paleoconservatism has broken through to the electoral mainstream, placing itself front and center in the conservative discourse.

Among the most important progenitors and disseminators of paleoconservative ideas, particularly their critique of global capitalism, have been Samuel Francis (1947–2005) and Patrick J. Buchanan (b. 1938). Francis was a key theoretician of paleoconservatism and published widely in conservative periodicals and journals, including the *National Review*, *Chronicles*, the *Washington Times*, and *VDARE*. His definition of what constitutes the "American identity" and his criticism of the managerial elite and of global capitalism and transnational corporations as contrary to conservatism have been at the core of paleoconservative political thought.[4] Francis also influenced paleoconservatism's most publicly recognized personality, Patrick Buchanan, and they frequently cited each other's work. Buchanan, an influential and prolific author in his own right, is more of a political practitioner, having worked for the Republican administrations of Richard Nixon, Gerald Ford, and Ronald Reagan. For decades he has been a television political pundit and a regular contributor to paleoconservative publications such as the *American Conservative*, which he cofounded, and *Chronicles*. Buchanan also ran for president in 1992 and 1996 as a Republican and in 2000 as the candidate of the Reform Party. He came closest to winning the Republican nomination in 1996 but was eventually defeated by Senator Robert Dole (R-Kans.). Buchanan's signature political moment came on August 17 at the 1992 Republican National Convention, where he gave what came to be known as "the culture war" speech. In apocalyptical terms, Buchanan argued that the United States was in the midst of a "religious war . . . for the soul" of the nation waged against the Clintons (Bill Clinton was seeking his first term for president), radical feminists (women who wanted to serve in the military without discrimination), and homosexuals.[5] The speech is significant for the terms in which Buchanan framed the political opposition as an enemy in a "war," ostensibly for America's survival. Following in Buchanan's footsteps, Trump's rhetoric about various individuals and groups, including President Barack Obama, Hillary Clinton, Latino immigrants, and refugees from war-torn countries mirrors Buchanan's rhetorical style and, as I argue later, paleoconservatives' ideas and public policy positions.[6]

Paleoconservatives have offered some of the most bitter criticisms of the contemporary American capitalist economy from the right, and the paleoconservative slogan, "America First," renewed its lease on life with Donald Trump's campaign to "Make America Great Again."[7] Both Trump and the paleoconservatives want to "take America back from the empire builders . . . international do-gooders . . . foreign lobbyist allies . . . career 'victims' . . . bureaucrats . . . special interests . . . politicians feeding at the public trough . . . and the corporate, professional, and managerial elites."[8] Indeed, Buchanan has written approvingly of Trump, outlining the parallels between paleoconservatism and Trumpism: "Patriotism, preserving and protecting the unique character of our nation and people, economic nationalism, America First, staying out of other nation's wars—these are as much the propellants of Trumpism as is the decline of the American working and middle class."[9] The paleoconservative alternative to global free-trade capitalism is a right-wing populism based on an economic and cultural nationalism rooted in white, Christian, English-speaking Americans. As Samuel Francis, a leading paleoconservative theorist himself, admitted, paleoconservatism in America today is nothing short of "counter-revolutionary."[10]

The paleoconservative label originated as a rejoinder to neoconservatism.[11] Beginning in the late 1970s, paleoconservative thought was formed by a loose group of conservative thinkers, journalists, academics, and political practitioners, including Patrick Buchanan and Samuel Francis, along with Clyde Wilson, Thomas Fleming, Paul Gottfried, Joseph Sobran, and the many others disgusted by the Republican leadership's moderation under Presidents Nixon and Ford.[12]

Then when Reagan appointed neoconservative William Bennett to chair the National Endowment for the Humanities rather than the paleoconservatives' preferred candidate, Southern traditionalist M. E. Bradford, they took that as a sign of betrayal and a marker of the ascendance of neoconservatism in the conservative mainstream. Repelled by the Republican Party's acceptance of the liberal welfare state and

the perceived takeover of American conservatism by a "neoconservative cabal" and transnational corporations, the paleoconservatives
committed themselves to reestablishing the "authentic conservatism"
that privileges limited government, states' rights, cultural conservatism, the dominance of the Christian Euro-American tradition, and
economic nationalism. Paleoconservatives were extremely critical of
George W. Bush, whose administration they believed was hijacked by
the neoconservatives. Indicative of the paleoconservatives' criticism
of George W. Bush's conservatism, George Carey declared,

> When a Republican administration, widely portrayed as perhaps the
> most conservative in our history, practices fiscal irresponsibility,
> promotes policies that expand the size of government, advances
> the centralization of federal authority, and launches a "preventive"
> war—that is, act in a manner one might expect of liberal Demo-
> cratic administrations—there is good reason to believe that some-
> thing is terribly amiss, that somehow and at some point in time
> those principles and tenets which once formed the core of conser-
> vatism have been altered and abandoned.[13]

For paleoconservatives, what passes for contemporary conservatism
is not conservative at all but is an ideology that has been "assimilated
by the regime of the Left."[14] In fact, in their view, modern America has
become so fundamentally deformed that there is precious little to conserve. Mainstream American conservatism, Francis argued, not only
has been culpable in the degeneration of America but also continues
to operate under the illusion that it is conserving something worthwhile. Instead of conserving the ideas of the Left and their "regime,"
Francis urged the rest of the conservative movement to join the paleoconservatives in a "counter-revolution."[15]

Paleoconservatism is part of and an outgrowth of the New Right,
which combines Christian thought and a nationalist populism.[16] Much
unites these two distinct strands of thought, including the paleoconservatives' belief in the United States as a Christian nation; opposition to legalized abortion, gay marriage, and other elements of the
culture wars; and hostility to the liberal welfare state. Unlike libertarians, paleoconservatives do not prioritize the unfettered market over

all other social goods and values. As Patrick Buchanan explained, "To worship the market is a form of idolatry no less than worshipping the state."[17] While both the Christian Right and paleoconservatives endorse the deregulation of business, lower taxes, and privatization and decentralization of social welfare, neither group would go so far as the libertarians to eliminate government from economic and social life and to construct a minimal "night-watchman" state.

Paleoconservatives differ from both libertarians and the Christian Right. For instance, in foreign policy, paleoconservatives generally are isolationists, seek to withdraw the United States from many international agreements, and are somewhat more reluctant to use U.S. military intervention abroad when it is not directly in defense of American interests and sovereignty. Many on the Christian Right welcomed American assertiveness under the administration of George W. Bush as a vehicle to spread the Christian (predominantly evangelical) mission to the rest of the world. Another point of difference is that while both paleoconservatives and the Christian Right believe that America's Christian institutions, culture, and heritage are under attack, the paleoconservatives emphasize the dangers to national identity posed by multiculturalism and the multiracial character of recent U.S. immigrants. As Edward Ashbee contends, paleoconservatism differs from the Christian Right in its focus on the regeneration of an American ethnic nationalism that goes beyond Christian identity.[18] Highlighting this distinction, Francis wrote:

> If they ever ended abortion, restored school prayer, outlawed sodomy and banned pornography, I suspect most of its followers [the Religious Right] would simply declare victory and retire. But having accomplished all of that, the Christian right would have done nothing to strip the federal government of the power it has seized throughout this century . . . stop the cultural and racial dispossession of the historic American people, or resist the absorption of the American nation into a multicultural and multiracial globalist regime.[19]

A final difference between the Christian Right and the paleoconservatives concerns capitalism. The Christian Right has largely been satisfied by the Christianization of the market by the likes of George

Gilder, Michael Novak, David Chilton, Ronald Nash, and others.[20] In their view, capitalism is an ethical system that bases its rewards (wealth) and punishments (poverty) on people's "free will" to work hard, save, and invest prudently. Consistent with the conservative perspective, poverty is the result of individual failings, a culture of poverty, and a dependence on government transfers. For the Christian Right, the pursuit of profit is God's mechanism to make fallen man productive. Paleoconservatives, in contrast, while defending the inequalities produced by capitalism as natural and merited, view global free-trade capitalism and its adjunct, permissive U.S. immigration policy, as threats to America's cultural heritage, its political and economic sovereignty, and the cause of the declining economic status and security of the nation's native-born population.[21]

Central to paleoconservatism is an ardent nationalism that has a decidedly white, European, and Christian orientation. Paleoconservatives reject multiculturalism and cosmopolitanism as undermining national identity and sovereignty, resulting in a life-and-death struggle between nations and their cultures. To Francis, the paleoconservatives' aim is to achieve national solidarity centered on white "Middle American Radicals" (MARs) who "seek the overthrow of the present elite and its replacement by themselves."[22]

Paleoconservatives do not reject the state. Instead, as Irving Kristol suggested and the paleoconservatives make plain, their counterrevolution is intended to reorient the state to protect and serve those defined as "deserving."[23] In the words of Patrick Buchanan, the culture war "is about power, it is about who determines the norms by which we live, and by which we define and govern ourselves." It is about "who decides what is right and wrong, moral and immoral, beautiful and ugly, healthy and sick . . . and whose beliefs shall form the basis of law."[24] Thus, for paleoconservatives, their cultural critiques of contemporary America are bound to an indictment of global capitalism that is eroding America's national identity.

The paleoconservative critique of capitalism is based on a combination of nationalist and populist sentiments. For the paleoconservatives, the members of the managerial elite control the nation's largest corporations and political institutions and are guided by profit maximization and the doctrines of egalitarianism, internationalism, and multiculturalism.[25] This elite is made up of the primary purveyors of the assault on America's national and cultural identity. Their ideas and adherents in business, government, the media, and academia are opposed to a common American culture, language, heritage, and, crucially, to an economic framework in which American economic independence and sovereignty are not at the mercy of foreign interests and the international market. In essence, the paleoconservative critique is a populist indictment of corporate-led free-trade capitalism, which it sees as weakening the economic foundations of America's national sovereignty and corrupting its cultural identity.

GLOBAL CAPITALISM AND AMERICAN NATIONAL IDENTITY: THE PALEOCONSERVATIVE CRITIQUE

According to paleoconservatives, several forces have contributed to America's degeneration: the managerial elite, the liberal welfare state, and global capitalism. The managerial elite is a concept that Francis adopted from James Burnham's theory of the managerial revolution, as described in *The Managerial Revolution* (1960) and developed in tandem with the growth and development of the large, bureaucratic corporation and administrative state.[26] The corporate elite cooperated with the political elite in breaking down the older, traditional, local and familial restraints on their respective scopes of power.[27] Then the political elite sought to remake the world in accordance with the egalitarian demands of progressive protest movements, beginning with workers' protests in the 1930s and the New Deal through the civil rights, women's liberation, and anti–Vietnam War movements of the 1960s. But it was not only the state, Francis observed, that was the purveyor of egalitarianism; the logic of capitalism and big corporations was at fault as well. In their narrow commitment to greater efficiency, increasing profits, and expanding market share, big corporations became agents of a particular kind of egalitarianism that was just as destructive of traditional institutional arrangements as the state was. In fact, although they were not driven by ideals of economic and political leveling, corporations were among the most destructive forces of local culture and institutions. Attracted by the pursuit of profit and expanded markets, corporations created homogenized wants and tastes by inculcating an "egalitarian ethic of universal consumption" that buying on credit had made possible. In the process, they ruined small-business owners, the economic bulwark of the traditional social order and of America's social, cultural, and political heritage. Like the conservative critics of capitalism before him, Francis believed that the capitalist drive for profits undercut the economic system itself. But unlike neoconservatives, who faulted American capitalists for not taking an ideological defense of capitalism seriously, Francis and the paleoconservatives view the capitalist system as being undermined by a creation of the system itself, namely, the transnational corporation.

> It is thus basic to the interests of the large corporation to erode social and cultural diversity and promote egalitarian uniformity, as well as to cooperate with and support political egalitarianism, the costs of which in increased unionization, protection of the labor force, regulation, civil rights legislation, and economic environmentalism, are ruinous to the smaller competitors of the corporations but much less harmful to those larger economies that can absorb such costs and pass them on to consumers.[28]

It is not only the corporate structure that is destroying tradition and community. In "Capitalism, the Enemy" (2000), an article criticizing the vote by South Carolina's House of Representatives to remove the Confederate battle flag from the state capitol building, Francis extended the populist critique of big business, stating that inherent in capitalism is a cosmopolitan and egalitarian ethic hostile to local communities and traditional institutions:

> Capitalism, an economic system driven only, according to its own theory, by the accumulation of profit, is at least as much the enemy of tradition as the NAACP or communism. . . . The hostility of capitalism toward tradition is clear enough in its reduction of all social issues to economic ones. Moreover, like communism, capitalism is based on an essential egalitarianism that refuses to distinguish

between one consumer's dollar and another. The reductionism and egalitarianism inherent in capitalism explains its destructive impact on social institutions.[29]

It was during the New Deal, paleoconservatives suggest, that the alliance between the corporate and the political elite was cemented through regulatory policies that benefited large corporations and through social welfare policies that brought down the hierarchy of traditional social organizations. This alliance of corporate and political elites has been strengthened over the years by the inherent dynamism of "managerial capitalism." "The dynamic of managerial capitalism," Francis stated, "involves a continuing erosion of the social and cultural fabric through the mass consumption and hedonism, social mobility, and dislocation that it promotes."[30] In the face of such political and economic power, the intermediate institutions and local communities that preserved established economic and racial hierarchies and checked centralized political and economic power were eroded.

As the national market turned into a global market, the once national managerial elite became a "transnational elite." Whereas the national managerial elite rode roughshod over local hierarchies, culture, tastes, traditions, and interests, the transnational elite, in an age of global free-trade capitalism, was doing the same to America's racial hierarchy and its national culture, heritage, and sovereign interests.[31] America has become a nation of consumers, and, in Francis's view, it has veered dangerously close to becoming a collection of strangers without a shared cultural identity binding them together as one people. Inevitably, Buchanan and Francis believe, such a divided nation will find itself in the midst of ethnic and racial conflict imperiling the culture and institutions that made America "exceptional" and a nation to be envied.[32]

America's strength, independence, and the opportunities it affords to its citizens, paleoconservatives contend, are largely based on a shared cultural identity and heritage fashioned by the Founding Fathers. Despite the regional variation and economic differences that existed in the United States during its earliest days, a shared Christian and European ancestry and an independent middle class formed the social foundation of the American polity.[33] The close connection between interpersonal relationships and a common culture and heritage fostered a republican citizenry that distrusted centralized power and prized personal independence and self-sufficiency. These shared cultural and political orientations, operating in an economic environment of small producers, helped promote a blend of individualism, populist republicanism, and Protestantism that made up a distinct American identity.

It was not only the racial, religious, and class homogeneity that transformed America from a young, vulnerable, ex-colony into a nation with a distinct identity and, ultimately, into the world's preeminent power. Buchanan and Francis credit the enlightened leadership of the Founding generation and of subsequent political elites such as Henry Clay, Abraham Lincoln, and Theodore Roosevelt, who crafted a strong nation founded on a distinct national identity.[34] They did so in no small part because of their commitment to a policy of economic nationalism as the basis for economic growth, development, and prosperity.[35] Buchanan highlights as central to America's economic independence, growth, and development the ideas of Alexander Hamilton in the "Report on Manufactures" and the protectionist policies that were put in place and were continued for more than a hundred years by successive administrations.[36] Hamilton's plan to impose tariffs on foreign goods and provide subsidies for domestic producers were necessary for U.S. manufacturers to develop and grow in order to compete with Britain and France on the international market. Buchanan contends that up to President Woodrow Wilson, American elites were not seduced by the free-trade doctrines that influenced policy on the European Continent throughout the nineteenth century. According to Buchanan's interpretation of the *Wealth of Nations*, even Adam Smith was reluctant to endorse global free trade in light of national interests, stopping short of the utopian free-trade vision of David Ricardo, Frederic Bastiat, Richard Cobden, and Jean-Baptist Say.[37] Resisting these "foreign doctrines," the American economy rested on the twin pillars of the "American system," a domestic free-trade zone and protectionism, which made the nation into an economic and military powerhouse. Yet according to Buchanan's reading, the course of American history was radically altered by the liberalism of Woodrow

Wilson, who was convinced that peace could be reached through free trade, which he thus incorporated into his Fourteen Points.

In Buchanan's historical narrative, America's corporate leaders also resisted the global free-trade doctrine in favor of protectionism. They did so because their economic interests still lay in the expanding domestic market and they feared foreign competition once tariffs on imported goods were lifted. Buchanan notes that the industrial titans of the Gilded Age—such as John D. Rockefeller, Cornelius Vanderbilt, and Henry Ford—saw themselves as "American patriots"[38] and have been erroneously portrayed in historical accounts of the age. The robber barons—the greedy and exploitative "malefactors of great wealth" whom Theodore Roosevelt and Brooks Adams believed needed to be guided toward nationalist goals by a strong central state—were instead, in Buchanan's view, committed patriots and stewards of their workers' well-being.[39] In the early 1900s Henry Ford famously paid his workers five dollars a day, which was double the wage earned by the average autoworker at that time.[40] However, as the global free-trade doctrine infiltrated liberal and conservative intellectual circles and was gradually implemented into public policy, the old bourgeoisie of the Gilded Age, those who owned and operated their businesses, gave way to a new breed of corporate elite, the managerial elite, who had little attachment to the place and the people they directed.[41]

In contrast to his rosy depiction of Gilded Age industrialists, Buchanan suggests that the corporate elite of global capitalism are guided only by profit. "If the bottom line commands the cashiering of loyal workers after years of service," he wrote about the new corporate elite, "it will be done with the same ruthless efficiency with which obsolete equipment is junked."[42] National corporations have become transnational corporations, and "patriotic" captains of industry have given way to a "rootless transnational elite who are without sentiment but the fittest alone survive" and who view "men and women not as family, friends, neighbors, fellow citizens, but 'customers' and 'factors of production.'"[43] The transnational corporation, Buchanan declared,

is a natural antagonist of tradition. With its adaptability and amorality, it has no roots; it can operate in any system. With efficiency its ruling principle, it has no loyalty to workers and no allegiance to any nation. With share price and stock options its reasons for being, it will sacrifice everything and everyone on the altar of profit.[44]

According to Francis and Buchanan, whereas America's corporate elite were once suspicious of free trade, today they embrace it. Out of a narrow commitment to profits and expanding markets for goods, services, and cheap labor, the new corporate elite subscribes to global free trade and mass immigration. Likewise, the nation's political and cultural elites are committed to egalitarianism, multiculturalism, and cosmopolitanism. The result is that the national interest has become defined by what is in the interest of the American consumer, whose interests and tastes are manipulated and defined by the corporation itself.[45]

A nation, paleoconservatives believe, is more than merely a collection of consumers buying and selling wares and services and reveling in imported consumerist luxuries. Instead, a nation provides individuals with a sense of belonging to a larger collective motivated by a purpose higher than that of liberal capitalist self-indulgence. "A nation's economic system," Buchanan wrote, "should reinforce the bonds of national unity . . . a nation is organic, alive; it has a beating heart. . . . The people or a nation are a moral community who must share values higher than economic interest, or their nation will not endure."[46] But in global capitalism, there are no national loyalties. "The Global Economy," Buchanan continued, "is rooted in the myth of Economic Man. . . . It elevates economics above all else."[47] As a result, multinational corporations—institutions without a national loyalty—trade with the nation's enemies, lay off workers, outsource work to foreign countries, and campaign for an open immigration policy that increases the labor supply, thereby putting downward pressure on wages and replacing white workers with less expensive immigrant workers of color.[48]

For paleoconservatives, the erosion of America's manufacturing sector is symptomatic of the triumph of global capitalism and is especially devastating to the nation's strength and independence. A nation without the capability to manufacture goods is perilously close to being unable to defend itself. "Manufacturing is the key to national power," Buchanan explained.[49] It is essential that a nation be able to supply its own "means of subsistence, habitation, clothing and defense" if it is to defend its liberty.[50] Buchanan suggests that a policy of free trade that results in corporations fleeing American shores for cheaper labor markets abroad has imperiled America's security. Because of free trade, the United States has ceded its sovereignty and, in the process, has become dependent on its trading partners and is vulnerable to their political whims and those of the international market. In an effort to ensure that its economy does not suffer, the United States has been forced to intervene in countries abroad, as it did in the Gulf War or when it bailed out the Mexican economy in 1995. As Buchanan argues in *The Great Betrayal*, the United States is no longer in control of its economic destiny, and it is no longer in control of its political destiny.

A further consequence of global capitalism is that it also imperils the nation's republican traditions. Paleoconservatives view the white middle and working classes as paramount to America's republican institutions. Drawing on the nation's long tradition of republicanism, particularly the Anti-Federalists' position during the debates over ratification of the U.S. Constitution, the paleoconservatives maintain that the republic requires a strong and relatively homogeneous middle class as its social basis. Through the growth of the welfare state and global capitalism, the managerial elite has wreaked havoc on the working class. An economic system in which capital and labor can move relatively freely from place to place lowers the economic status of workers. Capital is forced to look for inexpensive labor markets abroad and to import inexpensive workers from abroad. As immigrants from developing nations in the Caribbean, Latin America, Asia, and Africa enter the United States, many may not assimilate American dress, tastes, language, customs, traditions, and national identity. Rather, they transplant their ethnic and cultural customs to the United States and, as the paleoconservatives see it, instead force white Americans to adapt to them. Conservatives' insistence on using English only and their fearmongering regarding the imagined spread of *sharia* law in the United States are among the most obvious manifestations of the perceived threat to American cultural identity.

Outraged by this supposed economic, political, and cultural expropriation of the white middle and working classes, Francis insisted,

"Outsourcing and the whole jungle of globalization that goes with it can only accelerate that reaction (of middle and working class whites), as those who live on the receiving end of globalism experience the economic as well as the political, cultural, and racial dispossession it inflicts."[51] Paleoconservatives have been especially critical of the North American Free Trade Agreement (NAFTA) and other free-trade agreements. For them NAFTA is a clear expression of the economic and political elites' betrayal of American economic independence and its cultural heritage. By liberalizing trade among the United States, Canada, and, most disconcertingly, Mexico, the free-trade agreement invited U.S. manufacturers to outsource work or to relocate across the border. Indeed, much manufacturing, particularly assembly work, did take advantage of the low wages and minimal workplace and environmental protections in the *maquiladoras* located on the Mexican side of the U.S-Mexican border.[52] In those cases when the U.S.-based factories did not close their doors and move abroad, the owners increasingly threatened to do so in order to force wage and benefit concessions from their employees, thus contributing to not only a shrinking U.S. manufacturing sector but also declining median wages across much of the U.S. labor market.

Claiming to be the voice of the white working class and small businesses, paleoconservatives certainly have a point. The massive structural changes in the nation's economy since the early 1970s, among them NAFTA, have had a disastrous impact on the working class of all races, including whites.[53] The fact that when adjusted for inflation, wages and the median income have stagnated since the early 1970s indicates a legitimate source of frustration and resentment among the working class that paleoconservatives purport to represent.[54] For them, the threat to the economic independence for republican citizenship does not come from the widening inequality in wealth, the lack of democracy in the workplace, and the relationship of dominance and dependence that have resulted. Instead, for paleoconservatives, economic independence means that the white working class can seek employment in a domestic economy that is unencumbered by government regulations and strong labor unions, unburdened by costly welfare provision and regulations, and protected from competition by foreign labor. For paleoconservatives, there is no natural antagonism between capital and labor or in the relationship of domination and dependence in the domestic economy. Rather, class antagonism results from the intensity of competition wrought by global free trade, a liberal immigration policy, and redistributive government policies benefiting the "undeserving."[55] A government reoriented toward economic nationalism would restore to the United States its economic sovereignty and republican cultural heritage. Paleoconservatives believe that without government interference other than protectionism, the market would create the conditions for full employment and thus the economic independence necessary for republican citizenship.

As an alternative to global capitalism ruled by a cosmopolitan managerial elite, the paleoconservatives envision a policy of economic nationalism that carves out a significant role for the state in economic life and includes protectionism, subsidies, and redistribution. According to Joseph Scotchie, the paleoconservative task is to "balance American nationalism against the requirements of a free market and a free society, to present a radical and positive alternative to the right-wing social democrats who have taken over the conservative movement and hijacked the Republican Party."[56] This balance might be realized, Buchanan believes, by an economic vision that combines "the patriotism of Theodore Roosevelt" with the decentralizing, communitarian, "humane economic vision of Wilhelm Röpke."[57] This vision repudiates not only much of the welfare and regulatory state but also the free market and the "night-watchman" state.

The main goal is to strengthen the nation, which the paleoconservatives identify with the white middle and working classes, or Middle Americans. Perceiving themselves as the victims of global capitalism and an overbearing administrative state and conscious of their declining social status, the paleoconservatives contend, Middle Americans have begun to challenge the managerial elite by asserting the values of individualism, self-reliance, and a shared Christian, white, European heritage. Unlike Theodore Roosevelt's efforts to foster nationalism from the top down, the paleoconservative vision is a bottom-up mass movement focused on mobilizing ordinary "Middle American Radicals" (MARs).

Unlike libertarians, Francis believed that to maintain a distinct American identity, Middle Americans must not diminish the power of the state once they have gained control over it but must use it for their own benefit—just as the managerial elite does at present.

> [I]t is doubtful that the MAR coalition and its allies in the Sunbelt's entrepreneurial regions will continue to focus on this classical liberal principle [the free market]. . . . The central focus of MAR–New Right political economy is likely to be economic growth, a value often confused with, sometimes encompassing, but not identical to the free market.[58]

Francis readily conceded that the MARs see "little value in their adherence to a strict laissez-faire ideology."[59] Indeed, a paleoconservative political economy counts on an active role for the state, spurring economic growth on behalf of the antiestablishment, populist forces of Middle America. The goals of paleoconservative economic policy, according to Buchanan, might include full employment, wider and deeper distribution of property and prosperity, rising standards of living, and a living wage that enables one working parent to feed, clothe, house, and educate a large family. It might also include a tax system that leaves Americans with the largest share of the fruits of their labor of any industrial democracy; diminished dependence on foreign trade, especially for necessities; the restoration of America's lost sovereignty; self-sufficiency in all areas of industry and technology vital to national security; and maximum freedom for citizens and private institutions consistent with a moral community and the common good.[60]

As Francis pointed out, the paleoconservative "resentment of welfare, paternalism, and regulation is not based on a profound faith in the market but simply a sense of injustice that unfair welfare programs, taxes and regulation have bred."[61] The paleoconservative political economy focuses on economic growth, which requires the dismantling of government bureaucracy, deregulation, and a decentralization and privatization of economic forces.[62] Paleoconservatives argue that twentieth-century economic regulations were welcomed by large corporations as a means of stifling competition and ensuring corporate dominance over the domestic market. In paleoconservatives' view, these regulations are most burdensome to small businesses, as they discourage competition and benefit large, entrenched corporations. Deregulation is intended to reestablish a domestic free market without the burdensome rules and taxes that hinder entrepreneurs and small businesses from competing with their larger corporate competitors. Paleoconservatives admit, however, that dismantling the entire welfare state might not be desirable. Elements that are beneficial to MARs' interests, such as "the economic privileges of the elderly and unionized labor (where it now exists)" and the stronger regulation of East Coast banking and financial concerns would be maintained.[63]

After drastically restructuring the tax code and reducing the liberal welfare and regulatory state in the interest of Middle America, the paleoconservatives, using Hamilton's "Report on Manufactures" as a model, would repudiate global free trade and withdraw from global and regional trade treaties and organizations, including the World Trade Organization (WTO) and NAFTA. They would impose tariffs on imported goods and subsidies to domestic producers. These subsidies, Francis explained, would specifically target industries in the South and West, regions with strong bases of Middle American support. By subsidizing such enterprises as aerospace, defense, energy, and agriculture, the paleoconservatives would seek to transfer the center of America's economic vitality and prosperity from the East and the Frost Belt to Middle America and the Sun Belt.[64] These measures, they insist, would do much to prevent corporations from relocating to low-wage markets abroad and thus keep middle-class manufacturing jobs in the United States. The core of the paleoconservatives' economic nationalism is protectionism. By curtailing American economic interdependence with other nations, in their view, any necessary protectionism of and subsidies for American business would form the economic basis of a restored American middle class.

The final key public policy measure advocated by paleoconservatives and intended to restore the white working class to economic and cultural primacy is a restrictive immigration policy. Both Francis and Buchanan advocate what Chip Berlet and Matthew Lyons call "white racial nationalism."[65] According to Buchanan, "The central objection to the present flood of illegals [immigrants] is they are not English-speaking white people from Western Europe; they are Spanish-speaking brown and black people from Mexico, Latin America, and the Caribbean."[66] The liberal immigration policies implemented by the nation's elite have driven down wages and have "displaced" and "dispossessed" the native-born, white, Middle-American labor force.[67] In the paleoconservatives' narrative, unpatriotic corporations bent on generating greater profits conspired with liberal cosmopolitan elites in the government to enact permissive immigration policies and to relax border-control enforcement. As a result, undocumented immigrants, primarily from Mexico and Latin America, have flooded the United States. Not only have these immigrants not assimilated Anglo-American norms and practices, but they have forced previously American, English-speaking communities to change their customs and language to accommodate them. For paleoconservatives, this is nothing more than a cultural "reconquest" of the United States by Mexicans and a direct assault on America's European white heritage. Moreover, nonwhite immigrants have been especially successful at changing American culture because they, with the aid of government and corporations, have displaced white American workers.

As manufacturers have moved abroad and the U.S. economy has become more service oriented, especially in industries such as construction, hotels, and restaurants, more and more undocumented immigrants have been hired. Consequently, because immigrants agree to work for lower wages than American workers will, Buchanan blames them not only for driving down wages but also for being among the key forces responsible for the stagnation of wages over the last forty years. Buchanan's economic nationalism, combined with a restrictive immigration policy and a policy of deportation of undocumented immigrants (more than twelve million by recent counts) would, according to the paleoconservatives, relieve the downward pressure on wages, lower unemployment, curtail rising costs of Social Security and Medicare and would restore economic and cultural security to middle-class Americans.[68] For paleoconservatives, then, the counterrevolution in American culture that they envision would follow a counterrevolution in the structure and working of contemporary capitalism, along with an active and more expansive role for government. To turn back the rapid degeneration of the American identity under way, paleoconservatives offer drastic alternatives to current economic, social, and immigration policy.

THE PALEOCONSERVATIVE VISION GOES MAINSTREAM: DONALD TRUMP

The paleoconservative alternative to global capitalism and the free market is a populist economic nationalism drawing on resentment and racist, nativist, and nationalist thought, which has deep roots in American history. While there is much overlap among the paleoconservatives' and the other strains of contemporary conservative thinking on issues of taxation, deregulation, privatization, erosion of the welfare state, military strength, and the importance of religion and patriotism in public life, economic nationalism has not been as integral to libertarians, the neoconservatives, or the Christian Right as it has been for paleoconservatives. For many paleoconservatives, contemporary conservatives have variously reconciled themselves to the erosion of America's cultural foundations caused by free-trade capitalism. Indeed, free trade and immigration are among the most important issues that separate the paleoconservatives, the neoconservatives, and the Republican Party.[69]

For decades, paleoconservatives have tried unsuccessfully either to take over the Republican Party or to create a movement to displace it as the conservative electoral option. Along these lines, the Tea Party, although not explicitly a paleoconservative movement, is composed of the white middle and working classes that Francis regarded as the paleoconservatives' base.[70] Likewise, Buchanan believes that the Tea Party was "our last best hope" in the struggle against "globalism."[71] Even though it has not been successful in displacing the Republican "establishment," the Tea Party has been successful in pushing the Republican Party in a rightward direction.[72] Buoyed by the Tea Party's outsized influence over the Republican Party in recent years, paleoconservative ideas, albeit in Tea Party clothing, have emerged from the margins and have joined the mainstream.

The points shared by the paleoconservatives and the Tea Party are numerous enough to argue that the Tea Party draws on the right-wing populism of the same disaffected social base. Indeed, in the historical narrative of both Pat Buchanan and the Tea Party ideologue Glenn Beck, the Progressive era and Woodrow Wilson's administration are the origins of America's decline.[73] Likewise, both groups are critical of crony capitalism, illustrated by economic regulations that seemingly aid big corporations to the detriment of small business, as well as, most notably, the government bailouts of Wall Street.[74] Both oppose the liberal welfare state, including the regulatory regime, the minimum wage, and those elements of the welfare state that benefit those perceived to be "undeserving." Neither wants to eliminate the welfare state entirely but to reorient it toward the interests of those who they believe have worked to earn their benefits.[75]

The paleoconservative narrative regarding immigration and the threat to America's cultural heritage overlaps with that of the Tea Party. The Tea Party's ties with the Minutemen movement also suggests white ethnic nationalism.[76] Indeed, as Theda Skocpol, Vanessa Williamson, and, separately, Christopher Parker and others have demonstrated, Tea Party members' racial views show a decidedly more negative view of blacks than does the majority of the population.[77] For example, the Tea Party expresses many paleoconservative ideas in racially coded ways. Its insistence on "taking our country back," that America is being "taken over" by outsiders, and persistent calls for President Barack Obama to show his birth certificate, in which Donald Trump was the leading protagonist, indicate that the paleoconservatives' racial anxieties are core components of the Tea Party narrative.

After inserting paleoconservatism into the conservative mainstream, the Tea Party gave birth to the politics of Donald Trump. Paleoconservatism, the Tea Party, and now Donald Trump all are the outcome of a long-simmering belief among the American Right that the conservative intellectual and political establishment are part and parcel of the "rigged system" of crony capitalism, free trade, and open borders immigration that have sold out the white, native-born, American working class, which is the backbone of the American economy and the repository of its distinctive cultural identity. In part, the Tea Party was a reaction to the Big Government, imperial presidency of George W. Bush. But it is no coincidence that the Tea Party was founded just weeks after the inauguration of President Barack Obama in 2009 and that Trump's highest-profile foray into politics, before his 2016 presidential campaign, was a five-year crusade, beginning in 2011, to prove that President Obama is not a U.S. citizen and therefore ineligible to be president.[78] For paleoconservatives and the people that formed the constituency of the Tea Party, nothing symbolized their declining economic status and their perceived loss of America's cultural identity more than having a black man as president of the United States.[79]

With the exception of Trump's position on same-sex marriage and on abortion (he was prochoice but is now pro-life), many of his political positions on economic issues match those of the paleoconservatives and the Tea Party. Indeed, Buchanan praised Trump as "Middle America's Messenger."[80] Long before Trump promised to build a wall on the U.S.-Mexican border, Buchanan pushed for a fence. Likewise, Trump's demand to deport all twelve million undocumented immigrants has been a long-time position of Buchanan and the paleoconservatives. Trump's positions on political economy, including pulling out of free-trade pacts, instituting protectionism, abolishing the welfare state but preserving programs used by the "deserving," slashing taxes, and deregulating business and industry, as well as his rhetoric critical of Wall Street and the financial sector, all of which purport to "Make America Great Again," are in line with paleoconservative rhetoric and policy prescriptions. Trump's insistence on the "rigged system," his belief that America's allies in NATO and elsewhere are not fulfilling their obligations, and his charge that successive American administrations have been nefariously enabling Mexico and China to upend the American economy all highlight his seemingly total disregard for all political norms, institutions, and agreements since World War II and legitimize the paleoconservative view that the political and economic elites have been deliberately subverting the American nation. The whole gamut of Trump's criticisms of contemporary America may be summed up in his often repeated belief that "we don't have a country anymore."[81] This idea is not original to Trump, however; it mirrors paleoconservatives' views that these norms, institutions, and agreements are products of the managerial elite's attempts to undermine America's borders and domestic security, its economic sovereignty and independence, and its cultural identity. Trump's populism is consistent with the paleoconservatives' narrative that political and economic elites have used their power to reward themselves, the poor, and the "other"—variously defined as racial minorities, immigrants, refugees, women, or foreign interests, whether corporate or state agents. Furthermore, all this was done at the expense of the native-born Middle American.[82] Trump promises to "put America first" and to "no longer surrender this country or its people to the false song of globalism."[83]

As this chapter has shown, paleoconservatives' economic nationalism and populism—whether in the hands of Buchanan, Francis, or Trump—do not challenge the United States' class structure or the capitalist system, but they do offer the Right's most radical challenges to contemporary capitalism. The paleoconservatives' views illustrate how far conservatives have come in reconciling their various concerns for tradition and culture, on the one hand, and capitalism, on the other. Yet these views also show the limits of the conservatives' reconciliation and the tension remaining between them. Perhaps more than any other contemporary conservative critique of capitalism, the paleoconservatives seek the most drastic changes to the nation's political economy. While they do not repudiate capitalism, their rhetorical attacks on Wall Street and their more substantive calls for the United States to pull out of international economic institutions, to discard its free-trade agreements, to enact a protectionist trade policy, to seal America's borders from foreign labor and capital, and to deport millions of people believed to be here to do harm, as underscored by Trump's comment that Mexican immigrants are "criminals and rapists," promise a real counterrevolution.[84] For paleoconservatives, global capitalism is bringing the American nation to the brink of degeneration and ultimate extinction. Even though paleoconservatives embrace private enterprise and defend both capitalism and economic inequality at home, they see no solution to America's cultural and existential crisis in the context of contemporary capitalism. Rather, the only way to ensure the survival of the American nation is to curtail the expansionary nature of capitalism and harness it in the interest of the white, native-born, American nation.

CONCLUSION

Conservatism at a Crossroads

The betrayal of the Confederate flag by the Republicans and by the capitalism which so hypnotizes the GOP says plainly that neither institution can be counted on to defend either Southern traditions or national and civilizational ones . . . the Republican infatuation with capitalism, and the disengagement of capitalism from every other social institution in pursuit of its own profits and in antagonism to any institution that presents an obstacle to profits, pitches the usefulness of these alliances into the garbage dump of history.

Samuel Francis, "Capitalism the Enemy"

The free market has been sorting it out and
America has been losing.

Vice President–elect Mike Pence, *New York Times*, December 1, 2016

For nearly a century and a half, a diverse lot of conservatives have voiced skepticism of capitalism and the priority of economic interests over other social goods. They have wrestled with the tension between capitalism and the social goods that they value, which include the patriarchal family, traditional customs and mores, local social and economic institutions, a distinct American nation, and an American empire. In the process they have offered insightful critiques of our economic system and confronted the central challenge for conservative thought in America: Can capitalism be reconciled with a conservative social order? Conservatives as diverse as George Fitzhugh, Brooks Adams, John Crowe Ransom, Peter Viereck, Irving Kristol, and Patrick Buchanan have offered different answers and alternatives to this question. Conservatives in this intellectual strain in American political thought have always known that their values and institutions would be perennially challenged by capitalism and the instability it brought to tradition, culture, politics, the economy, and conservative social arrangements. For each of these thinkers, capitalist values were found wanting as the basis of a conservative social order. For them, capitalist values had to be subordinated to the noncapitalist values embodied in the slave plantation, a warrior-aristocrat–led nation-state, the yeoman farm, the Middle American nation, or an American empire.

The conservative critique evolved as capitalism grew and developed over a century and a half. With each structural change in capitalism, this critique shifted to address the threat to traditional elites and the social arrangements that protected established racial and class hierarchies. Each set of critics—whether defenders of slavery, warrior-aristocrats, or paleoconservatives—had its own redeemer class that was perceived to embody what conservatism is and ought to be. The social forces unleashed by capitalism were often led by new capitalist elites who did not appreciate the traditional bulwarks of the economic system that contained and repressed the laboring masses' demands for liberty, equality, and self-determination. For conservative critics, capitalism destroyed what they saw as more perfect forms of hierarchy and domination or, what conservatives sometimes euphemistically call, "community." Capitalism replaced these traditional arrangements with more tenuous forms of domination and control that were justified in material and economic terms or in what George Fitzhugh called "the cash nexus."

Needless to say, the conservative critique of capitalism and its values is not a critique of inequality. The overriding principle that unites these rather disparate conservatives, the defenders of slavery, the warrior-aristocrats, the Southern Agrarians, postwar conservatives, the neoconservatives, and the paleoconservatives as conservatives is their belief in inequality and hierarchy. Indeed, for conservatives—even those critical of capitalism—inequality and its manifestation in economic, social, and political power are both natural and necessary. The possibility of greater economic reward serves as an incentive to practice what Irving Kristol and the neoconservatives term "the bourgeois virtues." Likewise, progress advances when society is governed by its best people, and they are rewarded with privilege, influence, and power. Thus, despite their misgivings, conservatives have reconciled themselves to capitalism because the expansion of the market has also meant the growth of the private sphere of domination and control. The deregulation of business, privatization, and the transformation of the welfare state all are examples of their circumspection of the public sphere. That is, the purported freedom to choose what the market offers is nothing more than the freedom of those with wealth to expand their ability to extract from and to control those with lesser means. As it has developed in the United States, conservatism has not always been about the defense of the status quo, as many of the critics I have examined in this book make clear. Nor is it about economic laissez-faire or anti-statism. Rather, conservatism is about the freedom and ability of some people to dominate, control, and extract from others, which capitalist inequality and hierarchy make possible. Such arrangements are not only natural, conservatives argue, but also necessary, for they foster excellence and distinction, on which social order and progress depend.

Each of the thinkers considered here imagined the nation's political economy to extend beyond the polar choice between the liberal welfare state and economic laissez-faire. Accordingly, as the class structure and its dynamics changed, so did the critique. A key component in all the iterations of the conservatives' critique of economic laissez-faire is an emphasis on community. Moreover, while these conservatives pointed to other forces that undermined community, including the state, they were well aware that laissez-faire capitalism was an important force of change and an ongoing threat to conservative values, institutions, and communities. Conservative critics of capitalism were not anti-statists. Indeed, they turned to the state to preserve the economic and social relations of their preferred social order, to protect the institution of slavery and corporate property rights, to establish and preserve the Jim Crow system, to repress organized labor, to deport millions of immigrants, or to create an American empire. Conservatives who located the social basis of society in "the slave plantation South" or "the family farm" or "the Middle American nation" recognized that unleashing capitalism's pursuit of expansion and profit threatened the economic relations on which these social orders were based. In contrast, traditional social arrangements also were threatened by workers and racial minorities, especially when their movements made claims on the state. Thus, critical conservatives opposed both laissez-faire capitalism and the expansion of the democratic state.

Over the last four decades, American conservatism has undergone a discursive transformation, clearly articulated by the neoconservatives, in which the focus of their social and political critique moved to culture and the welfare state, thereby marginalizing the critique of capitalism. This discursive shift had significant political ramifications, as conservative ideas about the political economy have influenced public policy during the last forty years. Tax cutting, deregulation, privatization, and trimming of the welfare state have been the order of the day for both Republican and Democratic administrations, leading to an upward transfer of wealth to levels of wealth inequality not seen since before the Great Depression—as well as record lows in the public's trust in government.[1] At the present time, both contemporary capitalism and government are experiencing a crisis of legitimacy and a populist rising, not only in the United States but elsewhere, that may upend the entire framework of politics and the political economy by which the nations of the world have been operating since the end of World War II.

The deep economic crisis beginning in 2007/2008, along with eight years of a Democratic administration, has led conservative thinkers to begin reexamining the "deep structural problems" in the new capitalist economy, in order to pull the conservative discourse out of the static dualism between economic laissez-faire or welfare-state serfdom.[2] In this vein, David Frum, Ross Douthat, Reihan Salam, and David Brooks, among others, contend that if the Republican Party is to remain electorally competitive, it must offer a new, positive agenda that does not reject an activist government.[3]

According to this point of view, Republicans need to embrace pragmatic governance that does not categorically reject regulation and the welfare state but seeks to reform it to meet the needs of the economically and culturally insecure middle and working classes. As David Brooks and the authors of the conservative policy agenda *Room to Grow* have belatedly admitted—even though this was "uncomfortable for conservatives"—there is greater social mobility in Canada and Denmark than there is in the United States. To correct this problem, Brooks and others propose "programs that encourage local paternalism" and "disrupt local oligarchies and global autocracies" such as Wall Street, Washington, Big Energy, Big Agriculture, and Big Universities that "are dominated by interlocking elites who create self-serving arrangements for themselves."[4]

To "disrupt local oligarchies" and to foster decentralized, local businesses and institutions require an activist national government with the revenue and regulatory capacity to carry this out. For instance, Americans traveling abroad marvel at the ubiquity of small businesses throughout Europe, as opposed to the giant chain stores in the United States. But what often goes unnoticed is that in Europe, small and medium-size businesses benefit from government regulations that protect them from competition from large firms.[5] Among these regulations are workers' income-security benefits, which are a right rather than a benefit tied to a specific employer; generous subsidies specifically for small and medium-size businesses; as well as laws mandating "minimum price markups by retailers to prevent chains from undercutting mom-and-pop stores." Such government interventions in the free market may be unsettling to American conservatives, but the policies have netted good results, including the preservation of local communities and their cultural heritage in the context of a robust capitalist economy.

Despite these reformist signals by Brooks and others, the electoral energy in the contemporary conservative movement comes from those who recoil from the rest of the world, like those who look to the future and see nineteenth-century capitalism, complete with its xenophobia, nativism, and class, racial, and gender hierarchies. As Corey Robin argues, there is a strong current running through the conservative tradition, from Edmund Burke and Joseph de Maistre to Sarah Palin, Patrick Buchanan, and Donald Trump, that rejects moderation, prudence, and gradual change and instead embraces its opposites.[6]

There also is a counterrevolutionary strain in conservative thinking that seeks to restore the inequalities and hierarchies of the "old regime." Indeed, many of the conservatives whom I have discussed, despite using the language of restoration, have nonetheless pointed toward a new beginning. For instance, before the Civil War, George Fitzhugh called for the expansion of slavery to include the white working class. In creating an American empire, President Theodore Roosevelt sought to restore the vigor felt decades earlier in the conquest of the West. The Southern Agrarians wanted to re-create the customs of the Old South, but in a yeoman economic context. Through compassionate conservatism, the neoconservatives envisioned a conservative welfare state inspired by nineteenth-century models of poor relief. And in 2017, through the Republican president, Donald Trump, the paleoconservatives seek a society composed of a political economy and a cultural identity based on an America before the New Deal and the civil rights movement.[7]

If we take seriously ideas like freedom, equality, democracy, and community as not mere abstractions but as substantive values by which we organize our society, then economic inequality and the capitalism that produces it must be at the heart of the discussion. The prioritization of the market, of economic growth, and of wealth accumulation and profit over all other values has been repellent to progressives and to many conservatives as well. Indeed, although their perceptions of the crisis and their visions for an alternative are radically different, working- and middle-class supporters of Trump or the socialist senator from Vermont and Democratic presidential candidate Bernie Sanders expressed a genuine, widely felt frustration with the political and economic order that has brought them underemployment, foreclosure, stagnant wages, increasing economic insecurity, less upward social mobility, and a profound sense of hopelessness about the future.

Among conservatives, the Trump candidacy was deeply divisive. Many current and former Republican public servants refused to endorse him, with some even going as far as declaring they would vote for his Democratic opponent, former secretary of state Hillary Clinton. Conservative intellectuals, some of whom I have discussed here, were equally unsparing in their criticism of Trump. As Robert Kagan warned about a Trump presidency,

This is how fascism comes to America, not with jackboots and salutes (although there have been salutes, and a whiff of violence) but with a television huckster, a phony billionaire, a textbook egomaniac "tapping into" popular resentments and insecurities, and with an entire national political party—out of ambition or blind party loyalty, or simply out of fear—falling into line behind him.[8]

Similarly, David Brooks cautioned,

People will be judged by where they stood this time. Those who walked with Trump will be tainted forever after for the degradation of standards and the general election slaughter. The better course for all of us—Republican, Democrat and independent—is to step back and take the long view, and to begin building for that.[9]

The forty-fifth president of the United States will have to confront the corporate dominance of our political and economic system. The neoliberal status quo relationship between government and corporations has come under fire from both the Left and the Right. The populist pressure has brought capitalism back into mainstream political discussion, with questions about freedom, equality, hierarchy and their associated relations of power, domination, and control. For conservatives, this is yet another opportunity to confront the inherent tension in modern conservatism—between dynamic capitalism and the communities and values that conservatives wish to preserve. As David Brooks wrote, "We'll probably need a new national story. Up until now, America's story has been some version of the rags-to-riches story, the lone individual who rises from the bottom through pluck and work. But that story isn't working for people anymore, especially for people who think the system is rigged."[10] According to Brooks, America or conservatism or both will need a new story, and Donald Trump showed that Brooks was right.

NOTES

INTRODUCTION: CONSERVATIVES AGAINST CAPITALISM

1. Peter Dreier, "Is Capitalism on Trial?" *Dissent Magazine*, January 27, 2012, https://www.dissentmagazine.org/online_articles/is-capitalism-on-trial. In a Pew Research Center survey of public attitudes toward capitalism, 39 percent of self-identified "conservatives" had a negative view of capitalism ("Little Change in Public's Response to 'Capitalism,' 'Socialism,'" *Pew Research Center for the People and the Press* [December 28, 2011], http://pewresearch.org/pubs/2159/socialism-capitalism-occupy-wall-street-libertarian-liberal-conservative).

2. Among the few is the 2016 Republican president-elect, Donald Trump, who admitted to using his wealth to purchase political influence (Lee Fang, "Donald Trump Says He Can Buy Politicians, None of His Rivals Disagree," *The Intercept* [August 7, 2015], https://theintercept.com/2015/08/07/donald-trump-buy/).

3. While making exceptions for a handful of conservative thinkers, scholars of American conservatism presume that most conservatives are free-market enthusiasts. See Charles W. Dunn and J. David Woodward, *The Conservative Tradition in America* (Landham, Md.: Rowman & Littlefield, 2003); Gregory L. Schneider, ed., *Conservatism in America Since 1930: A Reader* (New York: New York University Press, 2003); George H. Nash, *The Conservative Intellectual Movement in America: Since 1945* (Wilmington, Del.: Intercollegiate Studies Institute, 1996); Stephen Eric Bonner, *Ideas in Action: Political Tradition in the Twentieth Century* (New York: Rowman & Littlefield, 1999); Stephen L. Newman, "Liberalism & the Divided Mind of the American Right," *Polity* 22, no. 1 (1989): 75–96.

4. The idea of an American conservative welfare state is different from its European formulation. Gosta Esping-Andersen characterized conservative

welfare states as "strongly corporatist," in which "a state edifice is perfectly ready to displace the market as provider of welfare" (*The Three Worlds of Welfare Capitalism* [Princeton, N.J.: Princeton University Press, 1990], 27). The idea of an American conservative welfare state is much closer to what Esping-Andersen characterized as a liberal welfare state, except that in conservatives' vision, the role of the market and traditional associations in providing welfare is even greater. According to Esping-Andersen, the liberal welfare state is a state in which "means tested assistance, modest universal transfers, or modest social insurance plans predominate" (26). In addition, "benefits cater mainly to the low-income working class, entitlement rules are strict and often associated with stigma, benefits are typically modest, and the state encourages the market, either passively, by guaranteeing only a minimum, or actively, by subsidizing private welfare schemes" (26).

5. Friedrich A. Hayek, "Why I Am Not a Conservative," in Schneider, ed., *Conservatism in America Since 1930*, 180–94.

6. Angus Burgin, *The Great Persuasion: Reinventing Free Markets Since the Depression* (Cambridge, Mass.: Harvard University Press, 2012), 15.

7. For a fascinating intellectual history of twentieth-century classical liberalism, its protagonists, their organizational development at times, their ambivalence regarding the free market, and their attempts to redevelop a social philosophy based on the free market, see Burgin, *The Great Persuasion.*

8. Burgin, *The Great Persuasion*; Nicholas Wapshott, *Keynes Hayek: The Clash That Defined Modern Economics* (New York: Norton, 2012); Brian Doherty, *Radicals for Capitalism: A Freewheeling History of the Modern American Libertarian Movement* (New York: Public Affairs, 2008); and Michael J. Thompson, *The Politics of Inequality: The Political History of the Idea of Economic Inequality in America* (New York: Columbia University Press, 2007), 118–74.

9. Patrick Allitt, *The Conservatives: Ideas and Personalities Throughout American History* (New Haven, Conn.: Yale University Press, 2009), 278 (italics in original).

10. Kim Phillips-Fein and others have written that the literature on conservatism has grown exponentially over the last twenty years. Despite the richness of contemporary research, Phillips-Fein contends that there remains a void in the scholarship. Among her suggestions for "moving the interpretive project forward" is studying the origins and the role of economic ideas in conservatism. Much of the recent scholarship on conservatism has centered on conservatism in Great Depression / New Deal era, on the rise of the post–World War II American Right, and on the resurgence of laissez-faire capitalism. In comparison, scholars of conservatism have suggested that relatively little scholarship has been done on the predecessors of post-1945 conservatism. I take up these challenges and offer a new perspective on the study of conservatism. See Kim Philips-Fein, "Conservatism: A State of the Field," *Journal of American History* (December 2011): 723–59; Kim Philips-Fein, "A Response,"

Journal of American History (December 2011): 771–73; Julian E. Zelizer, "Rethinking the History of American Conservatism," *Reviews in History* 38 (2010): 367–92; and Alan Brinkley, "The Problem of American Conservatism," *American Historical Review* 99 (April 1994): 409–29. On the resurgence of laissez-faire in conservatism, see Kim Philips-Fein, *Invisible Hands: The Businessmen's Crusade Against the New Deal* (New York: Norton, 2009); Philip Mirowski and Dieter Plehwe, eds., *The Road from Mont Pelerin: The Making of the Neoliberal Thought Collective* (Cambridge, Mass.: Harvard University Press, 2009); and Donald T. Critchlow, "Rethinking American Conservatism: Toward a New Narrative," *Journal of American History*, December 2011, 752–55.

11. I define capitalism as an economic system in which the means of production are privately held and operated for profit. It is a system of resource allocation in which prices are based on the law of supply and demand and is premised on the idea that self-interested individuals participate in a competitive market where they buy and sell their goods, services, and labor. As Adam Smith put it in *The Wealth of Nations*, "It is not from the benevolence of the butcher, the brewer, or the baker, that we expect our dinner, but from their regard to their own interest. We address ourselves, not to their humanity but to their self-love, and never talk to them of our own necessities but of their advantage" (*The Wealth of Nations* [New York: Modern Library, 2000], 14). Capitalism is a system in which the vast majority of people earn their living by selling their labor power for a wage to the owners of the means of production. The driving forces of the system are profit maximization, the accumulation of capital, and the incessant need to innovate and expand in order to remain competitive. In capitalism, writes Ellen Meiksins Wood, "the production of goods and services is subordinate to the production of capital and capitalist profit. The basic objective of the capitalist system, in other words, is the production and self-expansion of capital" (*The Origin of Capitalism: A Longer View* [1999; London: Verso, 2002], 2–3).

12. Alan Crawford, *Thunder on the Right: The "New Right" and the Politics of Resentment* (New York: Pantheon, 1980); Jerome L. Himmelstein, *To the Right: The Transformation of American Conservatism* (Berkeley: University of California Press, 1990); Corey Robin, "Endgame: Conservatives After the Cold War," *Boston Review*, February/March 2004, http://bostonreview.net/BR29.1/robin.html; Maurice Isserman and Michael Kazin, *America Divided: The Civil War of the 1960s* (Oxford: Oxford University Press, 2012); Paul Murphy, *Rebuke of History: The Southern Agrarians and American Conservative Thought* (Chapel Hill: University of North Carolina Press, 2001); Emily Bingham and Thomas Underwood, *The Southern Agrarians and the New Deal* (Charlottesville: University of Virginia Press, 2001); Michael Lind, *Up from Conservatism: Why the Right Is Wrong for America* (New York: Free Press, 1996); Eugene D. Genovese, *The Southern Tradition: The Achievement and Limitation of an American Conservatism*

(Cambridge, Mass.: Harvard University Press, 1994); Nash, *The Conservative Intellectual Movement in America*; and Allitt, *The Conservatives*.

13. Genovese, *The Southern Tradition*.

14. John Bellamy Foster, "Monopoly-Finance Capital," *Monthly Review* 58, no. 7 (2006), 1–14; Paul Baran and Paul Sweezy, *Monopoly Capital: An Essay on the American Economic and Social Order* (New York: Monthly Review Press, 1966); and John Bellamy Foster, "The Age of Monopoly-Finance Capital," *Monthly Review* 61, no. 9 (2010): 1–13.

15. Brinkley, "The Problem of American Conservatism," 414.

16. Nash, *The Conservative Intellectual Movement in America.*, xiii.

17. Russell Kirk, *The Conservative Mind: From Burke to Eliot* (1953; Chicago: Regnery Gateway, 1978). Other scholars of philosophical conservatism have come to similar conclusions regarding the elements of conservatism. See Stephen Rosskamm Shalom, *Which Side Are You On? An Introduction to Politics* (New York: Longman, 2003), 49–71; Terence Ball and Richard Dagger, *Political Ideologies and the Democratic Idea* (New York: Longman, 1999), 93–121; Lyman Tower Sargent, *Contemporary Political Ideologies* (Fort Worth, Tex.: Harcourt Brace, 1999), 102–10; and Godfrey Hodgson, *The World Turned Right Side Up: A History of the Conservative Ascendency in America* (New York: Houghton Mifflin, 1996).

18. Russell Kirk, "Conservatism: A Succinct Description." *National Review*, September 3, 1982, 1080–104.

19. John Micklethwait and Adrian Wooldridge, *The Right Nation: Conservative Power in America* (New York: Penguin, 2004), 13–14.

20. Clinton Rossiter, *Conservatism in America* (Cambridge, Mass.: Harvard University Press, 1982); Peter Viereck, *Conservatism Revisited: The New Conservatism—What Went Wrong* (1949; New York: Collier, 1962).

21. John Zumbrunnen and Amy Gangl, "Conflict, Fusion, or Coexistence? The Complexity of Contemporary American Conservatism," *Political Behavior* 30, no. 2 (2008): 199–221.

22. Nash, *The Conservative Intellectual Movement in America*, 160.

23. Robert B. Horwitz, *America's Right: Anti-Establishment Conservatism from Goldwater to the Tea Party* (Cambridge: Polity Press, 2013); Lisa McGirr, *Suburban Warriors: The Origins of the New American Right* (Princeton, N.J.: Princeton University Press, 2001); Jonathan M. Schoenwald, *A Time for Choosing: The Rise of Modern American Conservatism* (Oxford: Oxford University Press, 2001); and Nash, *The Conservative Intellectual Movement in America*.

24. Norberto Bobbio, *Left and Right: The Significance of a Political Distinction* (Chicago: University of Chicago Press, 1996), 66–67. It is important to note that for many on the left, "equality" does not mean sameness or equality for everyone in everything. Karl Marx's famous dictum "from each according to his ability to each according to his needs" illustrates this point.

25. Ibid., 66–67.

26. Corey Robin, *The Reactionary Mind: Conservatism from Edmund Burke to Sarah Palin* (Oxford: Oxford University Press, 2011), 16.

27. James Henry Hammond, "Speech of Hon. James Henry Hammond, of South Carolina, On the Admission of Kansas Under the Lecompton Constitution: Delivered in the Senate of the United States, March 4, 1858," *American Antiquarian*, http://www.americanantiquarian.org/Freedmen/Manuscripts/cottonisking.html.

28. Kirk, *The Conservative Mind*, 8.

29. Viereck, *Conservatism Revisited*, 134.

30. Ibid., 20, 134.

31. Ibid., 36–39.

32. Robert Nisbet, *The Quest for Community* (Oxford: Oxford University Press, 1973), 105.

33. Ibid., 68.

34. Ibid., 54.

35. Nash, *The Conservative Intellectual Movement in America*, 142.

36. Lind, *Up from Conservatism*, 54.

37. Ira Katznelson, *When Affirmative Action Was White: An Untold History of Racial Inequality in Twentieth Century America* (New York: Norton, 2005); and Jill Quadagno, *The Color of Welfare: How Racism Undermined the War on Poverty* (New York: Oxford University Press, 1994).

38. Michael Novak, *The Spirit of Democratic Capitalism* (Washington, D.C.: American Enterprise Institute, 1982); and George Gilder, *Wealth and Poverty* (New York: Basic Books, 1981).

39. Milton Friedman, *Capitalism and Freedom* (Chicago: University of Chicago Press, 1982). For a penetrating critique of Friedman's view of the absence of coercion in the capitalist market, see C. B. Macpherson, "Elegant Tombstones: A Note of Friedman's Freedom," *Democratic Theory: Essays in Retrieval* (Oxford: Clarendon Press, 1973), 143–56.

40. William Kristol and David Brooks, "What Ails Conservatism," *Wall Street Journal*, September 15, 1997, http://www.wsj.com/articles/SB874276753849168000.

41. William Kristol and Robert Kagan, "Toward a Neo-Reaganite Foreign Policy," *Foreign Affairs* (July/August 1996), https://www.foreignaffairs.com/articles/1996-07-01/toward-neo-reaganite-foreign-policy; and David Brooks, "A Return to National Greatness: A Manifesto for a Lost Creed," *Weekly Standard*, March 3, 1997.

42. Robin, "Endgame."

43. Kristol and Kagan, "Toward a Neo-Reaganite Foreign Policy."

44. Patrick Buchanan, "Inequality—Crisis of Scam?" *Human Events*, December 31, 2013, http://humanevents.com/2013/12/31/inequality-crisis-or-scam/.

45. Ibid.

46. John B. Judis, "Right-Wing Populism Could Hobble America for Decades: The Tea Party Is Going Down, Dysfunction Is Not," *New Republic*, October 27, 2013,

http://www.newrepublic.com/article/115332/tea-party-going-down-dysfunc
tion-not.

47. David Brooks, "If Not Trump, What?" *New York Times,* April 29, 2016, http://
www.nytimes.com/2016/04/29/opinion/if-not-trump-what.html?emc=eta1&_
r=0.

48. Richard M. Weaver, *Ideas Have Consequences* (1948; Chicago: University of
Chicago Press, 1984).

1. EMERGING CAPITALISM AND ITS CONSERVATIVE CRITICS

1. Eugene D. Genovese, *In Red and Black: Marxian Explorations in Southern and
Afro-American History* (New York: Pantheon, 1971), 317–18.

2. Excellent scholarship on the diversity of pro-slavery thinking includes Stan-
ley M. Elkins, *Slavery: A Problem in American Institutional and Intellectual Life*
(New York: Grosset & Dunlap, 1963); Eugene D. Genovese, *The Slaveholders
Dilemma: Freedom and Progress in Southern Conservative Thought, 1820–1860*
(Columbia: University of South Carolina Press, 1992); Drew Gilpin Faust, ed.,
The Ideology of Slavery: Proslavery Thought in the Antebellum South, 1830–1860
(Baton Rouge: Louisiana State University Press, 1981); Eric L. McKitrick, ed.,
Slavery Defended: The Views of the Old South (Englewood Cliffs, N.J.: Prentice-
Hall, 1963); David Donald, "The Proslavery Argument Reconsidered," *Journal
of Southern History* 37, no. 1 (1971): 3–18; and E. N. Elliot, ed., *Cotton Is King,
and Pro-Slavery Arguments: Comprising the Writings of Hammond, Harper, Cristy,
Stringfellow, Hodge, Bledsoe, and Cartwright on This Important Subject* (Oxford:
Benediction Classics, 2011).

3. For an excellent study situating the thought of Calhoun, Hammond, and
Fitzhugh in the intellectual currents in the antebellum South, see Michael
O'Brien, *Conjectures of Order: Intellectual Life and the American South, 1810–1860*
(Chapel Hill: University of North Carolina Press, 2004).

4. John C. Calhoun, *Disquisition on Government and Selections from the Discourse*
(Indianapolis: Bobbs-Merrill, 1953).

5. Eugene D. Genovese, *Roll, Jordan, Roll: The World the Slaves Made* (New York:
Vintage Books, 1972); and Charles Post, "Social-Property Relations, Class-
Conflict and the Origins of the US Civil War: Towards a New Social Interpre-
tation," *Historical Materialism* 19, no. 4 (2011): 129–68.

6. By 1860, attacks on Northern wage labor were common among pro-slavery
thinkers and a rejoinder to abolitionist arguments against Southern slavery
(Wilfred Carsel, "The Slaveholders' Indictment of Northern Wage Slavery,"
Journal of Southern History, November 1940, 504–20; and Richard N. Current,
"John C. Calhoun, Philosopher of Reaction," *Antioch Review,* summer 1943,
223–34).

7. George Fitzhugh, *Sociology for the South* (New York: Burt Franklin, 1965), 83–86; and James Henry Hammond, "Slavery in the Light of Political Science," in Elliot, ed., *Cotton Is King*.

8. George Fitzhugh, *Cannibals All! or Slaves Without Masters*, ed. C. Vann Woodward (1857; Cambridge, Mass.: Harvard University Press, 1960), 10.

9. Walter Johnson, *River of Dark Dreams: Slavery and Empire in the Cotton Kingdom* (Cambridge, Mass.: Harvard University Press, 2013); see also John Stauffer, "Fighting the Devil with His Own Fire," and Manisha Sinha, "Did the Abolitionists Cause the Civil War?" in *The Abolitionist Imagination*, ed. Andrew Delbanco (Cambridge, Mass.: Harvard University Press, 2012).

10. Josiah Nott, "Types of Mankind" and Samuel Cartwright, "The Prognathous Species of Mankind," both in McKitrick, ed., *Slavery Defended*.

11. Peter Kolchin, *American Slavery: 1619–1877* (New York: Hill & Wang, 1993), 191.

12. Faust, ed., *The Ideology of Slavery*, 5.

13. Ibid., 4, 9.

14. Stauffer, "Fighting the Devil with His Own Fire," and Sinha, "Did the Abolitionists Cause the Civil War?," both in Delbanco, ed., *The Abolitionist Imagination*; and Christopher Hayes, "The New Abolitionism," *The Nation* 298, no. 19 (2014): 12–18.

15. Eric Foner, *Give Me Liberty! An American History* (New York: Norton, 2006), 340.

16. Sven Beckert, *The Empire of Cotton: A Global History* (New York: Knopf, 2015), 103.

17. Robert E. May, *The Southern Dream of a Caribbean Empire, 1854–1861* (Athens: University of Georgia Press, 1989); and Matthew Karp, *This Vast Southern Empire: Slaveholders at the Helm of American Foreign Policy* (Cambridge, Mass.: Harvard University Press, 2016).

18. Albert G. Brown, "Speech at Hazlehurst," in *Speeches, Messages and Other Writings of the Hon. Albert G. Brown: A Senator in Congress from the State of Mississippi*, ed., Michael W. Cluskey (online, Ulan Press, 2012), 595.

19. There has been considerable scholarly dispute over whether the Old South was really all that distinct from the capitalist North, particularly whether, and to what extent, slave society was capitalist. See Barrington Moore, *Social Origins of Democracy and Dictatorship: Lord and Peasant in the Making of the Modern World* (Boston: Beacon Press, 1993); Immanuel Wallerstein, *The Modern World System: Capitalist Agriculture and the Origins of the European World-Economy in the Sixteenth Century* (New York: Academic Press, 1974); Robert William Fogel and Stanley L. Engerman, *Time on the Cross: The Economics of Negro Slavery* (New York: Norton, 1995); James Oakes, *The Ruling Race: A History of American Slaveholders* (New York: Knopf, 1982); James Oakes, *Slavery and Freedom: An Interpretation of the Old South* (New York: Norton, 1990); Elizabeth Fox-Genovese and Eugene D. Genovese, *Fruits of Merchant Capital: Slavery and Bourgeois Property in the Rise and Expansion of Capitalism* (New York: Oxford

University Press, 1983); John Ashworth, *Slavery Capitalism and Politics in the Antebellum Republic*, vol. 1, *Commerce and Compromise, 1820–1850* (Cambridge: Cambridge University Press, 1995); John Ashworth, *Slavery Capitalism and Politics in the Antebellum Republic*, vol. 2: *The Coming of the Civil War, 1850–1861* (Cambridge: Cambridge University Press, 2007); Kenneth Stampp, *The Peculiar Institution: Slavery in the Ante-Bellum South* (New York: Vintage, 1989); Kolchin, *American Slavery*; and Johnson, *River of Dark Dreams*.

20. Kolchin, *American Slavery*, 190–93.

21. Hammond, "Letter to an English Abolitionist," in Faust, ed., *The Ideology of Slavery*, 184.

22. Joseph G. Rayback, *A History of American Labor* (New York: Free Press, 1966), 50.

23. David R. Meyer, *The Roots of American Industrialization* (Baltimore: Johns Hopkins University Press, 2003), 27. Between 1800 and 1860, New York City grew from a city of 79,216 to an urban center of 1,174,779. Philadelphia's population grew from 61,559 to 565,529. Baltimore was a city of 26,514 inhabitants in 1800 and a city of 212,418 inhabitants in 1860. Boston's population grew from 24,937 to 177,840 in 1860.

24. Stanley Lebergott, "The Pattern of Employment Since 1800," in *American Economic History*, ed. Seymour E. Harris (New York: McGraw-Hill, 1961), 281–310.

25. Eric Foner, *The Story of American Freedom* (New York: Norton, 1998), 59.

26. Economic historians disagree on the precise year that the Industrial Revolution began in America. However, as Louis M. Hacker wrote, it is widely agreed that by 1860, the United States already was an industrialized nation. On competing theories of industrial development in the United States, see Louis M. Hacker, *The Course of American Economic Growth and Development* (New York: Wiley, 1970), 69.

27. Sven Beckert, *The Monied Metropolis: New York City and the Consolidation of the American Bourgeoisie, 1850–1896* (Cambridge: Cambridge University Press, 2001), 85–144.

28. Hammond, "Letter to an English Abolitionist," in Faust, ed., *The Ideology of Slavery*, 194.

29. See Philip Foner, *History of the Labor Movement in the United States* (New York: International Publishers, 1947), vol. 1; and Howard Zinn, *A People's History of the United States: 1492–Present* (New York: Harper Perennial, 2003), 211–51.

30. Edward Pessen, *Most Uncommon Jacksonians: The Radical Leaders of the Early Labor Movement* (Albany: State University of New York Press, 1967); Rayback, *A History of American Labor*; Michael J. Thompson, *The Politics of Inequality: A Political History of the Idea of Economic Inequality in America* (New York: Columbia University Press, 2007); Sean Wilentz, *Chants Democratic: New York City and the Rise of the American Working Class, 1788–1850* (New York: Oxford University Press, 1984).

31. Foner, *The Story of American Freedom*, 52.

32. Thompson, *The Politics of Inequality*, 57–98.

33. James Henry Hammond, "A Letter to an English Abolitionist," in Faust, ed., *The Ideology of Slavery*, 176.

34. For a fascinating and counterintuitive history of liberal defenses of slavery and oppression, see Domenico Losurdo, *Liberalism: A Counter-History* (London: Verso, 2014).

35. Fitzhugh, *Cannibals All!*, 190.

36. Hammond, "A Letter to an English Abolitionist," in Faust, ed., *The Ideology of Slavery*, 180–81.

37. Quoted in Harvey Wish, *Ante-Bellum Writings of George Fitzhugh and Hinton Rowan Helper on Slavery* (New York: Capricorn, 1960), 9.

38. For a classic statement about pro-slavery thinkers' inherent liberalism, see Louis Hartz, *The Liberal Tradition in America* (New York: Harcourt Brace Jovanovich, 1955).

39. *The Papers of John C. Calhoun*, vol. 13, *1835–1837*, ed. Clyde N. Wilson (Columbia: University of South Carolina Press, 1980), 66.

40. *The Papers of John C. Calhoun*, 13:395–96.

41. Calhoun, *Disquisition on Government*, 44.

42. James Henry Hammond, "Speech of Hon. James Henry Hammond, of South Carolina, On the Admission of Kansas Under the Lecompton Constitution: Delivered in the Senate of the United States, March 4, 1858," *American Antiquarian*, http://www.americanantiquarian.org/Freedmen/Manuscripts/cottonisking.html.

43. Quoted in Richard Hofstadter, *The American Political Tradition* (New York: Vintage, 1989), 105.

44. William J. Grayson, "The Hireling and the Slave," in McKitrick, ed., *Slavery Defended*, 60.

45. Edmund Ruffin, "The Political Economy of Slavery," in McKitrick, ed., *Slavery Defended*, 78.

46. Fitzhugh, *Cannibals All!*, 25.

47. Hammond, "Mud-Sill Speech," in McKitrick, ed., *Slavery Defended*, 123.

48. Grayson, "The Hireling and the Slave," in McKitrick, ed., *Slavery Defended*, 61.

49. Fitzhugh, *Sociology for the South*, 38.

50. C. Vann Woodward, *American Counterpoint: Slavery and Racism in the North-South Dialogue* (Boston: Little, Brown, 1971), 114–15.

51. Fitzhugh, *Cannibals All!*, 202–3.

52. Drew Gilpin Faust, "A Slave Owner in a Free Society: James Henry Hammond on the Grand Tour, 1836–1837," *South Carolina Historical Magazine*, July 1980, 189–206.

53. James Henry Hammond, "Slavery in the Light of Political Science—Letter II," in Elliot, ed., *Cotton Is King*, 679; and Carsel, "The Slaveholders' Indictment of Northern Wage Slavery," 513.

54. Fitzhugh, *Cannibals All!*, 17.

55. Ibid., 107.

56. Ibid., 17.
57. Fitzhugh, *Cannibals All!*, 15; also Post, "Social-Property Relations."
58. The slaveholders' narrative deemphasizing profitability and efficiency, or what may be called the "calculating spirit," has been debunked by scholars (Oakes, *The Ruling Race*).
59. Hammond, "A Letter to an English Abolitionist," in Faust, ed., *The Ideology of Slavery*, 184–85.
60. *The Papers of John C. Calhoun*, 13:396.
61. Eric Foner, *Give Me Liberty!*, 343.
62. Hammond, "Letter to an English Abolitionist," in Faust, ed., *The Ideology of Slavery*, 186–87.
63. Fitzhugh, *Cannibals All!*, 20.
64. Eric Foner, "Free Labor and Nineteenth Century Political Ideology," in *The Market Revolution in America*, ed. Melvyn Stokes and Stephen Conway (Charlottesville: University of Virginia Press, 1996), 105.
65. Fitzhugh, *Cannibals All!*, 32.
66. Fitzhugh, *Sociology for the South*, 20.
67. Kolchin, *American Slavery*, 120–27. See also Hammond, "A Letter to an English Abolitionist," in Faust, ed., *The Ideology of Slavery*, 182–83.
68. Fitzhugh, *Cannibals All!*, 30.
69. Fitzhugh, *Sociology for the South*, 38.
70. Ibid., 115–16.
71. Ibid., 35–36.
72. Genovese, *Roll, Jordan, Roll*, 6.
73. Theodore R. Marmor, "Anti-Industrialism and the Old South: The Agrarian Perspective of John C. Calhoun," *Comparative Studies in Society and History*, July 1967, 377–406.
74. *The Papers of John C. Calhoun*, vol. 24, *1846–1847*, ed. Clyde N. Wilson and Shirley B. Cook (Columbia: University of South Carolina Press, 1997), 190.
75. Hammond, "A Letter to an English Abolitionist," in Faust, ed., *The Ideology of Slavery*, 179.
76. Fitzhugh, *Cannibals All!*, 6.
77. Charles M. Wiltse, "A Critical Southerner: John C. Calhoun on the Revolutions of 1848," *Journal of Southern History*, August 1949, 299–310.
78. Calhoun, quoted in Marmor, "Anti-Industrialism and the Old South," 387.
79. Hammond, "A Letter to an English Abolitionist," in Faust, ed., *The Ideology of Slavery*, 177–78.
80. Indeed, pro-slavery thinkers, including Fitzhugh, suggested that socialists were generally correct in their critiques of capitalism but were wrong in trying to build an alternative system based on socialist values and view of human nature (Fitzhugh, *Cannibals All!*, 22–24).
81. Fitzhugh, *Sociology for the South*, 178.
82. Fitzhugh, *Cannibals All!*, 24.

83. *The Papers of John C. Calhoun*, 13:138.

84. Calhoun, *Disquisition on Government*, 36.

85. Hammond, "Speech of Hon. James Henry Hammond, of South Carolina, on the Admission of Kansas Under the Lecompton Constitution: Delivered in the Senate of the United States, March 4, 1858," *American Antiquarian*.

86. Fitzhugh, *Cannibals All!*, 245.

87. Jonathan M. Weiner, "Coming to Terms with Capitalism: The Postwar Thought of George Fitzhugh," *VaMHB* 87 (1979): 438–47.

88. Wish, *Ante-Bellum Writings*, 13–14.

89. Laura F. Edwards, "The Problem of Dependency: African Americans, Labor Relations, and the Law in the Nineteenth-Century South," *Agricultural History*, spring 1998, 313–40.

90. Eric Foner, *Reconstruction: American's Unfinished Revolution, 1863–1877* (New York: Harper & Row, 1988), 129–35; Beckert, *The Monied Metropolis*, 160–62; and Beckert, *The Empire of Cotton*.

91. W. E. B. Du Bois, *Black Reconstruction: An Essay Toward a History of the Part Which Black Folk Played in the Attempt to Reconstruct Democracy in America, 1860–1880* (New York: Harcourt, Brace & Co., 1935), 30.

2. IN SEARCH OF THE WARRIOR-STATESMAN

1. Jackson Lears, *Rebirth of a Nation: The Making of Modern America, 1877–1920* (New York: Harper, 2009), 4.

2. Robert H. Wiebe, *The Search for Order, 1877–1920* (New York: Hill & Wang, 1967).

3. Steven J. Diner, *A Very Different Age: Americans of the Progressive Era* (New York: Hill & Wang, 1998); Eric Foner, *The Story of American Freedom* (New York: Norton, 1998); Martin J. Sklar, *The Corporate Reconstruction of American Capitalism, 1890–1916: The Market, the Law, and Politics* (1988; New York: Cambridge University Press, 1997); Wiebe, *The Search for Order*; and Howard Zinn, *A People's History of the United States:1492–Present* (1980; New York: Harper Perennial, 2003).

4. Zinn, *A People's History*, 277; and Richard B. DuBoff, *Accumulation and Power: An Economic History of the United States* (Armonk, N.Y.: Sharpe, 1989), 71.

5. James A. Henretta, Rebecca Edwards, and Robert O. Self, *America: A Concise History*, vol. 2, *Since 1865*, 3rd ed. (New York: Worth, 1997), 665.

6. Ibid.

7. Historians and conservatives have debated for years whether Brooks Adams and Theodore Roosevelt can accurately be labeled conservative. Historians and scholars of American conservatism who count Roosevelt as a conservative are Daniel Aaron, *Men of Good Hope* (1951; New York: Oxford University Press, 1961); John Morton Blum, *The Republican Roosevelt* (Cambridge, Mass.: Harvard University Press, 1977); Melvyn Dubofsky, *The State and Labor in*

Modern America (Chapel Hill: University of North Carolina Press, 1994); *The Writings of Theodore Roosevelt*, ed. William H. Harbaugh (Indianapolis: Bobbs-Merrill, 1967); Richard Hofstadter, *The American Political Tradition* (1948; New York: Vintage, 1989); Gabriel Kolko, *The Triumph of Conservatism* (1963; New York: Free Press, 1977); and Clinton Rossiter, *Conservatism in America* (1955; Cambridge, Mass.: Harvard University Press, 1982). Regarding the conservatism of Brooks Adams, see, among others, Aaron, *Men of Good Hope*; Timothy Paul Donovan, *Henry Adams and Brooks Adams: The Education of Two American Historians* (Norman: University of Oklahoma Press, 1961); Charles W. Dunn and J. David Woodard, *The Conservative Tradition in America* (1996; Lanham, Md.: Rowman & Littlefield, 2003); Allen Guttmann, *The Conservative Tradition in America* (New York: Oxford University Press, 1967); Ronald Lora, *Conservative Minds in America* (Chicago: Rand McNally, 1971); Russell Kirk, *The Conservative Mind* (Chicago: Regnery, 1953); and Jay A. Sigler, *The Conservative Tradition in American Thought* (New York: Putnam, 1969).

8. Other prominent exponents include Henry Adams, John Hay, Henry Cabot Lodge, and Alfred Thayer Mahan. See John P. Mallan, "Roosevelt, Brooks Adams, and Lea: The Warrior Critique of Business Civilization," *American Quarterly*, autumn 1956, 216–30.

9. Aaron, *Men of Good Hope*; Arthur F. Beringause, *Brooks Adams: A Biography* (New York: Knopf, 1955); Charles Hirschfeld, "Brooks Adams and American Nationalism," *American Historical Review*, January 1964, 371–92; and William Appleman Williams, *History as a Way of Learning* (New York: New Viewpoints, 1973).

10. Mathew Josephson, *The President Makers: The Culture of Politics and Leadership in an Age of Enlightenment, 1896–1919* (1940; New York: Unger, 1964), 61.

11. Quoted in Hofstadter, *The American Political Tradition*, 300. For Brooks Adams's belief in conservatism through reform, see Brooks Adams, *The Theory of Social Revolutions* (New York: Macmillan, 1913).

12. Jackson Lears, *No Place for Grace: Antimodernism and the Transformation of American Culture, 1880–1920* (Chicago: University of Chicago Press, 1994), 100.

13. Lears, *Rebirth of a Nation*; Richard Hofstadter, *Social Darwinism in American Thought* (Boston: Beacon Press, 1959); and William Appleman Williams, *The Contours of American History* (Chicago: Quadrangle, 1966).

14. Cited in John P. Mallan, "Roosevelt, Brooks Adams, and Lea: The Warrior Critique of Business Civilization," *American Quarterly* 8, no. 3 (1956): 220.

15. For the emasculating character of commerce, see Albert O. Hirschman, *The Passions and the Interests: Political Arguments for Capitalism Before Its Triumph* (Princeton, N.J.: Princeton University Press, 1977); and J. G. A. Pocock, *The Machiavellian Moment: Florentine Political Thought and the Atlantic Republican Tradition* (Princeton, N.J.: Princeton University Press, 1975).

16. Patrick Allitt, *The Conservatives: Ideas and Personalities Throughout American History* (New Haven, Conn.: Yale University Press, 2009).

17. The classic statement on social Darwinism in the United States is by William Graham Sumner, *What Social Classes Owe Each Other* (New York: Arno, 1972).

18. Charles Beard, introduction to Brooks Adams, *The Law of Civilization and Decay* (1896; repr., New York: Knopf, 1943), 3.

19. Frederick Jackson Turner, *The Frontier in American History* (Ann Arbor: University of Michigan Press, 2008).

20. DuBoff, *Accumulation and Power*, 71.

21. Henry Adams, who was more famous than his brother Brooks, was much more fatalistic about the decline of civilization. For Brooks Adams's influence on the work of Henry Adams and on Theodore Roosevelt, see Williams, *History as a Way of Learning*, 25–38; and Henry Adams, *The Education of Henry Adams* (1907; New York: Oxford University Press, 1999).

22. Quoted in Aaron, *Men of Good Hope*, 262.

23. Brooks Adams, *The Law of Civilization and Decay*, 334.

24. Ibid., 326.

25. Theodore Roosevelt, "The Law of Civilization and Decay," *The Works of Theodore Roosevelt* (New York: Scribner, 1926), 13:242–60. The essay is available at http://www.theodore-roosevelt.com/images/research/treditorials/f6.pdf.

26. Williams, *History as a Way of Learning*, 25–38.

27. Quoted in Josephson, *The President Makers*, 98; See also Brooks Adams, *The Theory of Social Revolutions*, 3–6, 31–32.

28. Quoted in Aaron, *Men of Good Hope*, 270.

29. Brooks Adams, *The Theory of Social Revolutions*, 29.

30. Quoted in Aaron, *Men of Good Hope*, 258.

31. Brooks Adams, *The Theory of Social Revolutions*, 208.

32. Ibid., 208–9.

33. For Brooks Adams's relationship with Roosevelt and his influence on him, see Beringause, *Brooks Adams*, 143–70; Aaron, *Men of Good Hope*; Josephson, *The President Makers*, 26–27, 61–63, 98; and William A. Williams, "Brooks Adams and American Expansion," *New England Quarterly* 25, no. 2 (1952): 217–32.

34. Theodore Roosevelt, "The Strenuous Life," in *Theodore Roosevelt: An American Mind*, ed. Mario R. DiNunzio (1994; New York: Penguin, 1995), 185.

35. Roosevelt, "Address at San Francisco," and "The Minimum Wage," in Harbaugh, ed., *The Writings of Theodore Roosevelt*, 180–81, 289.

36. For details of the strike and Roosevelt's role in its resolution, see Dubofsky, *The State and Labor in Modern America*; and Edmund Morris, *Theodore Rex* (New York: Random House, 2001), 131–37, 150–69.

37. Quoted in Hofstadter, *The American Political Tradition*, 288.

38. Roosevelt, "Manhood and Statehood," in Theodore Roosevelt, *The Strenuous Life: Essays and Addresses* (New York: Century, 1901), 257. Also see "Letter to S. Stanwood Menken," in Harbaugh, ed., *The Writings of Theodore Roosevelt*, 383.

39. Brooks Adams was intensely anti-Semitic.

40. Roosevelt, "Brotherhood and the Heroic Virtues," in *The Strenuous Life,* 275–76.

41. Roosevelt, "Letter to S. Stanwood Menken," in Harbaugh, ed., *The Writings of Theodore Roosevelt,* 385.

42. Roosevelt, "America's Part of the World's Work," in DiNunzio, ed., *An American Mind,* 181.

43. See Arnaldo Testi, "The Gender of Reform Politics: Theodore Roosevelt and the Culture of Masculinity," *Journal of American History,* March 1995, 1509–33.

44. Theodore Roosevelt, "Theodore Roosevelt on Motherhood and the Welfare of the State," *Population and Development Review,* March 1987, 141–47.

45. Brooks Adams, *The Law of Civilization and Decay,* 338.

46. David H. Burton, *Theodore Roosevelt: Confident Imperialist* (Philadelphia: University of Pennsylvania Press, 1968), 142–43.

47. Brooks Adams, *America's Economic Supremacy* (1900; New York: Harper Bros., Publishers, 1947), 99.

48. Adams, *The Theory of Social Revolutions,* 207–8.

49. Ibid., 29–31.

50. Even conservative critics of capitalism like George Fitzhugh recognized that the seeds of revolutionary discord in the American North had been dissipated by the existence of the frontier.

51. It is worth noting that Roosevelt was a New Yorker.

52. Lears, *No Place for Grace,* 117.

53. Brooks Adams, *The Law of Civilization and Decay,* 35; and Williams, "Brooks Adams and American Expansion."

54. Brooks Adams, *The New Empire* (New York: Macmillan, 1902), xiii.

55. Similar arguments justifying American imperialism on economic grounds had been made by Henry Cabot Lodge, Alfred Thayer Mahan, and Albert Beveridge, among others. See Matthew Frye Jacobson, *Barbarian Virtues: The United States Encounters Foreign Peoples at Home and Abroad, 1876–1917* (New York: Hill & Wang, 2001).

56. Brooks Adams, *America's Economic Supremacy,* 87, 98.

57. Ibid., 72.

58. Quoted in David H. Burton, "The Influence of the American West on the Imperialist Philosophy of Theodore Roosevelt," *Arizona and the West,* spring 1962, 5.

59. Roosevelt, "The Indian Wars, 1784–1787," in DiNunzio, ed., *An American Mind,* 61–62.

60. Roosevelt, "America's Part of the World's Work," in DiNunzio, ed., *An American Mind,* 181; and Roosevelt, "National Duties," in *The Strenuous Life,* 293.

61. Roosevelt, "National Duties," in *The Strenuous Life,* 293.

62. Quoted in Jacobson, *Barbarian Virtues,* 226.

63. Roosevelt, "National Duties," in *The Strenuous Life,* 286.

64. Roosevelt's support for reform have led some scholars to underestimate the conservative principles behind the reforms and to characterize Roosevelt as a Progressive and a corporate liberal. See William E. Leuchtenburg, introduction

to Theodore Roosevelt's *The New Nationalism* (Englewood Cliffs, N.J.: Prentice-Hall, 1960); and Sklar, *The Corporate Reconstruction of American Capitalism.*

65. As president, however, Wilson soon turned away from the decentralization model and came to terms with centralized power.

66. Michael J. Sandel, *Democracy's Discontent: America in Search of a Public Philosophy* (Cambridge, Mass.: Harvard University Press, 1996.

67. Ibid., 218.

68. For a classic account of this view of republicanism, see Herbert J. Storing, *What the Anti-Federalists Were For: The Political Thought of the Opponents of the Constitution* (Chicago: University of Chicago Press, 1981), 15–23.

69. Roosevelt, "The Duties of American Citizenship," in Harbaugh, ed., *The Writings of Theodore Roosevelt*, 4–5.

70. Quoted in H. W. Brands, *T. R.: The Last Romantic* (New York: Basic Books, 1997), 773.

71. Hofstadter, *The American Political Tradition.*

72. Theodore Roosevelt, in *Politics and People: The Ordeal of Self-Government in America*, ed. Leon Stein (New York: Arno, 1974), 384.

73. Ibid.

74. Roosevelt, "First Annual Message to Congress," in DiNunzio, ed., *An American Mind*, 127.

75. Roosevelt, "The Menace of the Demagogue," in DiNunzio, ed., *An American Mind*, 116.

76. DiNunzio, ed., *An American Mind*, 116–17.

77. Quoted in Hofstadter, *The American Political Tradition*, 284.

78. Theodore Roosevelt, "Where We Cannot Work with Socialists," in Harbaugh, ed., *The Writings of Theodore Roosevelt*, 309.

79. Roosevelt, "Eighth Annual Message to Congress," in DiNunzio, ed., *An American Mind*, 136.

80. Hofstadter, *The American Political Tradition*, 288.

81. Roosevelt, "Conservation," in *The New Nationalism*, 56. Near the end of his life, Roosevelt continued to call for reform, including "a steeply graduated tax on excess profits, a bill of rights for returning soldiers, higher education for all men and women who desired it, the rights of workers to share in profits and in management, permanency of employment, day nurseries for children of working mothers, and a right to reasonable leisure" (Susan Dunn, "The TR Show," *New York Review of Books*, February 20, 2014, 28–30).

82. Richard Hofstadter wrote in *The American Political Tradition*: "It became his [Roosevelt's] obsession to "save" the masters of capital from their own stupid obstinacy" (286).

83. This idea that capitalists are not an effective ruling class can be found in the critiques of the defenders of slavery, Southern Agrarians, post–World War II conservative critics, and paleoconservatives. Likewise, this critique is also

common among those who do not identify themselves as conservatives, including Joseph Schumpeter, *Capitalism, Socialism, and Democracy* (1942; New York: Harper Bros., 1950), 135–39; and Arthur Schlesinger Jr., *The Vital Center: The Politics of Freedom* (1949; New Brunswick, N.J.: Transaction, 1998), 11–34.

84. See Hirschman, *The Passions and the Interests.*

85. Perry Anderson, "Imperium," *New Left Review* 83 (2013); and Leo Panitch and Sara Gindin, *The Making of Global Capitalism: The Political Economy of American Empire* (London: Verso, 2013).

3. THE AGRARIAN CRITIQUE OF CAPITALISM

1. L. S. Stavrianos, *Global Rift: The Third World Comes of Age* (New York: Morrow, 1981), 320–32.

2. Alfred D. Chandler Jr., *Scale and Scope: The Dynamics of Industrial Capitalism* (Cambridge, Mass.: Harvard University Press, 2009), 4, 47; Hugh Rockoff, "Until It Is Over, Over There: The US Economy in World War I," working paper no. 10580 (Washington, D.C.: National Bureau of Economic Research, 2004), www.nber.org/papers/w10580.

3. Quoted in James A. Henretta, Rebecca Edwards, and Robert O. Self, *America: A Concise History*, vol. 2, *Since 1865*, 3rd ed. (New York: Worth, 1997), 745.

4. Quoted in ibid., 740.

5. Richard B. DuBoff, *Accumulation and Power: An Economic History of the United States* (Armonk, N.Y.: Sharpe, 1989), 78–81.

6. Chandler, *Scale and Scope*, 86.

7. Stanley Aronowitz, *How Class Works: Power and Social Movement* (New Haven, Conn.: Yale University Press, 2003), 68.

8. DuBoff, *Accumulation and Power*, 88.

9. Christopher Clark, Nancy A. Hewitt, Roy Rosenzweig, and Nelson Lichtenstein (American History Project), *Who Built America? Working People and the Nation's History*, vol. 2, *1877 to the Present*, 3rd ed. (Boston: Bedford / St. Martin's Press, 2008), 343–44.

10. Between 1920 and 1930, the U.S. farm population dropped by 1.5 million people (*Historical Statistics of the United States: Colonial Times to 1970, Part 1* [Washington, D.C.: U.S. Department of Commerce, Bureau of the Census, 1975], 458).

11. Clark et al., *Who Built America?*, 2:347–48.

12. Clark et al., *Who Built America?*, 343–45; Irving Bernstein, *The Lean Years: A History of the American Worker, 1920–1933* (Baltimore: Penguin, 1966), 66–67.

13. DuBoff, *Accumulation and Power*, 86–92.

14. Kim Phillips-Fein, *Invisible Hands: The Making of the Conservative Movement from the New Deal to Reagan* (New York: Norton, 2009).

15. John Crowe Ransom et al., *I'll Take My Stand: The South and the Agrarian Tradition* (1930; Baton Rouge: Louisiana State University Press, 1977).

16. Paul V. Murphy, *The Rebuke of History: The Southern Agrarians and American Conservative Thought* (Chapel Hill: University of North Carolina Press, 2001), 62–67.

17. John J. Langdale, *Superfluous Southerners: Cultural Conservatism and the South, 1920–1990* (Columbia: University of Missouri Press, 2012).

18. Allen Tate, quoted in *The Southern Agrarians and the New Deal: Essays After I'll Take My Stand*, ed. Emily S. Bingham and Thomas A. Underwood (Charlottesville: University of Virginia Press, 2001), 8.

19. Frank Owsley, "The Pillars of Agrarianism," in *The Southern Agrarians and the New Deal: Essays After I'll Take My Stand*, ed. Emily S. Bingham and Thomas A. Underwood (Charlottesville: University of Virginia Press, 2001), 202.

20. Ibid., 201.

21. Paul K. Conklin, *The Southern Agrarians* (Knoxville: University of Tennessee Press, 1988); John L. Stewart, *The Burden of Time: The Fugitives and Agrarians* (Princeton, N.J.: Princeton University Press, 1965); and Patrick Allitt, *The Conservatives: Ideas and Personalities Throughout American History* (New Haven, Conn.: Yale University Press, 2009). For a counterargument suggesting that the Southern Agrarians were defending a real community, not an abstract theoretical one, see Christopher M. Duncan, *Fugitive Theory: Political Theory, the Southern Agrarians, and America* (Lanham, Md.: Lexington Books, 2000).

22. Eugene D. Genovese, *The Southern Tradition: The Achievements and Limitations of an American Conservatism* (Cambridge, Mass.: Harvard University Press, 1994); Murphy, *The Rebuke of History*.

23. In 1935, half of all American farmers were landless, and one-third of the South's cotton land was owned by absentee landlords. Jess Gilbert and Steve Brown, "Alternative Land Reform Proposals in the 1930s: The Nashville Agrarians and the Southern Tenant Farmers' Union," *Agricultural History* 55, no. 4 (1981): 351–69.

24. Ransom et al., "Introduction: A Statement of Principles," in *I'll Take My Stand*, xli.

25. Ibid., xl.

26. Critiques of the monotony and dulling of development of the total human personality by labor under industrial capitalism had been made for more than a century and by thinkers across the political spectrum, including Adam Smith, Alexis de Tocqueville, and Karl Marx.

27. John Crowe Ransom, "The South Defends Its Heritage," in *The Superfluous Men: Conservative Critics of American Culture, 1900–1945*, ed. Robert M. Crunden (Austin: University of Texas Press, 1977), 179.

28. Andrew Nelson Lytle, "The Small Farm Secures the State," in *The Southern Agrarians and the New Deal: Essays After I'll Take My Stand*, ed. Emily S. Bingham and Thomas A. Underwood (Charlottesville: University of Virginia Press, 2001), 154.

29. Ransom, "Reconstructed but Unregenerate," in *I'll Take My Stand*, 23; and Ransom, "The South Defends Its Heritage," 181.

30. Allen Tate, "Liberalism and Tradition," in *Reason in Madness: Critical Essays* (1941; Freeport, N.Y.: Books for Libraries Press, 1968), 230.

31. Lytle, "The Small Farm Secures the State," in Bingham and Underwood, eds., *The Southern Agrarians and the New Deal*, 155.

32. Conklin, *The Southern Agrarians*, 54; Murphy, *The Rebuke of History*, 23–24.

33. Ransom, "What Does the South Want?," in Bingham and Underwood, eds., *The Southern Agrarians and the New Deal*, 249.

34. Allitt, *The Conservatives*, 137.

35. Lyle H. Lanier, "A Critique of the Philosophy of Progress," in Ransom et al., *I'll Take My Stand: The South and the Agrarian Tradition* (1930; Baton Rouge: Louisiana State University Press, 1977), 146.

36. Irving Babbitt, cited in Clinton Rossiter, *Conservatism in America* (Cambridge, Mass.: Harvard University Press, 1982), 158; also see Allen Guttmann, *The Conservative Tradition in America* (New York: Oxford University Press, 1967), 135–41.

37. Ransom et al., "A Statement of Principles," in *I'll Take My Stand*, xliv (italics added).

38. Ransom, "The South Is a Bulwark," in Bingham and Underwood, eds., *The Southern Agrarians and the New Deal*.

39. Frank Owsley, "The Pillars of Agrarianism," in Bingham and Underwood, eds., *The Southern Agrarians and the New Deal*, 201.

40. Donald Davidson, "Agrarianism and Politics," *Review of Politics*, March 1939, 114–25.

41. Lanier, "A Critique of the Philosophy of Progress," in *I'll Take My Stand*, 140–41.

42. Allen Tate, *Jefferson Davis: His Rise and Fall* (New York: Minton, Blach, 1929), 43.

43. Stark Young, "Not in Memoriam, but in Defense," in Ransom et al., *I'll Take My Stand*, 328.

44. Tate, "Liberalism and Tradition," in *Critical Essays*, 209.

45. Ibid., 210.

46. Ibid., 209.

47. My understanding of the concept of market comes from the description by the renowned sociologist Georg Simmel: "The production for unknown purchasers who never appear in the actual field of vision of the producers themselves" ("The Metropolis and Mental Life," in *Sociological Theory in the Classical Era*, ed. Laura Desfor Edles and Scott Appelrouth [Thousand Oaks, Calif.: Sage, 2005], 292).

48. Clark et al., *Who Built America?*, 347–48.

49. The nine Scottsboro boys were African Americans accused of raping two white women in Paint Rock, Alabama. Eight of them were tried and sentenced to death. The International Labor Defense, a group associated with the Communist Party, handled the accused men's appeals.

50. Allen Tate, "Notes on Liberty and Property," in *Who Owns America? A New Declaration of Independence*, ed. Herbert Agar and Allen Tate (1936; Wilmington, Del.: ISI Books, 1999), 122.

51. Lyle H. Lanier, "Big Business in the Property State," in *Who Owns America?*, 29, 3. In addition to the eight Southern Agrarians and Agar, the contributors included English Distributists Doulas Jerrold and Hilaire Belloc; Catholic Agrarian John C. Rawe; and literary critic Cleanth Brooks.

52. Frank Owsley, "The Foundations of Democracy," in Bingham and Underwood, eds., *The Southern Agrarians and the New Deal*, 223–24.

53. Numan V. Bartley, "In Search of the New South: Southern Politics After Reconstruction," *Reviews in American History* 10, no. 4 (1982): 150–63; Howard N. Rabinowitz, *The First New South, 1865–1920* (Arlington Heights, Ill.: Harlan Davidson, 1992); and George Brown Tindall, *The Emergence of the New South, 1913–1945* (Baton Rouge: Louisiana State University Press, 1967).

54. Tate, "The Problem of the Unemployed: A Modest Proposal," in Bingham and Underwood, eds., *The Southern Agrarians and the New Deal*.

55. Owsley, "The Pillars of Agrarianism," in Bingham and Underwood, eds., *The Southern Agrarians and the New Deal*, 202.

56. Ibid., 205.

57. Ibid., 204.

58. Ibid.

59. Jonathan M. Wiener, "Class Structure and Economic Development in the American South, 1865–1955," *American Historical Review* 84, no. 4 (1979): 970–92.

60. Owsley, "The Pillars of Agrarianism," in Bingham and Underwood, eds., *The Southern Agrarians and the New Deal*, 206.

61. Ibid.

62. Ibid.

63. Quoted in Edward S. Shapiro, "Decentralist Intellectuals and the New Deal," *Journal of American History*, March 1972, 938–57.

64. Idus A. Newby, "The Southern Agrarians: A View After Thirty Years," *Agricultural History* 37, no. 3 (1963): 153.

65. Shapiro, "Decentralist Intellectuals and the New Deal," 938–57.

66. Edward Shapiro, "The Southern Agrarians and the Tennessee Valley Authority," *American Quarterly* 22, no. 4 (1970): 791–806.

67. Lanier, "A Critique of the Philosophy of Progress," in *I'll Take My Stand*, 142.

68. Wiener, "Class Structure and Economic Development," 989.

69. Frances Fox-Piven and Richard Cloward, *Poor People's Movements: Why They Succeed, How They Fail* (New York: Random House, 1979), 189–92.

70. Fox-Piven and Cloward, *Poor People's Movements*, 181–263; Clark et al., *Who Built America?*, 422–23.

71. Davidson. quoted in Murphy, *The Rebuke of History*, 201.

72. Ransom, "The South Defends Its Heritage."

73. Newby, "The Southern Agrarians," 150.

74. See Murphy, *The Rebuke of History*, 106–9, 199–201.

75. Conklin, *The Southern Agrarians*, 150–57.

76. Quoted in Murphy, *The Rebuke of History*, 106–7.

77. For fascinating accounts of how government action, not economic modernization, resulted in civil rights, see Gavin Wright, *Sharing the Prize: The Economics of the Civil Rights Revolution in the American South* (Cambridge, Mass.: Belknap Press, 2013); and Ira Katznelson, "The Great and Grudging Transformation," *New York Review of Books* 61, no. 6 (2014): 58–60. See also Fox-Piven and Cloward, *Poor People's Movements*, 181–263.

78. Davidson, quoted in Murphy, *The Rebuke of History*, 200.

79. Bingham and Underwood, eds., *The Southern Agrarians and the New Deal*, 19.

80. Donald Davidson, "That This Nation May Endure—The Need for Political Regionalism," in *Who Owns America?*, 173; Donald Davidson, "Where Regionalism and Sectionalism Meet," *Social Forces* 13, no. 1 (1934–1935): 23–31; Donald Davidson, "Political Regionalism and Administrative Regionalism," *Annals of the American Academy of Political and Social Science* 207 (1940): 138–43; and Donald Davidson, *The Attack on Leviathan: Regionalism and Nationalism in the United States* (Chapel Hill: University of North Carolina Press, 1938). For Owsley's fifth pillar (regionalism) of Agrarianism, see "The Pillars of Agrarianism," in Bingham and Underwood, eds., *The Southern Agrarians and the New Deal*; and Andrew Nelson Lytle, "John C. Calhoun," *Southern Review* 3 (1938): 529–30.

81. Albert E. Stone Jr., "Seward Collins and the American Review: Experiment in Pro-Fascism, 1933–37," *American Quarterly* 12, no. 1 (1960): 3–19. The Southern Agrarians rejected fascism and left the journal after Collins made his public declaration.

82. For the controversy surrounding the Southern Agrarians and Collins, as well as the parting of ways among Davidson, Ransom, and Tate, see Langdale's *Superfluous Southerners*.

83. The radicalism of the New Right, which I will discuss later, acknowledged as the intellectual heir of the Southern Agrarians, pales in comparison with both its critique of capitalism and the alternative that is offered (Genovese, *The Southern Tradition*, and Murphy, *The Rebuke of History*).

84. For a recent study of the influence of the Southern Agrarians on contemporary discourse, see Langdale, *Superfluous Southerners*; and Stephanie Houston Grey, "The Gospel of the Soil: Southern Agrarian Resistance and the Productive Future of Food," *Southern Communication Journal*, November/ December 2014, 387–406.

85. Davidson, "Agrarianism and Politics," 114–25; Donald Davidson, *Southern Writers in the Modern World* (Athens: University of Georgia Press, 1958); Davidson, "I'll Take My Stand: A History," in Bingham and Underwood, eds., *The Southern Agrarians and the New Deal*; Murphy, *The Rebuke of History*, 146, 168.

86. Richard M. Weaver, *Ideas Have Consequences* (Chicago: University of Chicago Press, 1948); Richard M. Weaver, *Southern Tradition at Bay: A History of*

Postbellum Thought, ed. George Core and M. E. Bradford (New Rochelle, N.Y.: Arlington House, 1968); Richard M. Weaver, "Agrarianism in Exile," *Sewanee Review* 58 (1950): 586–606; Richard M. Weaver, "The Tennessee Agrarians," *Shenandoah* 3 (1952): 3–10; and Richard M. Weaver, "The Southern Phoenix," *Georgia Review* 17 (1963): 6–17.

87. Murphy, *The Rebuke of History*, 167.

4. THE NEW CONSERVATIVES

1. For instance, see Robert Green McCloskey, *Conservatism in the Age of Enterprise* (Cambridge, Mass.: Harvard University Press, 1951).
2. Peter Viereck, "Will America Prove Marx Right?," *Antioch Review*, autumn 1952, 333.
3. Russell Kirk, *The Conservative Mind: From Burke to Eliot* (1953; Chicago: Regnery Gateway, 1978), 199.
4. Peter Viereck, *Shame and Glory of Intellectuals: Babbitt Jr. vs. the Rediscovery of Values* (Boston: Beacon Press, 1953), 251.
5. Russell Kirk, *Program for Conservatives* (Chicago: Regnery, 1962).
6. For the importance of anti-Communism as the glue bringing together economic libertarians and traditionalists in a conservative fusion, see George H. Nash, *The Conservative Intellectual Movement in America: Since 1945* (1976; Wilmington, Del.: Intercollegiate Studies Institute, 1996); and Jonathan M. Schoenwald, *A Time for Choosing: The Rise of Modern American Conservatism* (Cary, N.C.: Oxford University Press, 2001).
7. Many civil rights leaders, including A. Phillip Randolph and Martin Luther King Jr., were accused of being Communists as a means of discrediting their leadership and struggle. For J. Edgar Hoover's red-baiting of King, see Taylor Branch, *Parting the Waters: America in the King Years, 1954–1963* (New York: Simon & Schuster, 1989).
8. Among the nonacademic sources, especially those funded and patronized by the business community, suggesting an affinity between the liberal welfare state and Communism, see Kim Phillips-Fein, *Invisible Hands: The Making of the Conservative Movement from the New Deal to Reagan* (New York: Norton, 2009). The academic exponents of the liberal welfare state's "creeping totalitarianism" argument were many, perhaps none more influential than Friedrich von Hayek and his influential *The Road to Serfdom* (Chicago: Chicago University Press, 1944).
9. Tony Judt, *Postwar: A History of Europe Since 1945* (New York: Penguin, 2005); and Alfred E. Eckes Jr., *Opening America's Market: U.S. Foreign Trade Policy Since 1776* (Chapel Hill: University of North Carolina Press, 1995).
10. Odd Arne Westad, *The Global Cold War: Third World Interventions and the Making of Our Times* (Cambridge: Cambridge University Press, 2007); Perry

Anderson, "Imperium," *New Left Review* 83 (2013), http://newleftreview.org/II/83/perry-anderson-imperium; Leo Panitch and Sam Gindin, *The Making of Global Capitalism: The Political Economy of American Empire* (London: Verso, 2013); Warren I. Cohen, *The Cambridge History of American Foreign Relations*, vol. 4, *America in the Age of Soviet Power, 1945–1991* (Cambridge: Cambridge University Press, 1993); and Eric Hobsbawm, *The Age of Extremes: A History of the World, 1914–1991*(New York: Vintage, 1996).

11. Nelson Lichtenstein, *American Capitalism: Social Thought and Political Economy in the 20th Century* (Philadelphia: University of Pennsylvania Press, 2006), 5; Daniel Bell, ed., *The End of Ideology: On the Exhaustion of Political Ideas in the Fifties* (New York: Free Press, 1962); and C. Wright Mills, *White Collar: The American Middle Class* (New York: Galaxy, 1956).

12. Franklin Delano Roosevelt, "1944 State of the Union Message to Congress," January 11, 1944, http://www.fdrlibrary.marist.edu/archives/address_text.html.

13. The GI Bill was an important piece of social legislation that, among other things, expanded housing and employment opportunities for millions of military veterans. For its broad social effect, see Joshua Freeman, *American Empire: The Rise of a Global Power, the Democratic Revolution at Home, 1945–2000* (New York: Penguin, 2012), 32–35; and Ira Katznelson, *When Affirmative Action Was White: An Untold History of Racial Inequality in Twentieth Century America* (New York: Norton, 2005).

14. Lisa McGirr, *Suburban Warriors: The Origins of the New American Right* (Princeton, N.J.: Princeton University Press, 2001), 8.

15. Richard B. DuBoff, *Accumulation and Power: An Economic History of the United States* (Armonk, N.Y.: Sharpe, 1989), 99.

16. For employment and wage statistics during this time period, see DuBoff, *Accumulation and Power*; and Marc Allen Eisner, *The American Political Economy: Institutional Evolution of Market and State* (New York: Routledge, 2011). For the term *golden age of capitalism* as applied to 1945 to the early 1970s, see Jack Metzger, *Striking Steel: Solidarity Remembered* (Philadelphia: Temple University Press, 2000), 210; and Ira Katznelson, *The Politics of Power: A Critical Introduction to American Government*, 7th ed. (New York: Norton, 2014), 76.

17. Kevin Mattson, *Rebels All!: A Short History of the Conservative Mind in Postwar America* (New Brunswick, N.J.: Rutgers University Press, 2008), 32.

18. In a brilliant history of the Republican Party in the 1950s and early 1960s, Geoffrey Kabaservice wrote that the GOP was composed of several factions, of which the smallest, at the 1960 Republican Convention, was made up of those we would identify as conservatives today (*Rule and Ruin: The Downfall of Moderation and the Destruction of the Republican Party, from Eisenhower to the Tea Party* [New York: Oxford University Press, 2012], 18–26).

19. Frank S. Meyer, *What Is Conservatism?* (New York: Holt, Rinehart & Winston, 1964); Frank S. Meyer, *The Conservative Mainstream* (New Rochelle, N.Y.: Arlington House, 1969); and Jeffrey Hart, *The Making of the American Conservative Mind: National Review and Its Times* (Wilmington, Del.: ISI Books, 2007).

20. Jennifer Burns, "Liberalism and the Conservative Imagination," in *Liberalism for a New Century*, ed. Neil Jumonville and Kevin Mattson (Berkeley: University of California Press, 2007), 58–72; and Mark Thomas Edwards, *The Right of the Protestant Left: God's Totalitarianism* (New York: Palgrave Macmillan, 2012) 146–58.

21. Peter Viereck, *Conservatism Revisited: The Revolt Against Ideology* (1949; New York: Collier Books, 1962), 134.

22. Frank S. Meyer, "Counterfeit at a Popular Price," in *The Conservative Mainstream*, 67–70.

23. Nash, *The Conservative Intellectual Movement in America*, 60.

24. Nash, *The Conservative Intellectual Movement in America*, 60; Claes G. Ryn, "Peter Viereck: Unadjusted Man of Ideas," *Political Science Reviewer* 7 (1977): 326–66; Marie Henault, *Peter Viereck* (New York: Twayne, 1969); Irving Louis Horowitz, "Peter Viereck: European-American Conscience—1916–2006," *Society* 44, no. 2 (2007): 60–63; and Tom Reiss, "The First Conservative," *New Yorker*, October 24, 2005, http://newyorker.com/archive/2005/10/24/051024fa_fact1?printable=true.

25. Cited in Reiss, "The First Conservative."

26. Russell Kirk, "Libertarians: Chirping Sectaries," in *The Essential Russell Kirk: Selected Essays*, ed. George A. Panichas (Wilmington, Del.: ISI Books, 2007), 382.

27. William H. Honan, "Russell Kirk Is Dead at 75; Seminal Conservative Author," *New York Times*, April 30, 1994, http://www.nytimes.com/1994/04/30/obituaries/russell-kirk-is-dead-at-75-seminal-conservative-author.html.

28. Mattson, *Rebels All!*, 46.

29. Robert Nisbet, *The Present Age: Progress and Anarchy in Modern America* (New York: Harper & Row, 1988), 42, 50; and Gerald J. Russello, *The Postmodern Imagination of Russell Kirk* (Columbia: University of Missouri Press, 2007), 110.

30. Kirk, *The Conservative Mind*. It is important to note that as sketched out by Viereck, advocates of economic laissez-faire also were absent from the conservative tradition (Viereck, *Conservatism Revisited*; and Clinton Rossiter, *Conservatism in America* [Cambridge, Mass.: Harvard University Press, 1955]).

31. Quotation from Ronald Reagan is cited in W. Wesley McDonald, *Russell Kirk and the Age of Ideology* (Columbia: University of Missouri Press, 2004), 3.

32. Robert Nisbet, *Twilight of Authority* (New York: Oxford University Press, 1975), 198, 209.

33. Brad Lowell Stone, *Robert Nisbet: Communitarian Traditionalist* (Wilmington, Del.: ISI Press, 2000); J. David Hoeveler Jr., *Watch on the Right: Conservative Intellectuals in the Reagan Era* (Madison: University of Wisconsin Press, 1991), 177–205.

34. Brad Lowell Stone, "Robert Nisbet and the Conservative Intellectual Tradition," in *The Dilemmas of American Conservatism*, ed. Kenneth L. Deutch and Ethan Fishman (Lexington: University of Kentucky Press, 2010), 77–96.

35. Robert Thomas, "Robert Nisbet, 82, Sociologist and Conservative Champion," *New York Times*, September 12, 1996, http://www.nytimes.com/1996/09/12/world/robert-nisbet-82-sociologist-and-conservative-champion.html.

36. Stone, "Robert Nisbet and the Conservative Intellectual Tradition," 87–88.

37. Richard M. Weaver, who was briefly discussed in chapter 3, located the beginning of degeneration with the nominalism of the fourteenth-century thinker William of Occam (*Ideas Have Consequences* [Chicago: University of Chicago Press, 1948]).

38. For liberal praise for Viereck, see Burns, "Liberalism and the Conservative Imagination."

39. Louis Hartz, *The Liberal Tradition in America: An Interpretation of American Political Thought Since the Revolution* (New York: Harcourt Brace, 1955); and Gunnar Myrdal, *An American Dilemma: The Negro Problem and American Democracy* (New York: Harper Bros., 1944).

40. Viereck was not the only postwar conservative of the 1950 and 1960s to write favorably of the New Deal, most prominent among whom was the historian Clinton Rossiter.

41. Viereck, "Will America Prove Marx Right?," 336.

42. Peter Viereck, "Liberals and Conservatives, 1789–1951," *Antioch Review*, winter 1951, 387–96.

43. Peter Viereck, *The Unadjusted Man, A New Hero for Americans: Reflections on the Distinctions Between Conforming and Conserving* (New York: Capricorn, 1962), 232–35.

44. William F. Buckley Jr., "Our Mission Statement," *National Review*, November 19, 1955, http://www.nationalreview.com/article/223549/our-mission-statement-william-f-buckley-jr.

45. Peter Viereck, "The Rootless 'Roots': Defects in the New Conservatism," *Antioch Review*, summer 1955, 220.

46. Viereck, *Shame and Glory*, 192.

47. Ibid., 263.

48. Peter Viereck, "But I'm a Conservative!," *Atlantic*, April 1940, http://www.theatlantic.com/magazine/archive/1969/12/but-i-apos-m-a-conservative/4434/.

49. Viereck, *Shame and Glory*, 192.

50. Viereck, *Conservatism Revisited*, 124.

51. Ibid., 125.

52. Viereck, *Conservatism: From John Adams to Churchill* (Princeton, N.J.: Van Nostrand, 1956), 18.

53. Viereck, *The Unadjusted Man*, 232.

54. Viereck, *Shame and Glory*, 275–76, and *The Unadjusted Man*, 232–33.

55. Viereck, *Shame and Glory*, 270.

56. Viereck, *The Unadjusted Man*, 232.

57. Viereck, *Conservatism Revisited*, 133.

58. Ibid., 137.

59. Ibid., 135.

60. Ibid., 137.

61. Ibid., 135.

62. Ibid., 135.

63. Ibid., 126.

64. Viereck, *Conservatism Revisited*, 123. Russell Kirk rejected the Declaration of Independence as utopian.

65. Viereck, *Conservatism Revisited*, 142.

66. Ibid.

67. Viereck, "The Rootless 'Roots,' " 228.

68. Viereck, *Conservatism Revisited*, 32.

69. Viereck, *Shame and Glory*, 134.

70. Ibid., 252.

71. Viereck, *Conservatism Revisited*, 38.

72. Viereck, *Shame and Glory*, 221.

73. Robert Nisbet, *The Quest for Community* (1953; New York: Oxford University Press, 1973) ; and George F. Will, *Statecraft as Soulcraft: What Government Does* (New York: Simon & Schuster, 1983).

74. Frank S. Meyer, "Counterfeit at a Popular Price," *National Review* 2, August 11, 1956, 18.

75. Russell Kirk, *The American Cause* (Chicago: Regnery, 1957), 125.

76. Russell Kirk, "Is Capitalism Still Viable?," *Journal of Business Ethics*, November 1982, 277–80; and Kirk, *The American Cause*, 108.

77. Quoted in David Frum, "The Legacy of Russell Kirk," *New Criterion*, December 1994, https://www.newcriterion.com/articles.cfm/The-legacy-of-Russell-Kirk-5053.

78. Kirk, *Program for Conservatives*, 152.

79. John Attarian, "Russell Kirk's Political Economy," *Modern Age*, winter 1998, 87–97.

80. Kirk, "Is Capitalism Still Viable?," 278.

81. Kirk, *Program for Conservatives*, 147.

82. Ibid.

83. Ibid.

84. Ibid., 148.

85. Kirk, *The Conservative Mind*, 198–99.

86. Kirk, *Program for Conservatives*, 149.

87. Ibid., 152.

88. Ibid., 151.

89. Ibid., 155.

90. Russell Kirk, "American Conservative Action," *Chicago Review*, fall 1955, 65–75.

91. Quoted in Kirk, *Program for Conservatives*, 153.

92. According to the 1960 U.S. Census, 63.1 percent of the population lived in urban areas and 36.9 percent lived in rural areas (U.S. Census Bureau, "Population:

1790 to 1990, United States Urban and Rural," https://www.census.gov/popu
lation/censusdata/table-4.pdf).

93. According to Michael Lind, Kirk died still believing that traditional conservatism had more in common with socialists than with libertarians (*Up from Conservatism: Why the Right Is Wrong for America* [New York: Free Press, 1996], 54).

94. Robert Nisbet, *Prejudices: A Philosophical Dictionary* (Cambridge, Mass.: Harvard University Press,1982), 295–96.

95. Nash, *The Conservative Intellectual Movement in America*, 47.

96. Robert Nisbet, *Social Philosophers: Community and Conflict in Western Thought*
(New York: Crowell, 1973), 213–14; and Robert Nisbet, *Conservatism: Dream and
Reality* (Minneapolis: University of Minnesota Press, 1986), 9–10.

97. Nisbet, *Twilight of Authority*, 196–97; Nisbet, *Prejudices*, 51–53.

98. Nisbet, *The Quest for Community*, 278.

99. Ibid., 237.

100. Ibid.

101. Ibid., 239.

102. Ibid., 240.

103. Ibid., 279 (italics added).

104. Karl Marx and Friedrich Engels, "Manifesto of the Communist Party," in *The
Marx-Engels Reader*, 2nd ed., ed. Robert C. Tucker (1972; New York: Norton,
1978), 469–500; Karl Polanyi, *The Great Transformation* (New York: Farrar and
Rinehart, 1944); Barrington Moore Jr., *Social Origins of Dictatorship and Democ-
racy: Lord and Peasant in the Making of the Modern World* (Boston: Beacon
Press, 1966); and Mark A. Martinez, *The Myth of the Free Market: The Role of the
State in a Capitalist Economy* (Sterling, Va.: Kumarian Press, 2009).

105. Nisbet, *The Quest for Community*, 288 (italics added).

106. Kirk, *Program for Conservatives*, 160.

107. Nisbet, *Twilight of Authority*, 272, 276.

108. Nisbet, *The Quest for Community*, 270.

109. Ibid., 270–71 (italics added).

110. Viereck, *The Unadjusted Man*, 91.

111. John J. Miller, "Veering Off Course," *National Review*, October 25, 2005, http://
www.nationalreview.com/article/215772/veering-course-john-j-miller.

5. THE NEOCONSERVATIVE CRITIQUES OF AND RECONCILIATION WITH CAPITALISM

1. In 1973/1974, the total share of U.S income that went to the top 1 percent of
earners was 8.9 percent, the lowest in the twentieth century. Likewise, in the
mid-1970s, the top 1 percent of wealthiest Americans owned about 24 percent
of the total wealth in the United States, also the lowest percentage in the

twentieth century (Emmanuel Saez and Gabriel Zucman, "Wealth Inequality in the United States Since 1913: Evidence from Capitalized Income Tax Data," working paper 20625, National Bureau of Economic Research, October 2014, https://gabriel-zucman.eu/files/SaezZucman2014.pdf.

2. Quoted in Leo Panitch and Sam Gindin, *The Making of Global Capitalism: The Political Economy of American Empire* (London: Verso, 2013), 143.

3. Quoted in ibid., 143.

4. Kim Phillips-Fein, *Invisible Hands: The Making of the Conservative Movement from the New Deal to Reagan* (New York: Norton, 2009), 163–64.

5. As Lisa McGirr notes, pre–World War II conservatives were "far more flexible in their ideas about the economy" ("Now That Historians Know So Much About the Right, How Should We Best Approach the Study of Conservatism?" *Journal of American History*, December 2011, 769). See also Michael J. Thompson, ed., *Confronting the New Conservatism: The Rise of the Right in America* (New York: New York University Press, 2007); Patrick Allitt, *The Conservatives: Ideas and Personalities Throughout American History* (New Haven, Conn.: Yale University Press, 2009); and Michael Lind, *Up from Conservatism: Why the Right Is Wrong for America* (New York: Free Press, 1996).

6. Irving Kristol, *Two Cheers for Capitalism* (New York; Basic Books, 1978); and Daniel Bell, *The Cultural Contradictions of Capitalism* (1976; New York: Basic Books, 1996). Note that Daniel Bell, unlike other thinkers, never accepted the neoconservative label. In his 1978 foreword to his *Cultural Contradictions of Capitalism*, he maintained that he "is a socialist in economics, a liberal in politics, and a conservative in culture." Nevertheless, he is widely considered to be an original neoconservative thinker.

7. David Hoeveler Jr., *Watch on the Right: Conservative Intellectuals in the Reagan Era* (Madison: University of Wisconsin Press, 1991), 94.

8. James Piereson, "Investing in Conservative Ideas," *Commentary*, May 2005, 51.

9. Irving Kristol, "When Virtue Loses All Her Loveliness—Some Reflections on Capitalism and the 'Free Society,'" in *Two Cheers for Capitalism*, 239–53.

10. For the importance of Irving Kristol to the paradigm shift in American conservatism, see Robert B. Horwitz, *America's Right: Anti-Establishment Conservatism from Goldwater to the Tea Party* (Boston: Polity Press, 2013), 112–56.

11. Francis Fukuyama, *The End of History and the Last Man* (New York: Perennial, 2002).

12. Robert Kagan and William Kristol, *Present Dangers: Crisis and Opportunity in American Foreign and Defense Policy* (San Francisco: Encounter Books, 2000); David Brooks, "A Return to National Greatness: A Manifesto for a Lost Creed," *Weekly Standard*, March 3, 1997, http://www.weeklystandard.com/a-return-to-national-greatness/article/9480; and Corey Robin, "Endgame: Conservatives After the Cold War," *Boston Review*, February 2, 2004, http://www.bostonreview.net/us/corey-robin-endgame.

13. Gary Dorrien, "Benevolent Global Hegemony: William Kristol and the Politics of American Empire," *Logos* 3, no. 2 (2004), http://www.logosjournal.com/dorrien.htm.

14. Robert Kagan and William Kristol, "What to Do About Iraq: For the War on Terror to Succeed, Saddam Hussein Must Be Removed," *Weekly Standard* 8, no. 18 (2002), www.weeklystandard.com/print/Content/Public/Articles/000/000/000/768pylwj.asp.

15. Indicative of the intellectual shift away from Keynesian policies, two laissez-faire enthusiasts, Friedrich Hayek and Milton Friedman, won the Nobel Prize in Economics in 1974 and 1976, respectively (Eric Hobsbawm, *The Age of Extremes: A History of the World, 1913–1991* [New York: Vintage, 1996], 409).

16. Bruce Schulman, *The Seventies: The Great Shift in American Culture, Society, and Politics* (New York: Free Press, 2001); Joseph E. Lowndes, *From the New Deal to the New Right: Race and the Southern Origins of Modern Conservatism* (New Haven, Conn.: Yale University Press, 2008); Jefferson Cowie, *Stayin' Alive: The 1970s and the Last Days of the Working Class* (New York: New Press, 2010); Judith Stein, *Pivotal Decade: How the United States Traded Factories for Finance in the Seventies* (New Haven, Conn.: Yale University Press, 2010); and Maurice Isserman and Michael Kazin, *America Divided: The Civil War of the 1960s* (New York: Oxford University Press, 2012).

17. Walter Goodman, "Irving Kristol: Patron Saint of the New Right," *New York Times Magazine*, December 6, 1981, 90; and Bruce Schulman and Julian E. Zelizer, eds., *Rightward Bound: Making America Conservative in the 1970s* (Cambridge, Mass.: Harvard University Press, 2008), 160–61.

18. For discussion of Reagan's cuts to the welfare state, see Peter Dreier, "Reagan's Legacy: Homelessness in America," *National Housing Institute*, May/June 2004, http://www.nhi.org/online/issues/135/reagan.html; and Jill Quadagno, *The Color of Welfare: How Racism Undermined the War on Poverty* (New York; Oxford University Press, 1994), 162, 178.

19. Barry Gewen, "Irving Kristol, Godfather of Modern Conservatism, Dies at 89," *New York Times*, September 19, 2009, http://www.nytimes.com/2009/09/19/us/politics/19kristol.html.

20. Some of Kristol's neoconservative works on foreign policy referred to later were written with Robert Kagan (1958–), a historian and a professor at Yale University. He is a member of several think tanks, including the Council on Foreign Relations, the Brookings Institution, and the Project for a New American Century. He has advised leaders of both parties on foreign policy, including Democrat Barack Obama and Republican Mitt Romney.

21. The neoconservatives were not the only ones writing critically of capitalism's cultural crisis, nor were they the only ones to point out that its cultural energy had turned against the system itself. For other examples in this genre, see Christopher Lasch, *The Culture of Narcissism: American Life in an*

Age of Diminishing Expectations (New York: Warner, 1979); and Erich Fromm, *The Heart of Man: Its Genius for Good and Evil* (New York: Harper & Row, 1980).

22. Bell, *The Cultural Critique of Capitalism.*

23. Irving Kristol, *Two Cheers for Capitalism,* 128–30.

24. Bell, *The Cultural Critique of Capitalism,* 82.

25. Irving Kristol, *Two Cheers for Capitalism,* 247.

26. Ibid., 60.

27. Bell, *The Cultural Critique of Capitalism,* xx.

28. Bell, *The Cultural Critique of Capitalism,* 21, 293; and Irving Kristol, *Two Cheers for Capitalism,* 82.

29. Bell, *The Cultural Critique of Capitalism,* 293.

30. Hoeveler, *Watch on the Right,* 95. For the role of advertising in creating a consumer culture, see Stuart Ewen, *Captains of Consciousness: Advertising and the Social Roots of the Consumer Culture* (1976; New York: Basic Books, 2001).

31. Irving Kristol, *Two Cheers for Capitalism,* 82.

32. Bell, *The Cultural Critique of Capitalism,* 338.

33. Irving Kristol, *Two Cheers for Capitalism,* 82.

34. Kristol, "When Virtue Loses All of Her Loveliness," *Two Cheers for Capitalism,* 246.

35. Irving Kristol, *Neo-Conservatism: The Autobiography of an Idea* (New York: Free Press, 1995), 103.

36. Ibid., 128.

37. Hoeveler, *Watch on the Right,* 104.

38. Irving Kristol, "Pornography, Obscenity, and the Case for Censorship," in *The Neocon Reader,* ed. Irwin Stelzer (New York: Grove Press, 2004), 169–80.

39. Kristol, *Two Cheers for Capitalism,* 83.

40. Ibid., 3–22.

41. Jude Wanniski, *The Way the World Works: How Economies Fall—and Succeed* (New York: Basic Books, 1978).

42. Reagan's 1981 tax cut slashed the top marginal tax bracket from 70 to 50 percent. Although he was forced to increase taxes several times during his eight years in office, by the time he left the top marginal tax rate had plummeted from 70 to 33 percent ("Federal Individual Income Tax Rates History, 1913–2013," http://taxfoundation.org/sites/default/files/docs/fed_individual_rate_history_nominal.pdf).

43. Hoeveler, *Watch on the Right,* 101.

44. Frank S. Meyer attempted to resolve the tension in conservatism between laissez-faire capitalism and a morally conservative traditional society in what he called "conservative fusion" (*The Conservative Mainstream* [New Rochelle, N.Y.: Arlington House, 1969]). Fusion became the conservatism of William F. Buckley Jr. and the *National Review,* but traditionalists like Russell Kirk were never persuaded by "fusionism" and remained skeptical of the compatibility

of laissez-faire capitalism and a traditional society (Lind, *Up from Conservatism*, 54).

45. U.S. Department of Labor, Office of Policy Planning and Research, *The Negro Family: The Case for National Action* (Washington, D.C.: U.S. Department of Labor, 1965), https://www.dol.gov/oasam/programs/history/webid-meynihan.htm.

46. Throughout the 1970s and 1980s, the neoconservative magazine the *Public Interest* was full of such criticisms of the welfare state.

47. Irving Kristol, "The Death of the Socialist Idea," *Saturday Evening Post*, March 1979, 56.

48. Irving Kristol, "A Conservative Welfare State," in Stelzer, ed., *The Neocon Reader*, 145.

49. Irving Kristol, "The Two Welfare States," *Wall Street Journal*, October 19, 2000, A29.

50. Ibid., A29.

51. Hobsbawm, *The Age of Extremes*; and Roy Rosenzweig, Nelson Lichtenstein, Joshua Brown, and David Jaffee, *Who Built America? Working People and the Nation's History, 1877–Present* (New York: Bedford / St. Martin's, 2008).

52. For a discussion of racial and gender discrimination in New Deal programs, see Ira Katznelson, *When Affirmative Action Was White: An Untold History of Racial Inequality in Twentieth-Century America* (New York: Norton, 2005); and Suzanne Mettler, *Dividing Citizens: Gender and Federalism in New Deal Public Policy* (Ithaca, N.Y.: Cornell University Press, 1998). For a discussion of the U.S. economy in the postwar era and particularly the roots of the economic crisis in the early to mid-1970s, see Richard B. DuBoff, *Accumulation and Power: An Economic History of the United States* (Armonk, N.Y.: Sharpe, 1989), 125–28; Paul M. Sweezy, "The Crisis of American Capitalism," *Monthly Review* 32, no. 5 (1980): https://archive.monthlyreview.org/index.php/mr/article/view/MR-032-05-1980-09_1; and Panitch and Gindin, *The Making of Global Capitalism*.

53. DuBoff, *Accumulation and Power*, 113–39; Sweezy, "The Crisis of American Capitalism"; and Fred Magdoff and John Bellamy Foster, "Stagnation and Financialization: The Nature of the Contradiction," *Monthly Review* 66, no. 1 (2014), http://monthlyreview.org/2014/05/01/stagnation-and-financialization/.

54. Martin Luther King Jr., *Where Do We Go from Here: Chaos or Community?* (1967; Boston: Beacon Press, 2010), 5–6.

55. For how African Americans were deliberately excluded and marginalized from New Deal social programs, see Ira Katznelson, *When Affirmative Action Was White: An Untold History of Racial Inequality in Twentieth-Century America* (New York: Norton, 2005); Quadagno, *The Color of Welfare*; and Frances Fox-Piven and Richard Cloward, *Poor People's Movements: Why They Succeed and How They Fail* (New York: Vintage, 1978).

56. Cowie, *Stayin' Alive*.

57. Pete Hamill, "Wallace," in *Takin' It to the Streets*, ed. Alexander Bloom and Wini Breines (New York: Oxford University Press, 1995), 348–51; and Michael Novak, "Why Wallace?," in *Takin' It to the Streets*, 352–54.

58. Martin Gilens, "How the Poor Became Black: The Racialization of American Poverty in the Mass Media," in *Race and the Politics of Welfare Reform*, ed. Sanford F. Schram et al. (Ann Arbor: University of Michigan Press, 2003), 101–30.

59. *Washington Star*, " 'Welfare Queen' Becomes Issue in Reagan Campaign," *New York Times*, February 15, 1976, 51.

60. Irving Kristol, "A Conservative Welfare State," *Neocon Reader*, 145.

61. Quoted in Herb Kutchins, "Neither Alms nor a Friend: The Tragedy of Compassionate Conservatism," *Social Justice*, spring 2001, 14.

62. George W. Bush, "Remarks on Compassionate Conservatism in San Jose, California," *Weekly Compilation of Presidential Documents*, April 30, 2002, 717.

63. While the idea that social welfare ought to be the function of civil society rather than the state has a very long history in the conservative tradition, its influence among contemporary conservative political leaders such as Bush, Gingrich, John Ashcroft, and many others can be attributed to Marvin Olasky. Olasky served as an adviser to Bush, and Bush wrote the foreword and appendix to Olasky's *Compassionate Conservatism*, calling Olasky "compassionate conservatism's leading thinker." For a short biography of Marvin Olasky, see www.nndb.com. Olasky coined the term *compassionate conservatism* and wrote numerous books and articles on the subject. Among the most important for conservatives is *The Tragedy of American Compassion*, a historical study of welfare in America in which Olasky claims that the poor were better taken care of before the development of the welfare state in the twentieth century when social welfare was largely the responsibility of families, churches, and voluntary associations (*The Tragedy of American Compassion* [Lanham, Md.: Regnery Gateway, 1992]). See also Marvin Olasky, *Compassionate Conservatism: What It Is, What It Does, and How It Can Transform America* (New York: Free Press, 2000). Despite the questionable historical accuracy of Olasky's study, his depiction of private welfare provision from the colonial era to the nineteenth century serves as the model for conservatives' alternative to the liberal welfare state.

64. Bush, "Remarks on Compassionate Conservatism," 718.

65. Stephen Goldsmith, "What Compassionate Conservatism Is—and Is Not," *Hoover Digest*, April 30, 2000, http://www.hoover.org/research/what-compassionate-conservatism-and-not.

66. Ibid.

67. Compassionate conservatism, or the conservative welfare state, has two interlinked conservative goals. First, it is indeed Big Government conservatism, as both advocates and detractors suggest. But conservatives have succeeded in changing the welfare state to deliver the benefits and services that the American people have come to expect, but not directly from the government. This transformation of the welfare state has had a number of effects. It

has obscured the role of the government in providing essential services and benefits that deliver a decent standard of living. As Suzanne Mettler has written, whereas formerly the government's provision of services and benefits was "visible" through clearly defined government program such as the GI Bill and Social Security, over the last thirty years the state has retreated from universalistic government programs and instead has opted to provide social welfare such as housing, education, and health care through the use of tax credits and the private market. As her research indicates, most people who receive benefits through what Mettler calls a *submerged state*, do not realize that they have been recipients of government aid at all ("20,000 Leagues Under the State," *Washington Monthly* 43, no. 7 [2011]: 29–34). Hence, many Americans mistakenly believe that their taxes are going to pay for the benefits of undeserving "moochers" and that hard-working taxpayers get little from the government. This perception in turn feeds into the neoconservatives' critique of the "unintended consequences" of the liberal welfare state and justifies their reasoning that the government does not have the capability to solve collective social problems.

The second goal of the conservative welfare state is that by shifting the provision of welfare state services and benefits to the private market, the power of corporate elites is restored. The devolution of social provision from the federal government to state and local governments and to market actors like charter schools and HMOs expands the sphere of private domination and control over recipients of social welfare. Constrained by budgetary pressures, which are a product of conservatives' tax cutting, state and local governments might curtail eligibility and impose burdensome requirements on benefit recipients. A good example of this is the transformation of Aid to Families with Dependent Children (AFDC) into Temporary Assistance to Needy Families (TANF). As Juliet F. Gainsborough explained in regard to TANF, a number of states have given control and spending to county and regional governments and governing boards. These entities have exercised broad discretion over a number of decisions, including work requirements, sanctions, and time limits, which have the effect of controlling and disciplining labor in accordance with the needs of local social and economic elites. Indeed, in most of the states that have handed over control of TANF to county and local officials, at least half the governing boards are composed of members of the local business community ("To Devolve or Not to Devolve? Welfare Reform in the States," *Policy Studies Journal* 31, no. 4 [2003]: 603–23). For data on the drop in the number of families on assistance since TANF and the absence of impact on the decline in poverty rates, see Greg Kaufmann, "This Week in Poverty: Revealing the Real TANF," *Nation Blog*, February 8, 2013, www.thenation.com/blog/172767/week-poverty-revealing-real-tanf#. The conservative reorientation of the welfare state, however, served only to perpetuate poverty and increase the economic insecurity of the most vulnerable populations. This placed them at the mercy of local political and economic elites to exploit their labor and to use their economic hardship as a weapon against the working and middle classes, who themselves have suffered decades of increasing unemployment, stagnant wages, falling employer-provided benefits, speedups and production increases, and precarious employment security (Mike Davis, *City of Quartz: Excavating the Future in Los Angeles* [New York: Vintage,1992]; and John R. Logan and Harvey L. Molotch, *Urban Fortunes: The Political Economy of Place* [Berkeley: University of California Press, 1987]).

68. Compassionate conservatism has its critics, even among those considered solidly in the conservative camp, including former supporters such as Marvin Olasky, John DiIulio, and David Kuo. In a 2007 article Olasky expressed his frustration with how compassionate conservatism had been "distorted," regarded as a "political gambit" or "rhetorical device," and used for political expediency ("The Test of Time," *Texas Monthly*, March 2007). DiIulio and Kuo, both of whom worked in the Bush administration to make the faith-based component of compassionate conservatism a pillar of federal social welfare policy, were ultimately disappointed. Despite Bush's rhetoric to "harness the armies of compassion," DiIulio and Kuo believe that Bush was more interested in prosecuting the wars in Afghanistan and Iraq and enacting tax cuts than in pressing Congress to come up with innovative ways to create and fund partnerships between the federal government and faith-based agencies (John DiIulio Jr., *Godly Republic: A Centrist Blueprint for America's Faith-Based Future* [Berkeley: University of California Press, 2007]; and David Kuo, *Tempting Faith: An Inside Story of Political Seduction* [New York: Free Press, 2007]).

69. Irving Kristol, "A New Look at Capitalism," *National Review*, April 17, 1981, 414–15.

70. Tod Lindberg, "Neoconservatism's Liberal Legacy," in *Varieties of Conservatism in America*, ed. Peter Berkowitz (Stanford, Calif.: Hoover Institution Press, 2004), 145.

71. Brooks, "A Return to National Greatness."

72. Francis Fukuyama, "Francis Fukuyama Says Tuesday's Attack Marks the End of 'American Exceptionalism,' " *Financial Times*, September, 15, 2001, 1.

73. David Brooks, "Facing Up to Our Fears," *Newsweek*, October, 22, 2001, http://web.a.ebscohost.com.bcc.ezproxy.cuny.edu:2048/ehost/detail/detail?vid=14&sid=8f7b517a-99e8-4334-a56d-3da6be07fa5d%40sessionmgr4008&hid=4104&bdata=JnNpdGU9ZWhvc3QtbGl2ZQ%3d%3d#AN=5343966&db=a9h.

74. Irving Kristol, *Reflections of a Neoconservative: Looking Back, Looking Ahead* (New York: Basic Books, 1983), 29.

75. Robin, "Endgame."

76. William Kristol and Robert Kagan, "Toward a Neo-Reaganite Foreign Policy," *Foreign Affairs*, July/August 1996, 27.

77. Not all neoconservatives were as melancholy about the prospect of peace at the end of the Cold War. As Daniel Patrick Moynihan wrote about some of his

neoconservative colleagues, "they wished for a military posture approaching mobilization; they would create or invent whatever crises were required to bring this about" (*Pandaemonium: Ethnicity in International Politics* [New York: Oxford University Press, 1993], 36).

78. Irving Kristol, "A Post-Wilsonian Foreign Policy," *AEI Online*, August 2, 1996.

79. Robin, "Endgame."

80. The rhetoric of George W. Bush and, more recently, the campaign rhetoric of Republican president-elect Donald Trump have taken the rhetoric of fear to new dangerous lows.

81. Kagan and Kristol, "What to Do About Iraq."

82. Hart Seely, "The Poetry of D. H. Rumsfeld," *Slate*, April 2, 2003, http://www.slate.com/articles/news_and_politics/low_concept/2003/04/the_poetry_of_dh_rumsfeld.html.

83. Kristol and Kagan, "Toward a Neo-Reaganite Foreign Policy," 31.

84. Tod Lindberg, "Valor and Victimhood After September 11," in *The Weekly Standard: A Reader: 1995–2005*, ed. William Kristol (New York: HarperCollins, 2005), 258.

85. It is rather ironic that neoconservatives were almost united in their opposition to Donald Trump's presidential candidacy, for his determination to abolish established U.S. foreign policy norms and treaties, especially with regard to international trade, NATO, and America's allies in the Middle East (William Kristol, NR Symposium, "Conservatives Against Trump," *National Review*, January 21, 2016, http://www.nationalreview.com/article/430126/donald-trump-conservatives-oppose-nomination).

86. Barack Obama, "Nobel Peace Prize Speech," *New York Times*, December 10, 2009, http://www.nytimes.com/2009/12/11/world/europe/11prexy.text.html.

87. There have been moments when President Obama has repudiated, at least rhetorically, the narrative of American exceptionalism. For example,

> I believe in American exceptionalism, just as I suspect that the Brits believe in British exceptionalism and the Greeks believe in Greek exceptionalism. I'm enormously proud of my country and its role and history in the world. . . . Now, the fact that I am very proud of my country and I think that we've got a whole lot to offer the world does not lessen my interest in recognizing the value and wonderful qualities of other countries, or recognizing that we're not always going to be right, or that other people may have good ideas, or that in order for us to work collectively, all parties have to compromise and that includes us. . . . And so I see no contradiction between believing that America has a continued extraordinary role in leading the world towards peace and prosperity and recognizing that that leadership is incumbent, depends on, our ability to create partnerships because we create partnerships because we can't solve these problems alone ("News Conference by President

Obama," White House: Office of the Press Secretary [Strasbourg, France, April 4, 2009], www.whitehouse.gov/the-press-office/news-conference-president-obama-4042009).

88. Steven Rosenfeld, "U.S. Economy Increasingly Dominated by Monopolies as 2015 Corporate Mergers Continue," *AlterNet*, November 17, 2015, http://www.alternet.org/economy/us-economy-increasingly-dominated-monopolies-2015-corporate-mergers-continue.

89. "Little Change in Public's Response to 'Capitalism,' 'Socialism,'" Pew Research Center for the People and the Press, December 28, 2011, http://pewresearch.org/pubs/2159/socialism-capitalism-occupy-wall-street-libertarian-liberal-conservative; and Peter Dreier, "Is Capitalism on Trial?," *Dissent*, January 27, 2012.

6. THE PALEOCONSERVATIVE CRITIQUE OF GLOBAL CAPITALISM

1. Sara Diamond, *Roads to Dominion: Right-Wing Movements and Political Power in the United States* (New York: Guilford, 1995).

2. Samuel T. Francis, *Beautiful Losers: Essays on the Failure of American Conservatism* (Columbia: University of Missouri Press, 1993); and Justin Raimondo, *Reclaiming the American Right* (1993; Wilmington, Del.: ISI Books, 2008).

3. Clyde N. Wilson, "Citizens or Subjects?," in *The New Right Papers*, ed. Robert W. Whitaker (New York: St. Martin's Press, 1982), 127.

4. Many paleoconservatives exhibit nativism, anti-Semitism, and racism that go beyond maintaining cultural identity. In fact, a strong current in paleoconservative thinking ties American identity explicitly to the white race. Writing in this vein, Francis suggested that there is no reason to believe that American civilization "can be successfully transmitted to a different people" (Leonard Zeskind, *Blood and Politics: The History of the White Nationalist Movement from the Margins to the Mainstream* (New York: Farrar, Straus and Giroux, 2009), 368–69). Paleoconservatives' advocacy for strict immigration laws, support for the mass deportation of illegal immigrants, and, for some like Samuel Francis, opposition to miscegenation points to a belief in biological racism. Francis's ideas have been extremely controversial, even in conservative circles. He called for the United States to withdraw from the United Nations, the World Trade Organization, the International Monetary Fund, and NAFTA, and he insisted that U.S. officials and public leaders "must reflect Christian beliefs and values." Francis also saw miscegenation and affirmative action as efforts to "destroy and denigrate the European-American heritage" ("Council of Conservative Citizens: Statement of Principles," Council of Conservative Citizens [2005], http://conservative-headlines.com/introduction/statement-of-principles/). In 1995 Francis was fired from the *Washington Times* after giving a racially charged speech at the American Renaissance conference, where he

stated, "We as whites under assault need to . . . reassert our identity and our solidarity and we need to do so in explicitly racial terms, through the articulation of a racial consciousness as whites. . . . The civilization that we as whites created in Europe and America could not have developed apart from the genetic endowments of the creating people" (quoted in Chip Berlet and Matthew N. Lyons, *Right-Wing Populism in America: Too Close for Comfort* [New York: Guilford, 2000], 284). Francis also edited and contributed to several collections on conservative thought, including Francis, *Beautiful Losers* (1994); Samuel T. Francis and Jerry Woodruff, *Revolution from the Middle* (Raleigh, NC: Middle American Press, 1997); Peter B. Gemma, ed., *Shots Fired: Sam Francis on America's Culture War* (Vienna, Va.: FGF Books, 2006); Samuel T. Francis, ed., *Race and the American Prospect: Essays on the Racial Realities of Our Nation and Our Time* (Atlanta: Occidental Press, 2006); and Samuel T. Francis, *Essential Writings on Race* (Oakton, Va.: New Century Foundation, 2007). Francis's essays have appeared in numerous readers on conservative thought in America, and he wrote two books on the thought of James Burnham, whose theory of the managerial revolution is a central theme of his right-wing populism: Samuel T. Francis, *Power and History: The Political Thought of James Burnham* (Lanham, Md.: University Press of America, 1984); and Samuel T. Francis, *James Burnham: Thinkers of Our Time* (New York: Claridge, 1999).

5. Patrick Buchanan, "1992 Republican National Convention Speech," *Patrick Buchanan Blog*, August 17, 1992, http://buchanan.org/blog/1992-republican-national-convention-speech-148.

6. There are many examples of Trump suggesting that individuals or groups are intent on undermining the United States. A glaring example of this is Trump stating that President Obama and Hillary Clinton were the "founder and cofounder" of the Islamic State of Syria (ISIS), a fundamentalist Muslim terrorist organization (Nick Corasaniti, "Donald Trump Calls Obama 'Founder of ISIS' and Says It Honors Him," *New York Times*, August 10, 2016, http://www.nytimes.com/2016/08/11/us/politics/trump-rally.html). In another speech, Trump characterized Mexican immigrants as "rapists" and "killers," a comment obviously implying that immigrants are coming to the United States to endanger public safety (Carolina Moreno, "9 Outrageous Things Donald Trump Has Said About Latinos," *Huffington Post*, August 31, 2015, http://www.huffingtonpost.com/entry/9-outrageous-things-donald-trump-has-said-about-latinos_us_55e483a1e4b0c818f618904b).

7. Patrick Buchanan, "At Last, America First," *Patrick Buchanan Blog*, April 28, 2016, http://buchanan.org/blog/last-america-first-125165?doing_wp_cron=1474 158305.5969491004943847656250.

8. Raimondo, *Reclaiming the American Right*, 294.

9. Patrick Buchanan, "What Trump Has Wrought," *American Conservative*, April 5, 2016, http://www.theamericanconservative.com/buchanan/what-trump-has-wrought/.

10. Francis, *Beautiful Losers*.
11. Joseph Scotchie, *The Paleoconservatives: New Voices of the Old Right* (New Brunswick, N.J.: Transaction, 1999), 1.
12. According to Paul Gottfried and Thomas Fleming's 1993 account of the rise of the New Right, Richard A. Viguerie, a founding member, dated the formation of the New Right movement to August 1974 and President Gerald Ford's nomination of the liberal Republican Nelson Rockefeller as vice president (*The Conservative Movement* [New York: Twayne, 1993]). At its inception, the New Right's most prominent members were Paul Weyrich, Howard Phillips, Terry Dolan, and Richard A. Viguerie. See also Buchanan's autobiography: *Right from the Beginning* (Boston: Little, Brown, 1988).
13. George W. Carey, introduction to Justin Raimondo, *Reclaiming the American Right*, 2nd ed. (Intercollegiate Studies Institute, 2008), xii.
14. Francis, *Beautiful Losers*, 231.
15. Samuel Francis, "Message from MARs: The Social Politics of the New Right," in *Conservatism in America: Since 1930*, ed. Gregory L. Schneider (New York: New York University Press, 2003), 300–317.
16. According to Joseph Scotchie, the label *paleoconservative* originated in the 1980s as a rejoinder to neoconservatism (*The Paleoconservatives*, 1).
17. Patrick J. Buchanan, *The Great Betrayal: How American Sovereignty and Social Justice Are Being Sacrificed to the Gods of the Global Economy* (Boston: Little, Brown, 1998), 288.
18. Edward Ashbee, "Politics of Paleoconservatism," *Society*, March/April 2000, 75–84.
19. Ibid.
20. See George F. Gilder, *Wealth and Poverty* (New York: Basic Books, 1981); Michael Novak, *Toward a Theology of the Corporation* (Washington, D.C.: American Enterprise Institute, 1981); Michael Novak, *The Spirit of Democratic Capitalism* (Washington, D.C.: American Enterprise Institute, 1982); David Chilton, *Productive Christians in an Age of Guilt-Manipulators* (Tyler, Tex.: Institute for Christian Economics, 1981); and Roland Nash, *Poverty and Wealth: The Christian Debate Over Capitalism* (Westchester, Ill.: Crossway Books, 1986).
21. Patrick Buchanan, "Equality: American Idol," *Human Events*, July 4, 2013, http://www.humanevents.com/2013/07/04/equality-american-idol/; and Patrick Buchanan, "Inequality—Crisis or Scam?," *Human Events*, December 31, 2013, http://www.humanevents.com/2013/12/31/inequality-crisis-or-scam/.
22. Samuel T. Francis, "Message from MARs," 308.
23. Scotchie, *The Paleoconservatives*, 194–98; and Francis, "Message from MARs."
24. Quoted in Leonard Zeskind, *Blood and Politics*, 283.
25. Joseph Scotchie, *The Paleoconservatives*, 193; and Francis, "Message from MARs."
26. James Burnham, *The Managerial Revolution* (Bloomington: Indiana University Press, 1960). For a critique of the elite from ideological perspectives different from those of Burnham and Francis, see C. Wright Mills, *The Power Elite* (1956;

New York: Oxford University Press, 2000); and Christopher Lasch, *The Revolt of the Elites and the Betrayal of Democracy* (New York: Norton, 1995).

27. Francis, *Beautiful Losers*, 98.
28. Francis, *Beautiful Losers*, 219. Francis's view that Big Business has been an agent or, at the very least, an accomplice to progressive public policy is suspect (Kim Phillips-Fein, *Invisible Hands: The Making of the Conservative Movement from the New Deal to Reagan* [New York: Norton, 2009]).
29. Samuel T. Francis, "Capitalism, the Enemy," *Chronicles*, July 3, 2000, http://www.chroniclesmagazine.org/2000/August/24/8/magazine/article/10828498/.
30. Francis, *Beautiful Losers*, 104.
31. Francis, "Francis on Free Trade," *VDare*, January 3, 2002, http://www.vdare.com/francis/free_trade.htm.
32. In an article entitled "Why Immigrants Kill," Francis used several high-profile acts of violence perpetrated by immigrants, including a multiple homicide in Wisconsin by a Hmong immigrant, to suggest that immigrants "lacking roots in the society and civilization" (that is, non-European immigrants) "feel little obligation to it" and therefore are more prone to violence than are people born in the United States ("Why Immigrants Kill," *VDare*, November 29, 2004, http://www.vdare.com/francis/041129_kill.htm).
33. Francis, "Nationalism, Old and New," in *The Paleoconservatives*, 191–92.
34. Whereas paleoconservatives see the weakening of American sovereignty and strength as the product of increasing domestic multiculturalism, Theodore Roosevelt regarded the internal sources of America's decline as the product of class conflict.
35. Buchanan, *The Great Betrayal*, 93, 288; and Francis, *Beautiful Losers*, 203.
36. Patrick J. Buchanan, "Death of Manufacturing," *American Conservative*, April 11, 2003, http://www.amconmag.com/article/2003/aug/11/00007/.
37. Buchanan, *The Great Betrayal*, 174–76.
38. Ibid., 93–94.
39. Ibid., 93.
40. Ford did so not out of generosity or commitment to his workers, or so that his employees could afford to buy the automobiles that they built. Instead, the five-dollar wage was a measure meant to discipline his workers and stem the high employee turnover at Ford's plants, which disrupted production and threatened profits (Tim Worstall, "The Story of Henry Ford's $5 a Day Wages: It's Not What You Think," *Forbes*, March 4, 2012, http://www.forbes.com/sites/timworstall/2012/03/04/the-story-of-henry-fords-5-a-day-wages-its-not-what-you-think/#ec6a51c1c96d).
41. Buchanan's narrative ignores American corporations' demands for an expanded global market, which paralleled Theodore Roosevelt's and other warrior-aristocrats' imperial vision, as discussed in chapter 2. Buchanan also overlooks the fact that by the early 1900s, many of the largest firms were not directed by their owners but by well-paid corporate managers. An infamous

example is Andrew Carnegie's absence (albeit support of) during Henry C. Frick's brutal suppression of striking steelworkers at the Homestead plant in Pennsylvania in 1892.

42. Buchanan, *The Great Betrayal*, 55.

43. Ibid., 97.

44. Patrick J. Buchanan, *The Death of the West: How Dying Populations and Immigrant Invasions Imperil Our Country and Civilization* (New York: St. Martin's Griffin, 2002), 229.

45. Francis, *Beautiful Losers*, 208–21.

46. Buchanan, *The Great Betrayal*, 287.

47. Ibid.

48. Buchanan view of United States' economic history is found in *The Great Betrayal* and *The Death of the West.*

49. Buchanan, "Death of Manufacturing," http://www.theamericanconservative.com/articles/death-of-manufacturing/.

50. Ibid.

51. Samuel T. Francis, "Outsourcing—The Economic Equivalent of Ethnic Cleansing," June 10, 2004, www.vdare.com.

52. Lori Wallach, "NAFTA at 20: One Million U.S. Jobs Lost, Higher Income Inequality," *World Post*, January 6, 2014, www.huffingtonpost.com/lori/wallach/nafta-at-20-one-million-u-b_4550207.html.

53. Nancy Isenberg, *White Trash: The 400-Year Untold History of Class in America* (New York: Viking, 2016).

54. Dave Gilson, "Overworked America: 12 Charts That Will Make Your Blood Boil," *Mother Jones*, July/August 2011, www.motherjones.com/politics/2011/06/speedup-americans-working-harder-charts. See also the charts and graphs in the Economic Policy Institute, *The State of Working America*, January 9, 2013, stateofworkingamerica.org.

55. Patrick Buchanan, "Speech on Free Trade," Council on Foreign Relations, November 18, 1998, http://www.chuckbaldwinlive.com/read.freetrade.html.

56. Quoted in Raimondo, *Reclaiming the American Right*, 297.

57. Buchanan, *The Great Betrayal*, 288.

58. Francis, "Message from MARs," 310.

59. Ibid., 311.

60. Buchanan, *The Great Betrayal*, 289.

61. Francis, "Message from MARs," 310.

62. Ibid., 315.

63. Francis, "Message from MARs," 310. Kevin Phillips, one of the founders of the New Right, admitted that the regulation of Wall Street might not be such a bad idea ("Why I Am No Longer a Conservative," *American Conservative*, October 7, 2002, http://www.theamericanconservative.com/articles/why-i-am-no-longer-a-conservative/. Buchanan supports unionized workers as long as their demands are limited to keeping manufacturing jobs in the United States. But

he steadfastly opposes unionized labor advocating for wages and benefits, workplace conditions, or, more broadly, greater economic equality. In particular, conservatives—and Buchanan is no exception—are hostile to public-sector unions ("Why Scott Walker Must Win," *Patrick Buchanan Blog*, March 1, 2011, Buchanan.org/blog/why-scott-walker-must-win-4613). See also Harold Meyerson, "St. Pat's Day," *Metro*, March 21, 1996, http://www.metroarchive.com/papers/metro/03.21.96/buchanan-9612.html; and Patrick Buchanan, "The Toyota Republicans," *Human Events*, December 16, 2008, http://www.freere public.com/focus/news/2149673/posts.

64. Francis, "Message from MARs," 310.

65. Berlet and Lyons, *Right-Wing Populism in America*, 280.

66. Quoted in Berlet and Lyons, *Right-Wing Populism in America*, 280.

67. Patrick Buchanan, "End of the Line for the Welfare State?," *Human Events*, February 11, 2014, http://www.humanevents.com/2014/02/11/end-of-the-line-for-the-welfare-state/; and Patrick Buchanan, "Inequality—Crisis or Scam?," *Human Events*, December 31, 2013, http://humanevents.com/2013/12/31/inequality-crisis-or-scam/.

68. Patrick Buchanan, "How Free Trade Is Killing Middle America," *American Conservative*, January 24, 2014, http://www.the americanconservative.com/free-trade-middle-america/.

69. While many leftists also oppose free-trade agreements like NAFTA, the Left's opposition differs from that of the paleoconservatives on a number of points. The Left does not oppose free trade on principle. Its opposition to free-trade agreements is not rooted in racism, nativism, or a belief in American cultural supremacy but in the belief that free-trade pacts as currently negotiated are detrimental to workers (wherever they live and work) and their communities, the environment, and democracy.

70. John B. Judis, "Right-Wing Populism Could Hobble America for Decades: The Tea Party Is Going Down, Dysfunction Is Not," *New Republic*, October 27, 2013, https://newrepublic.com/article/115332/tea-party-going-down-dysfunction-not; and Robert B. Horwitz, *America's Right: Anti-Establishment Conservatism from Goldwater to the Tea Party* (New York: Polity, 2013), http://www.newrepub lic.com/article/115332/tea-party-going-down-dysfunction-not.

71. Patrick Buchanan, "The Tea Party: America's Last Best Hope," *Free Republic*, December 24, 2009, http://www.freerepublic.com/focus/f-news/2415155/posts. For Buchanan's view that the Tea Party represents what he calls white "ethnonationalism," see Patrick Buchanan, "The Tea Party Tribe," *American Conservative*, April 19, 2010, http://www.amconmag.com/blog/2010/04/19/the-tea-party-tribe/.

72. For a thorough historical analysis of the Republican Party's rightward shift, see Geoffrey Kabaservice, *Rule and Ruin: The Downfall of Moderation and the Destruction of the Republican Party* (New York: Oxford University Press, 2012).

73. Sean Wilentz, "Confounding Fathers: The Tea Party's Cold War Roots," *New Yorker*, October 18, 2010, www.newyorker.com/reporting/2010/10/18/101018fa_fact_wilentz; and Matthew Continetti, "The Two Faces of the Tea Party: Rick Santelli, Glenn Beck, and the Future of the Populist Insurgency," *Weekly Standard*, June 28, 2010, http://www.weeklystandard.com/articles/two-faces-tea-party.

74. Paul Ryan, "Down with Big Business," *Forbes Magazine*, December 11, 2009, http://www.forbes.com/2009/12/11/business-government-politics-reform-opinions-contributors-paul-ryan.html.

75. As Skocpol and Williamson have shown, the rank-and-file Tea Party members' views are much closer to the paleoconservatives' economic and welfare-state views than they are to those of the Tea Party's leading lights, including Ron Paul, Rand Paul, and Paul Ryan, whose views tend to be much more economic libertarian. While rank-and-file Tea Party members certainly want to deregulate business (but not Wall Street), drastically lower taxes, and fundamentally curtail the welfare state (especially those whom they consider to be "undeserving"), they do not want to eliminate it entirely. Neither the rank and file nor the paleoconservatives are committed to free-market principles. Instead, they differentiate among welfare-state programs that benefit the "deserving," or those who have worked and earned their benefits. Thus the rank and file would like to see programs like Social Security, Medicare, and veterans' benefits preserved. In contrast, they want to eliminate those welfare-state measures that Tea Party members view as primarily benefiting the "undeserving," or those whom they perceive as "freeloaders" who have not earned them. The Tea Party associates Temporary Assistance for Needy Families (TANF), food stamps, and a whole host of other income-support measures with the excesses of the liberal welfare state, and so it is viscerally opposed to them (Theda Skocpol and Vanessa Williamson, *The Tea Party and the Remaking of American Conservatism* [New York: Oxford University Press, 2012], 68–72).

76. David Holthouse, "Dangerous Levels of Overlap Between Xenophobic 'Minutemen' Movement and Tea Party," May 29, 2011, Alternet, www.alternet.org/story/151070/dangerous_levels_of_overlap_between_xenophobic_'minutemen'_movement_and_tea_party; and David Holthouse, "Minutemen Welcome Tea Partiers to the Border," August 15, 2010, teaparty.org, www.teaparty.org/minutemen-welcome-tea-partiers-to-the-border-380/.

77. Skocpol and Williamson, *The Tea Party*, 68–72; and Christopher Parker et al., "2010 Multi-State Survey of Race and Politics," University of Washington Institute for the Study of Ethnicity, Race, and Sexuality, May 5, 2011, http://depts.washington.edu/uwiser/racepolitics.html.

78. On September 16, 2016, Trump publicly admitted that Obama was born in the United States.

79. The decline in wages, income, and savings and the greater prevalence of economic hardship and insecurity for the working classes of all races have

several causes, none of which has to do with President Obama's race. The decimation of labor unions; the changes in the tax code for the benefit of corporations and the wealthy; and the deregulation of finance and business, not to mention the curtailment of the welfare state, all have contributed to the increased economic inequality between the top 1 percent of wealthy Americans and everyone else and has led to the political and economic disempowerment of the American working and middle classes. The myriad policies that the paleoconservatives have adopted, whether opposition to raising the minimum wage; opposition to regulating business; an antilabor position, including opposition to the Family Leave Act; support for Ronald Reagan's firing of striking air-traffic controllers; and opposition to the Strikers' Replacement Bill—just to name a few examples—as well as support for tax cuts for the wealthy and corporations, have themselves done much to create the economic insecurities that plague the white working class that the paleoconservatives claim to represent. Indeed, to obscure that fact, paleoconservatives have erected a ready-made scapegoat: the undocumented immigrant.

80. Patrick Buchanan, "Trump, Middle America's Messenger," *American Conservative*, February 23, 2016, http://www.theamericanconservative.com/buchanan/trump-middle-americas-messenger/.

81. Marc Fisher and Michael Kranish, "The Trump We Saw: Populist, Frustrating, Naïve, Wise, Forever on the Make," *Washington Post*, August 12, 2016, https://www.washingtonpost.com/politics/the-trump-we-saw-populist-frustrating-naive-wise-forever-on-the-make/2016/08/11/35efe458–58ee-11e6–9aee-807599 3d73a2_story.html.

82. Throughout his presidential campaign, Trump did not court any constituencies other than wealthy donors and the white working and middle classes. Instead, he insulted women, Latinos, refugees, blacks, and the disabled; he alluded to and accepted violence at his rallies; and he gave his approval to his supporters' xenophobia and racism (James E. Freeman and Peter Kolozi, "Trumpism Is Conservatism: The New Conservative Mainstream," *Logos* 15, no. 1 (2016): http://logosjournal.com/2016/freeman_kolozi/).

83. Donald Trump, "Transcript: Donald Trump's Foreign Policy Speech," *New York Times*, April 27, 2016, http://www.nytimes.com/2016/04/28/us/politics/transcript-trump-foreign-policy.html.

84. Moreno, "9 Outrageous Things Donald Trump Has Said About Latinos."

CONCLUSION: CONSERVATISM AT A CROSSROADS

1. Pew Research Center, "Trust in Government: 1958–2015," in *Beyond Distrust: How Americans View Their Government*, November 23, 2015, http://www.people-press.org/2015/11/23/1-trust-in-government-1958–2015/.

2. David Brooks, "The New Right," *New York Times*, June 9, 2014, http://www.nytimes.com/2014/06/10/opinion/brooks-the-new-right.html?hp&rref=opinion

&_r=0; and Peter Wehner et al., *Room to Grow: Conservative Reforms for a Limited Government and a Thriving Middle Class* (YG Network, 2014), ygnetwork.org/wp-content/uploads/2014/05/Room-To-Grow.pdf.

3. David Frum, *Comeback: Conservatism That Can Win Again* (New York: Doubleday, 2008); Ross Douthat and Reihan Salam, *Grand New Party: How Republicans Can Win the Working Class and Save the American Dream* (New York: Doubleday, 2008); David Brooks, "The Republican Collapse," *New York Times*, October 5, 2007; David Brooks, "Ceding the Center," *New York Times*, October 26, 2008; and Wehner et al., *Room to Grow*.

4. Brooks, "The New Right."

5. Steve Coll, "Citizen Bezos," *New York Review of Books*, July 10, 2014, 28–32.

6. Corey Robin, "Conservatives and Counterrevolution," *Raritan*, summer 2010, 1–17.

7. Trump's constituency is overwhelmingly white, although only 58 percent of white, non-Hispanic voters voted for him. According to postelection exit polls, Trump garnered a mere 8 percent of the African American vote and 28 percent of the Latino vote (Alec Tyson and Shiva Maniam, "Behind Trump's Victory: Divisions by Race, Gender, Education," *Pew Research Center*, November 9, 2016, http://www.pewresearch.org/fact-tank/2016/11/09/behind-trumps-victory-divisions-by-race-gender-education/).

8. Robert Kagan, "This Is How Fascism Comes to America," *Washington Post*, May 18, 2016, https://www.washingtonpost.com/opinions/this-is-how-fascism-comes-to-america/2016/05/17/c4e32c58–1c47–11e6–8c7b–6931e66333e7_story.html?utm_term=.e21f2923d5f9.

9. David Brooks, "If Not Trump, What?," *New York Times*, April 29, 2016, http://www.nytimes.com/2016/04/29/opinion/if-not-trump-what.html?_r=0.

10. Ibid.

INDEX